Aubrey St. John Clerke

The Law and Practice under the Settled Land Acts

1882 - 1890

Aubrey St. John Clerke

The Law and Practice under the Settled Land Acts
1882 - 1890

ISBN/EAN: 9783744667111

Printed in Europe, USA, Canada, Australia, Japan

Cover: Foto ©ninafisch / pixelio.de

More available books at **www.hansebooks.com**

THE LAW AND PRACTICE

UNDER THE

SETTLED LAND ACTS,

1882 TO 1890.

WITH

THE STATUTES AND THE RULES AND FORMS ISSUED
UNDER THE SETTLED LAND ACT, 1882.

BY

AUBREY ST. JOHN CLERKE, B.A.,

OF THE MIDDLE TEMPLE, BARRISTER-AT-LAW.

SECOND EDITION.

LONDON:
SWEET & MAXWELL, LIMITED, 3, CHANCERY LANE,
Law Publishers.
MEREDITH, RAY, & LITTLER, MANCHESTER;
C. F. MAXWELL, MELBOURNE AND SYDNEY.
1891.

PREFACE
TO THE SECOND EDITION.

During the eight years that have elapsed since the Settled Land Act came into operation, the Courts have in many important cases determined the construction, and elucidated the principles of this important measure. The decisions, however, which have found their way into the Reports are few in number compared with the multitude of cases decided day by day under the Act in the Chambers of the Judges. Many of these Chamber-cases are, no doubt, formal applications, involving no question of general interest, and dealing merely with matter of administrative detail; but their number is in itself conclusive testimony that the Act is largely employed for the management of Settled Estates. No Statute of modern times has effected a more sweeping change in the Land Laws of England than the Settled Land Act of 1882—a change which has been judicially described as amounting to a " revolution."

Whether the innovations introduced by the Statute are regarded as a "revolution" or merely a "reform," it certainly has been welcomed and utilized by large numbers of distressed or incumbered landowners. No small boon has been conferred upon them by the provisions of the Act, which enable them either to sell the Settled Land and replace it by an income-bearing fund, or else to effect necessary improvements at the expense of Capital money. Still more advantageous in particular cases has been found the isolated section which authorizes the tenant for life, with the consent of the Court, to sell heirlooms and to apply the proceeds of sale in some remunerative manner. Under this Statutory power the works of Ancient Masters have been sacrificed in order to supply a system of drainage; and Presentation Plate, annexed as an heirloom to a Baronetcy, has been sold to provide an income for the impoverished Baronet.

Regarded as a measure of Conveyancing Reform, the Settled Land Act has achieved considerable success. The Powers of Sale and Exchange, and other powers, now inalienably conferred upon the tenant for life by the Statute itself, were formerly, by the express terms of the Settlement, vested in the Trustees; and the omission of these cumbrous clauses has materially reduced the length of all such instruments.

The Act has been on its trial for eight years and upwards; and its Author may be congratulated on the very few imperfections or omissions which have since been discovered in its details, and on the almost total absence of verbal ambiguity in its many complicated sections.

Four amending Statutes have been passed since 1882, but those of 1887 and 1889 are of trivial importance, while those of 1884 and 1890, with a few exceptional provisions, supplement the Principal Act only in matters of detail. The Act of 1884 increased the already large powers of the tenant for life by relaxing the stringency of the previously existing provisions as to notices to the Trustees of the Settlement, and corrected the hasty legislation of the former Act with reference to Settlements by way of trust for sale. The Act of 1890, among other enactments, authorizes the creation of easements on an exchange or partition of the Settled Land, enables the tenant for life to grant short leases without communicating with the Trustees of the Settlement, replaces s. 15 of the Act of 1882 by a more intelligible restriction on the alienation of the Principal Mansion House, and confers power on the tenant for life of raising money by Mortgage for the discharge of incumbrances. The most important amendments, however, introduced by the last-mentioned Act, are contained in the two sections relating to Trustees; one of which materially extends the definition of "The Trustees of the Settlement," while the other applies to the appointment, discharge, and retirement of such trustees all the provisions of the Conveyancing and Law of Property Act, 1881.

In the preparation of the present Edition, the utmost care has been taken to avoid the omission of any reported case decided under the Act, or bearing however remotely on the construction of any of its sections; and it is hoped that in this respect the present work will be found to be a complete index to the Case law on these important Statutes.

LINCOLN'S INN,
26th February, 1891.

CONTENTS.

	PAGE
TABLE OF CASES CITED WITH REFERENCES TO ALL THE REPORTS	xvii
TABLE OF STATUTES	xxix

INTRODUCTORY CHAPTER.

Scheme of the Act	1
Settled Land	3
Powers of tenant for life	6
Checks for security of remaindermen	7
Trustees of the settlement	8
The Court	11
The Board of Agriculture	12
Capital money arising under the Act	13
Investment and application of capital money	14
Position of a purchaser under the Act	17
Incumbrances	17
Limited owners who may exercise the powers	19
Effect upon existing settlements	20
Effect upon the Settled Estates Act	21
Exclusion of the Act	22

THE SETTLED LAND ACT, 1882.

I.—PRELIMINARY.

SECT.
1. Short title; commencement; extent	24

II.—DEFINITIONS.

2. Definition of settlement, tenant for life, &c.	24

III.—Sale; Enfranchisement; Exchange; Partition.

General Powers and Regulations.

SECT. | PAGE
3. Powers to tenant for life to sell, &c. 38
4. Regulations respecting sale, enfranchisement, exchange and partition 44

Special Powers.

5. Transfer of incumbrances on land sold, &c. . . . 48

IV.—Leases.

General Powers and Regulations.

6. Power for tenant for life to lease for ordinary or building or mining purposes 49
7. Regulations respecting leases generally 51

Building and Mining Leases.

8. Regulations respecting building leases 54
9. Regulations respecting mining leases 56
10. Variation of building or mining lease according to circumstances of district 59
11. Part of mining rent to be set aside 60

Special Powers.

12. Leasing powers for special objects 63

Surrenders.

13. Surrender and new grant of leases 66

Copyholds.

14. Power to grant to copyholders licences for leasing 68

V.—Sales, Leases, and other Dispositions.

Mansion and Park.

15. Restriction as to mansion-house, park, &c. 69

Streets and Open Spaces.

16. Dedication for streets, open spaces, &c. 71

Surface and Minerals apart.

SECT.
17. Separate dealings with surface and minerals with or without way-leaves, &c. 73

Mortgage.
18. Mortgage for equality money, &c. 75

Undivided Share.
19. Concurrence in exercise of powers as to undivided share . . 76

Conveyance.
20. Completion of sale, lease, &c., by conveyance 77

VI.—INVESTMENT OR OTHER APPLICATION OF CAPITAL TRUST MONEY.

21. Capital money under Act; investment, &c., by trustees or Court . 83
22. Regulations respecting investment, devolution, and income of securities, &c. 92
23. Investment in land in England 94
24. Settlement of land purchased, taken in exchange, &c. . . . 95

VII.—IMPROVEMENTS.

Improvements with Capital Trust Money.
25. Description of improvements authorized by Act 98
26. Approval by Land Commissioners of scheme for improvement and payment thereon 103
27. Concurrence in improvements 106
28. Obligation on tenant for life and successors to maintain, insure, &c. 106

Execution and Repair of Improvements.
29. Protection as regards waste in execution and repair of improvements 111

Improvement of Land Act, 1864.
30. Extension of 27 & 28 Vict. c. 114, s. 9 112

VIII.—CONTRACTS.

31. Power for tenant for life to enter into contracts . . . 114

IX.—MISCELLANEOUS PROVISIONS.

SECT.		PAGE
32.	Application of money in Court under Lands Clauses and other Acts	118
33.	Application of money in hands of trustees under powers of settlement	120
34.	Application of money paid for lease or reversion	122
35.	Cutting and sale of timber, and part of proceeds to be set aside	124
36.	Proceedings for protection or recovery of land settled or claimed as settled	125
37.	Heirlooms	126

X.—TRUSTEES.

38.	Appointment of trustees by Court	129
39.	Number of trustees to act	132
40.	Trustees' receipts	133
41.	Protection of each trustee individually	134
42.	Protection of trustees generally	135
43.	Trustees' reimbursement	136
44.	Reference of differences to Court	137
45.	Notice to trustees	137

XI.—COURT; LAND COMMISSIONERS; PROCEDURE.

46.	Regulations respecting payments into Court, applications, &c.	140
47.	Payment of costs out of settled property	143
48.	Constitution of Land Commissioners; their powers, &c.	144
49.	Filing of certificates, &c., of Commissioners	146

XII.—RESTRICTIONS, SAVINGS, AND GENERAL PROVISIONS.

50.	Powers not assignable; contract not to exercise powers void	146
51.	Prohibition or limitation against exercise of powers void	149
52.	Provision against forfeiture	150
53.	Tenant for life trustee for all parties interested	151
54.	General protection of purchasers, &c.	154
55.	Exercise of powers; limitation of provisions, &c.	154
56.	Saving for other powers	155
57.	Additional or larger powers by settlement	158

XIII.—LIMITED OWNERS GENERALLY.

58.	Enumeration of other limited owners to have powers of tenant for life	159

XIV.—INFANTS; MARRIED WOMEN; LUNATICS.

SECT.		PAGE
59.	Infant absolutely entitled to be as tenant for life	166
60.	Tenant for life, infant	167
61.	Married woman, how to be affected	169
62.	Tenant for life, lunatic	171

XV.—SETTLEMENT BY WAY OF TRUSTS FOR SALE.

63.	Provision for case of trust to sell and re-invest in land	173

XVI.—REPEALS.

64.	Repeal of enactments in schedule	178

XVII.—IRELAND.

65.	Modifications respecting Ireland	178
	SCHEDULE	181

THE SETTLED LAND ACT, 1884.

1.	Short title	182
2.	Interpretation	182
3.	Construction of the Act	182
4.	Fine on a lease to be capital money	182
5.	Notice under the Act of 1882	182
6.	Consents of tenants for life	183
7.	Powers given by s. 63 to be exercised only with leave of the Court	184
8.	Curtesy to be deemed to arise under settlement	186

THE SETTLED LAND ACT, 1887.

1.	Amendment of s. 21 of the Act of 1882	187
2.	Section 28 of the Act of 1882 to apply to improvements within foregoing section	188
3.	Short title	188

THE SETTLED LAND ACT, 1889.

SECT.	PAGE
1. Construction and short title	189
2. Option of purchase in building lease	189
3. Price to be capital money	190

THE SETTLED LAND ACT, 1890.

Preliminary.

1. Short title	191
2. Acts to be construed together	191
3. Interpretation	191

Definitions.

4. Instrument in consideration of marriage, &c., to be part of settlement	191

Exchanges.

5. Creation of easements on exchange or partition	192

Completion of Contracts.

6. Power to complete predecessor's contract	192

Leases.

7. Provision as to leases for twenty-one years	193
8. Provisions as to mining leases	193
9. Power to reserve a rent-charge on a grant in fee simple	194

Mansion and Park.

10. Restriction on sale of mansion	195

The Raising of Money.

11. Power to raise money by mortgage	195

Dealings as between tenant for life and the Estate.

12. Provision enabling dealings with tenant for life	197

Application of Capital Money.

SECT.		PAGE
13.	Application of capital money	197
14.	Capital money in Court may be paid out to trustees	198
15.	Court may order payment for improvements executed	198

Trustees.

16.	Trustees for the purposes of the Act	199
17.	Application of the Conveyancing Act, 1881, to appointment of trustees	200
18.	Extension of meaning of "working classes" in the Housing of the Working Classes Act	201
19.	Power to vacate registration of writ	201

RULES UNDER THE SETTLED LAND ACT, 1882. 203

APPENDIX OF FORMS 209

INDEX 221

TABLE OF CASES.

WITH REFERENCES TO ALL THE REPORTS.

	PAGE
ALEXANDER v. Mills, L. R. 6 Ch. 125; 19 W. R. 310; 40 L. J. Ch. 73; 24 L. T. 206	148
Allen v. Allen, 2 Dru. & W. 307	163
Allwood v. Heywood, 1 H. & C. 745; 11 W. R. 291; 32 L. J. Ex. 153; 7 L. T. 640; 1 N. R. 289; 9 Jur. N. S. 108	82
Andrew v. Williams, 52 L. T. 41	108
Arabin's Trusts, *Re*, 52 L. T. 728	119
Arnold, *Re*, 31 S. J. 560	120
Askew v. Woodhead, 14 Ch. D. 27; 28 W. R. 874; 49 L. J. Ch. 320; 42 L. T. 567	123
Aspden v. Seddon, L. R. 10 Ch. 394; 23 W. R. 580; 44 L. J. Ch. 359; 32 L. T. 415; S. C. 1 Ex. D. 496; 24 W. R. 828; 46 L. J. Ex. 353; 34 L. T. 906	75
Atkinson, *Re*, 31 Ch. D. 577; 34 W. R. 445; 55 L. J. Ch. 49; 54 L. T. 403	31, 32, 144, 160
Attorney-General v. Marlborough, 3 Mad. 498	161
—— v. Tomline, 5 Ch. D. 750; 25 W. R. 803; 46 L. J. Ch. 654; 36 L. T. 684	37
—— v. Welsh Granite Company, 35 W. R. 617	37
Atwell v. Atwell, L. R. 13 Eq. 23; 20 W. R. 108; 41 L. J. Ch. 23; 25 L. T. 526	121
Austerberry v. Corporation of Oldham, 29 Ch. D. 750; 33 W. R. 807; 55 L. J. Ch. 633; 53 L. T. 543	47, 72, 73
Aylesford's (Earl of) Settled Estates, *Re*, 32 Ch. D. 162; 34 W. R. 410; 55 L. J. Ch. 523; 54 L. T. 414	36, 125
BAGOT v. Bagot, 32 Beav. 509; 12 W. R. 35; 33 L. J. Ch. 116; 9 L. T. 217; 9 Jur. N. S. 1022	61
Baker v. Sebright, 13 Ch. D. 179; 28 W. R. 177; 49 L. J. Ch. 65; 41 L. T. 614	109
Barber's Settled Estates, *Re*, 18 Ch. D. 624; 29 W. R. 909; 50 L. J. Ch 769; 45 L. T. 433	123, 163
Barnes v. Dowling, 44 L. T. 809	108
Barrell, *Ex parte*, L. R. 10 Ch. 512; 23 W. R. 846; 33 L. T. 115	115
Barrs-Haden's Settled Estates, *Re*, 32 W. R. 194; 49 L. T. 661	22, 41, 156
Bartram v. Whichcote, 6 Sim. 86	43
Basset v. Basset, Amb. 843	58

TABLE OF CASES.

	PAGE
Batthyany v. Walford, 36 Ch. D. 269; 35 W. R. 815; 56 L. J. Ch. 881 .	110
Beaumont's Settled Estates, Re, 58 L. T. 916	129
Beck, Re, 24 Ch. D. 608; 31 W. R. 910; 52 L. J. Ch. 815; 49 L. T. 95 .	91
	137, 153
Beioley v. Carter, L. R. 4 Ch. 230; 17 W. R. 300; 38 L. J. Ch. 283; 20 L. T. 381	28
Bell v. Wilson, L. R. 1 Ch. 303; 14 W. R. 493; 35 L. J. Ch. 337; 14 L. T. 115; 12 Jur. N. S. 263	37
Berkeley's (Earl) Will, Re, L. R. 10 Ch. 56; 23 W. R. 195; 44 L. J. Ch. 3; 31 L. T. 531	126
Berry v. White, Bridg. 82	148
Bethlehem and Bridewell Hospitals, Re, 30 Ch. D. 541; 34 W. R. 148; 54 L. J. Ch. 1143; 53 L. T. 558	119
Bethlem Hospital, Re, L. R. 19 Eq. 457; 23 W. R. 644; 44 L. J. Ch. 406	120
Bidder v. North Staffordshire Ry. Co., 4 Q. B. D. 412; 27 W. R. 540; 48 L. J. Q. B. 248; 40 L. T. 801	59
Blackburn and District Benefit Building Society, Re, 42 Ch. D. 343; 38 W. R. 178; 59 L. J. Ch. 183; 61 L. T. 745; 5 T. L. R. 565 . .	195
Blore v. Sutton, 3 Mer. 237	117
Bolton Estate Act, 1863, Re, 52 L. T. 728	118, 162
Bolton's Lease, Re, L. R. 5 Ex. 82; 18 W. R. 351; 39 L. J. Ex. 51; 21 L. T. 720	56
Bradshaw v. Eyr, Cro. Eliz. 570	48
Brigstocke v. Brigstocke, 8 Ch. D. 357; 47 L. J. Ch. 817; 38 L. T. 760 .	65
Broadwater Estate, Re, 33 W. R. 738; 54 L. J. Ch. 1104; 53 L. T. 745 .	101, 104, 142
Broadwood's Settled Estates, Re, 1 Ch. D. 438; 24 W. R. 108; 45 L. J. Ch. 168	90
Browne v. Collins, 62 L. T. 567	128
Brown's Will, Re, 27 Ch. D. 179; 32 W. R. 894; 53 L. J. Ch. 921; 51 L. T. 156	70
Bryant and Barningham's Contract, Re, 44 Ch. D. 218; 38 W. R. 469; 59 L. J. Ch. 636; 63 L. T. 20	41
Buckingham's (Duke of) Estate, Re, see Re Clitheroe Estate.	
Buckley v. Howell, 29 Beav. 546; 9 W. R. 544; 30 L. J. Ch. 524; 4 L. T. 172; 7 Jur. N. S. 536	74
Bulwer Lytton's Will, Re, 38 Ch. D. 20; 36 W. R. 420; 57 L. J. Ch. 340; 59 L. T. 12	105
Burchell v. Clark, 2 C. P. D. 88; 25 W. R. 334; 46 L. J. C. P. 115; 35 L. T. 690	54
Burden's Will, Re, 5 Jur. N. S. 1378; 7 W. R. 711; 28 L. J. Ch. 840; 2 L. T. 70	28
Burke v. Gore, 13 L. R. Ir. 367	122, 131
Burnaby's Settled Estates, Re, 42 Ch. D. 621; 58 L. J. Ch. 464; 61 L. T. 22	82
Bute (Marquis of) v. Thompson, 13 M. & W. 487; 14 L. J. Ex. 95 . .	58
Butler's Will, Re, L. R. 16 Eq. 479	90
Byron's Charity, Re, 23 Ch. D. 171; 31 W. R. 517; 53 L. J. Ch. 152; 48 L. T. 515	86, 119

	PAGE
CALDECOTT v. Brown, 2 Hare, 144 ; 7 Jur. 693	103
Calton's Will, Re, 25 Ch. D. 240 ; 32 W. R. 167 ; 53 L. J. Ch. 329 ; 49 L. T. 566	119
Camden v. Murray, 16 Ch. D. 161 ; 29 W. R. 190 ; 50 L. J. Ch. 282 ; 43 L. T. 661	31
Campbell v. Leach, Amb. 740	50, 58
Cardigan v. Curzon-Howe, 30 Ch. D. 531 ; 33 W. R. 836 ; 55 L. J. Ch. 71 ; 53 L. T. 704	41, 152
Cardigan v. Curzon-Howe, 41 Ch. D. 375 ; 37 W. R. 521 ; 58 L. J. Ch. 177 ; 60 L. T. 723 . . . . 90, 93, 148, 153
Carr, Re, 9 W. R. 766	60
—— v. Benson, L. R. 3 Ch. 524 ; 16 W. R. 744 ; 18 L. T. 696 . .	37
Cartington Estate, Re, see Re Beck.
Cartwright, Re, 41 Ch. D. 532 ; 37 W. R. 613 ; 58 L. J. Ch. 590 ; 60 L. T. 891 ; 5 T. L. R. 482	51, 108
Cecil v. Langdon, 54 L. T. 418.	60
Chaytor's Settled Estate Act, Re, 25 Ch. D. 651 ; 32 W. R. 517 ; 53 L. J. Ch. 312 ; 50 L. T. 88 . . . . 39, 40, 86, 142, 150, 156
Chelsea Waterworks Company, Re, 56 L. J. Ch. 640 ; 56 L. T. 421 . .	119
Chesham (Lord), Re, 31 Ch. D. 466 ; 34 W. R. 321 ; 55 L. J. Ch. 401 ; 54 L. T. 154	128
Cheshunt College, Re, 1 Jur. N. S. 995 ; 3 W. R. 638	120
Cholmeley v. Paxton, 3 Bing. 207 ; 10 B. & Cr. 564 . . .	46, 125
Christie v. Gosling, L. R. 1 H. L. 279 ; 35 L. J. Ch. 667 ; 15 L. T. 40 .	97
Clark, Re, L. R. 1 Ch. 292 ; 13 L. T. 732	28
—— v. Seymour, 7 Sim. 67	42
Clarke v. Thornton, 35 Ch. D. 307 ; 35 W. R. 603 ; 56 L. J. Ch. 302 ; 56 L. T. 294 . . . . 15, 89, 93, 94, 121, 152
Clavering v. Clavering, 2 P. Wms. 388	61
Clay v. Rufford, 5 De G. & Sm. 768	45
Cleveland (Duchess of) v. Meyrick, 16 W. R. 104 ; 37 L. J. Ch. 125 ; 17 L. T. 233	37
Clifford v. Watts, L. R. 5 C. P. 577 ; 18 W. R. 925 ; 40 L. J. C. P. 36 ; 22 L. T. 717	58
Clitheroe Estate, Re, 31 Ch. D. 135 ; 34 W. R. 169 ; 55 L. J. Ch. 107 ; 53 L. T. 733 . . . . 31, 32, 158, 164, 165
Cockerell v. Cholmeley, 1 R. & My. 418 ; 1 Cl. & F. 60 . . .	46, 125
Collett v. Collett, L. R. 2 Eq. 203	28
Collinge's Settled Estates, Re, 36 Ch. D. 516 ; 36 W. R. 264 ; 57 L. J. Ch. 219 ; 57 L. T. 221 . . . . 30, 31, 36, 77
Constable v. Constable, 32 Ch. D. 233 ; 34 W. R. 470 ; 55 L. J. Ch. 491 ; 54 L. T. 608	34, 128
Conway v. Fenton, 40 Ch. D. 512 ; 37 W. R. 156 ; 58 L. J. Ch. 282 ; 59 L. T. 928	100
Cook v. Cook, 15 P. D. 116 ; 38 W. R. 656 ; 59 L. J. P. D. 69 ; 62 L. T. 667	202
Cooke v. Chilcott, 3 Ch. D. 694 ; 34 L. T. 207	47
Cookes v. Cookes, 34 Ch. D. 498 ; 35 W. R. 402 ; 56 L. J. Ch. 397 ; 56 L. T. 159 . . . . 90, 93, 133, 134, 198
Cookes' Settled Estates, Re, W. N. 1885, 177	32, 164

TABLE OF CASES.

	PAGE
Cooper and Allen's Contract, *Re*, 4 Ch. D. 802; 25 W. R. 301; 46 L. J. Ch. 133; 35 L. T. 890	47, 77, 83
Cooper *v.* Denne, 4 Bro. C. C. 80	55
Copper Mining Company *v.* Beach, 13 Beav. 478	65
Cottrell *v.* Cottrell, 28 Ch. D. 628; 33 W. R. 361; 54 L. J. Ch. 417; 52 L. T. 486	122, 123
Courtier, *Re*, 34 Ch. D. 136; 35 W. R. 85; 56 L. J. Ch. 350; 55 L. T. 574	108
Cross's Charity, *Re*, 27 Beav. 592	60
Currey, *Re*, 35 W. R. 326	171
Cust *v.* Middleton, 3 De G. F. & J. 33; 9 W. R. 242; 30 L. J. Ch. 260; 3 L. T. 718; 7 Jur. N. S. 151	56, 64
DANCE *v.* Goldingham, L. R. 8 Ch. 902; 21 W. R. 761; 42 L. J. Ch. 777; 29 L. T. 166	47
D'Angibau, *Re*, 15 Ch. D. 228; 28 W. R. 930; 49 L. J. Ch. 756; 43 L. T. 135	167, 169
Davies *v.* Davies, 38 Ch. D. 499; 36 W. R. 399; 57 L. J. Ch. 1093; 58 L. T. 514	51
Davis *v.* Harford, 22 Ch. D. 128; 31 W. R. 61; 52 L. J. Ch. 61; 47 L. T. 540	64
De Beauvoir *v.* De Beauvoir, 3 H. L. Cas. 524	121
De Grey's (Earl) Entailed Estate, *Re*, 32 S. J. 108	120
De La Warr's (Earl) Estates, *Re*, 16 Ch. D. 587; 29 W. R. 350; 50 L. J. Ch. 383; 44 L. T. 56	126
Dent *v.* Dent, 30 Beav. 363; 10 W. R. 375; 31 L. J. Ch. 436	103
Depree *v.* Bedborough, 4 Giff. 479; 12 W. R. 191; 33 L. J. Ch. 134; 9 L. T. 532; 3 N. R. 187; 9 Jur. N. S. 1317	115
D'Eyncourt *v.* Gregory, 3 Ch. D. 635; 24 W. R. 424; 45 L. J. Ch. 741	127
Dicconson *v.* Talbot, L. R. 6 Ch. 32; 19 W. R. 138; 24 L. T. 49	153, 172
Dixon *v.* Jackson, 25 L. J. Ch. 588; 4 W. R. 450	120
—— *v.* Peacock, 3 Drew. 288	103
—— *v.* White, 8 App. Cas. 833	75
Doe *v.* Bettison, 12 East, 305	53, 65, 193
—— *v.* Earl of Burlington, 5 B. & Ad. 507	69
—— *v.* Radcliffe, 10 East, 278	53
—— *v.* Stephens, 6 Q. B. 208	193
Doran *v.* Wiltshire, 3 Sw. 699	125
Drake *v.* Trefusis, L. R. 10 Ch. 364; 23 W. R. 762; 33 L. T. 85	100
Dudley's (Countess of) Contract, *Re*, 35 Ch. D. 338; 35 W. R. 492; 56 L. J. Ch. 478; 57 L. T. 10	10, 167, 168
—— Settled Estates, *Re*, 26 S. J. 359	62
Dugdale *v.* Meadows, L. R. 6 Ch. 501; 40 L. J. Ch. 140; 24 L. T. 113	82
Dunne *v.* Dunne, 7 De G. M. & G. 207; 3 W. R. 380; 25 L. T. 60; 1 Jur. N. S. 1056	103
Dunn's Settled Estates, *Re*, W. N. 1877, 39	113
Durrant and Stoner, *Re*, 18 Ch. D. 106; 30 W. R. 37; 45 L. T. 363	36
Dyas *v.* Cruise, 2 Jo. & Lat. 460	53
Dyke's Estate, *Re*, L. R. 7 Eq. 337; 17 W. R. 658; 20 L. T. 292	64, 115

	PAGE
EARLE and Webster's Contract, *Re*, 24 Ch. D. 144; 31 W. R. 887; 52 L. J. Ch. 828; 48 L. T. 961 . . . . 157, 176, 183	
Easton *v.* Pratt, 2 H. & C. 676; 12 W. R. 805; 33 L. J. Ex. 31; 9 L. T. 342; 10 Jur. N. S. 732 55	
Eaton *v.* Hewitt, 2 Dr. & Sm. 184 163	
Edwards, *Re*, 10 Ch. D. 605; 27 W. R. 611; 48 L. J. Ch. 233; 40 L. T. 113 172	
Egmont's (Lord) Settled Estates, *Re*, 45 Ch. D. 395; 38 W. R. 762; 59 L. J. Ch. 768; 63 L. T. 608; 6 T. L. R. 461 87	
Eisdale *v.* Hammersly, 31 Beav. 255; 6 L. T. 706 148	
Errington *v.* Metropolitan District Ry. Co., 19 Ch. D. 559; 30 W. R. 663; 51 L. J. Ch. 305; 46 L. T. 443 36	
Esdaile *v.* Esdaile, 54 L. T. 637 . . . . 36, 88	
Etches *v.* Etches, 3 Drew. 441; 4 W. R. 307 163	
Eyton's Settled Estates, *Re*, W. N. 1888, 254 91	

FERRAND *v.* Wilson, 4 Hare, 344; 9 Jur. 860 46
Ferrer's (Earl) Case, 2 Eden. 373 127
Ford *v.* Peering, 1 Ves. jun. 72 82
Ford's Settled Estates, *Re*, L. R. 8 Eq. 309 67
Fowler, *Re*, 16 Ch. D. 723; 29 W. R. 891; 44 L. T. 99 . . . 108
Frewen, *Re*, 38 Ch. D. 383; 36 W. R. 840; 57 L. J. Ch. 1052; 59 L. T. 131 88
Frith and Osborne, *Re*, 3 Ch. D. 618; 24 W. R. 1061; 45 L. J. Ch. 780; 35 L. T. 146 44
Fry *v.* Tapson, 28 Ch. D. 268; 33 W. R. 113; 54 L. J. Ch. 224; 51 L. T. 326 135

GAITSKELL, *Re*, 40 Ch. D. 416; 58 L. J. Ch. 262 . . . 77, 172
Gamston, Rector of, *Ex parte*, 1 Ch. D. 477; 24 W. R. 359; 33 L. T. 803 120
Gandy *v.* Gandy, 30 Ch. D. 57; 33 W. R. 803; 54 L. J. Ch. 1154; 53 L. T. 306 63
Garner *v.* Hannyngton, 22 Beav. 627 82
Garnett Orme and Hargreave's Contract, *Re*, 25 Ch. D. 595; 32 W. R. 313; 53 L. J. Ch. 196; 49 L. T. 655 . . . . 34, 132, 140
Gaskin *v.* Balls, 13 Ch. D. 324; 28 W. R. 552 47
Gas Light and Coke Company *v.* Towse, 35 Ch. D. 519; 56 L. J. Ch. 889; 56 L. T. 602 . . . . 52, 53, 65, 116
Goodright *v.* Cator, Doug. 460 147
Goodwin's Settled Estates, *Re*, 3 Giff. 620; 10 W. R. 612; 6 L. T. 530; 8 Jur. N. S. 1170 28
Gowan *v.* Christie, L. R. 2 H. L. Sc. 273 58
Great Western Railway Company *v.* Rous, L. R. 4. H. L. 650; 23 L. T. 360 . . . . 58, 59
Greenville Estate, *Re*, 11 L. R. Ir. 138 168
Griffith's Will, *Re*, 49 L. T. 161 123

	PAGE
Hale and Clark, Re, 34 W. R. 624 ; 55 L. J. Ch. 550 ; 55 L. T. 151	31, 148
Hall-Dare's Contract, Re, 21 Ch. D. 41 ; 30 W. R. 556 ; 51 L. J. Ch. 671 ; 46 L. T. 755	21
Hallett to Martin, 24 Ch. D. 624 ; 32 W. R. 112 ; 52 L. J. Ch. 804 ; 48 L. T. 894	52, 53
Hanbury, Re, 52 L. J. Ch. 687 ; 31 W. R. 784	120
—— v. Litchfield, 2 My. & K. 629	68
Harding's Settled Estates, Re, 1891, 1 Ch. 60 ; 39 W. R. 118 ; 63 L. T. 539	157, 176, 183, 185
Hardwicke (Earl of), Ex parte, 17 L. J. Ch. 422	120
Hardy v. Reeves, 4 Ves. 466	69
Hare v. Burges, 4 K. & J. 45 ; 6 W. R. 144 ; 27 L. J. Ch. 86 ; 3 Jur. N. S. 1294	65
Hargreave's Trust, Re, 58 L. T. 367	119, 120
Harrington v. Harrington, L. R. 5 H. L. 87 ; 40 L. J. Ch. 716	97
Harris v. Barnes, 4 Burr. 2157	163
Harrop's Trusts, Re, 24 Ch. D. 717 ; 53 L. J. Ch. 137 ; 48 L. T. 937	86, 120, 131
Hatten v. Russell, 38 Ch. D. 334 ; 36 W. R. 317 ; 57 L. J. Ch. 425 ; 58 L. T. 271	40, 136, 137, 140, 152, 154
Haynes, Re, 37 Ch. D. 306 ; 36 W. R. 321 ; 57 L. J. Ch. 519 ; 58 L. T. 14	150, 151
Haywood v. Brunswick Benefit Building Society, 8 Q. B. D. 403 ; 30 W. R. 209 ; 51 L. J. Q. B. 73 ; 45 L. T. 699	47
Hazle's Settled Estates, Re, 29 Ch. D. 78 ; 33 W. R. 759 ; 54 L. J. Ch. 628 ; 52 L. T. 947	149, 162
Head's Trustees and Macdonald's Contract, Re, 45 Ch. D. 310 ; 38 W. R. 657 ; 59 L. J. Ch. 604 ; 63 L. T. 21	41
Healey v. Corporation of Batley, L. R. 19 Eq. 375	73
Hext v. Gill, L. R. 7 Ch. 699 ; 20 W. R. 957 ; 41 L. J. Ch. 761 ; 27 L. T. 291	37
Hibbert v. Cooke, 1 S. & S. 552	103
Hickman v. Upsal, 4 Ch. D. 144 ; 25 W. R. 175 ; 46 L. J. Ch. 245 ; 35 L. T. 919	153
Higginbotham v. Hawkins, L. R. 7 Ch. 676 ; 20 W. R. 955 ; 41 L. J. Ch. 828	109
Higgins v. Rosse, 3 Bli. 112	55
Hindle v. Taylor, 5 De G. M. & G. 577 ; 3 W. R. 62 ; 25 L. J. Ch. 78 ; 1 Jur. N. S. 1029	97
Hodges v. Blagrove, 18 Beav. 404	65
Holdsworth v. Goose, 29 Beav. 111 ; 9 W. R. 443 ; 30 L. J. Ch. 188 ; 4 L. T. 196 ; 7 Jur. N. S. 301	148
Hollier v. Burne, L. R. 16 Eq. 163 ; 21 W. R. 805 ; 42 L. J. Ch. 789 ; 28 L. T. 531	123
Honywood v. Honywood, L. R. 18 Eq. 306 ; 22 W. R. 749 ; 43 L. J. Ch. 652 ; 30 L. T. 671	109, 124
Horlock v. Smith, 17 Beav. 472 ; 2 W. R. 117	103
Horn's Settled Estates, Re, 29 L. T. 830	28
Horne's Settled Estates, Re, 39 Ch. D. 84 ; 37 W. R. 69 ; 57 L. J. Ch. 790 ; 59 L. T. 580	142, 165, 166, 168, 177

TABLE OF CASES.

	PAGE
Hotchkin's Settled Estates, *Re*, 35 Ch. D. 41 ; 35 W. R. 463 ; 56 L. J. Ch. 445 ; 56 L. T. 244	104, 105, 198
Houghton *v.* Koenig, 10 C. B. 235	53
Houghton Estate, *Re*, 30 Ch. D. 102 ; 33 W. R. 869 ; 55 L. J. Ch. 37 ; 53 L. T. 196	30, 100, 128
Howard *v.* Ducane, T. & R. 81	153
Howe *v.* Smith, 27 Ch. D. 89 ; 32 W. R. 802 ; 53 L. J. Ch. 1055 ; 50 L. T. 573	94, 115
Hurst *v.* Hurst, 16 Beav. 372 ; 22 L. J. Ch. 538	148
Hutchinson, *Re*, 14 L. T. 129	149
ISAAC *v.* Hughes, L. R. 9 Eq. 191 ; 39 L. J. Ch. 379 ; 22 L. T. 11	148
JACKSON, *Re*, 21 Ch. D. 786	100
James, *Re*, 32 W. R. 898 ; 51 L. T. 596	162
Jefferys *v.* Fairs, 4 Ch. D. 448 ; 25 W. R. 227 ; 46 L. J. Ch. 113 ; 36 L. T. 10	58
Jeffreys *v.* Conner, 28 Beav. 328 ; 8 W. R. 572	123
Jenner *v.* Morris, L. R. 1 Ch. 603 ; 3 De G. F. & J. 45 ; 14 W. R. 1003	82
Jesse *v.* Lloyd, 48 L. T. 656	103
Jesus College, Cambridge, *Ex parte*, 50 L. T. 583	119
Johnstone, *Re*, 17 L. R. Ir. 172	34
Jones, *Re*, 26 Ch. D. 736 ; 32 W. R. 735 ; 53 L. J. Ch. 807 ; 50 L. T. 466	7, 31, 32, 142, 160, 164
KANE, *Re*, 21 L. R. Ir. 112	130
Keates *v.* Lyon, L. R. 4 Ch. 218 ; 17 W. R. 338 ; 38 L. J. Ch. 357 ; 20 L. T. 255	48
Kemp's Settled Estates, *Re*, 24 Ch. D. 485 ; 31 W. R. 930 ; 52 L. J. Ch. 950 ; 49 L. T. 231	131
Kennaway, *Re*, W. N. 1889, 70	131
Kentish Town Estate, *Re*, 1 J. & H. 230	64
Kirksmeaton (Rector of), *Ex parte*, 20 Ch. D. 203 ; 30 W. R. 539 ; 51 L. J. Ch. 581	120
Knatchbull's Settled Estates, *Re*, 29 Ch. D. 588 ; 33 W. R. 569 ; 54 L. J. Ch. 1168 ; 53 L. T. 284	3, 87, 104, 137
Knowles' Settled Estates, *Re*, 27 Ch. D. 707 ; 33 W. R. 364 ; 54 L. J. Ch. 264 ; 51 L. T. 655	28, 131
LANGDALE (Lady) *v.* Briggs, 8 De G. M. & G. 391 ; 4 W. R. 703	82
Leathes *v.* Leathes, 5 Ch. D. 221 ; 25 W. R. 492 ; 46 L. J. Ch. 562 ; 36 L. T. 646	82
Lee's (Sir Richard) Case, 1 And. 67	155
Lefroy *v.* Walsh, 1 Ir. C. L. Rep. N. S. 313	68
Leinster's (Duke of) Settled Estates, *Re*, 23 L. R. Ir. 152	87
Lewis *v.* Fothergill, L. R. 5 Ch. 103	58
Life Association of Scotland *v.* Siddal, 3 De G. F. & J. 58 ; 9 W. R. 541 ; 4 L. T. 311 ; 7 Jur. N. S. 785	154

	PAGE
Llewellin, Re, 37 Ch. D. 317 ; 36 W. R. 347; 57 L. J. Ch. 316 ; 58 L. T. 152	91, 125, 153
Lloyd, Re, 54 L. T. 643	86
London and South-Western Ry. Co. v. Gomm, 20 Ch. D. 562; 30 W. R. 620 ; 51 L. J. Ch. 193 ; 45 L. T. 505	47
London Bridge Acts, Re, 13 Sim. 176	83
Love v. Bell, 9 App. Cas. 286; 32 W. R. 725 ; 53 L. J. Q. B. 257 ; 51 L. T. 1	75
Lowndes v. Norton, 6 Ch. D. 139 ; 25 W. R. 826 ; 46 L. J. Ch. 613	124
Lowther v. Heaver, 41 Ch. D. 248; 37 W. R. 465 ; 58 L. J. Ch. 482; 60 L. T. 310	116

MABERLY, Re, 33 Ch. D. 455 ; 34 W. R. 771 ; 56 L. J. Ch. 54 ; 55 L. T. 164	16, 86, 121
Mackenzie v. Childers, 43 Ch. D. 265 ; 38 W. R. 243; 59 L. J. Ch. 188 ; 62 L. T. 98	47
Mackenzie's Trusts, Re, 23 Ch. D. 750 ; 31 W. R. 948; 52 L. J. Ch. 726 ; 48 L. T. 936	29, 121, 122, 137
Maddy v. Hale, 3 Ch. D. 327 ; 45 L. J. Ch. 791 ; 35 L. T. 134	123
Madgwick, Re, 25 Ch. D. 371 ; 32 W. R. 512; 53 L. J. Ch. 333; 49 L. T. 560	119
Maidstone and Ashford Railway Company, Re, 25 Ch. D. 168; 32 W. R. 181 ; 53 L. J. Ch. 127 ; 49 L. T. 777	119
Manchester, &c., Ry. Co., Re, 21 Beav. 162	120
Mansel's Settled Estates, Re, W. N. 1884, 209	148
Marlborough (Duke of) v. Sartoris, 32 Ch. D. 616 ; 35 W. R. 55 ; 56 L. J. Ch. 70 ; 55 L. T. 506	139
Marlborough's (Duke of) Settlement, Re, 32 Ch. D. 1 ; 34 W. R. 377 ; 55 L. J. Ch. 339 ; 55 L. T. 914	86, 93, 94, 128, 151
Marsh v. Wells, 2 S. & S. 87	108
Martelli v. Holloway, L. R. 5 H. L. 532	97
Master v. Hansard, 4 Ch. D. 718 ; 34 L. T. 719	48
Mellers v. Devonshire (Duke of), 16 Beav. 252 ; 1 W. R. 44 ; 22 L. J. Ch. 210	58
Mellor v. Watkins, L. R. 9 Q. B. 400	67
Mercer's Company, Ex parte, 10 Ch. D. 481 ; 27 W. R. 424 ; 48 L. J. Ch. 384	120
Mette's Estate, Re, L. R. 7 Eq. 72 ; 38 L. J. Ch. 445	123
Midland Ry. Co. v. Checkley, L. R. 4 Eq. 19 ; 15 W. R. 671 ; 36 L. J. Ch. 380 ; 16 L. T. 260	37
—— v. Haunchwood Brick and Tile Co., 20 Ch. D. 552 ; 51 L. J. Ch. 778 ; 46 L. T. 301	37
Mill's Estate, Re, 34 Ch. D. 24 ; 35 W. R. 65 ; 56 L. J. Ch. 60 ; 55 L. T. 465	120
Minet v. Leman, 20 Beav. 269 ; 7 De G. M. & G. 340 ; 3 W. R. 580 ; 1 Jur. N. S. 692 ; 3 Eq. Rep. 783	43
Moir, Re, 25 Ch. D. 605 ; 32 W. R. 377 ; 53 L. J. Ch. 474 ; 50 L. T. 10	150
Money's Trusts, Re, 2 Dr. & Sm. 94 ; 10 W. R. 399 ; 31 L. J. Ch. 496	123
More v. More, 37 W. R. 414 ; 60 L. T. 626	126

TABLE OF CASES.

Morgan, *Re*, 24 Ch. D. 114; 31 W. R. 948; 53 L. J. Ch. 85; 48 L. T. 964 . . . . 160, 162, 166
Mundy's Settled Estates, *Re*, 63 L. T. 311; 39 W. R. 209   28, 29, 101, 122

Navan and Kingscourt Ry. Co., *Re*, 21 L. R. Ir. 369 86
Naylor and Spendla's Contract, *Re*, 34 Ch. D. 217; 35 W. R. 219; 56 L. J. Ch. 453; 56 L. T. 132 81
Newcastle's (Duke of) Estates, *Re*, 24 Ch. D. 129; 31 W. R. 782; 52 L. J. Ch. 645; 48 L. T. 779 . . 34, 61, 75, 93, 121, 156, 157, 167
Newman, *Re*, 3 Ch. D. 494; 25 W. R. 261 110
Newton's Settled Estates, *Re*, 61 L. T. 787 . . . . 87, 100
Norris *v.* Harrison, 2 Mad. 268 109
Norton *v.* Johnstone, 30 Ch. D. 649; 34 W. R. 13; 55 L. J. Ch. 222   41, 152, 164
Nottingham Brick and Tile Co. *v.* Butler, 16 Q. B. D. 778; 34 W. R. 405; 55 L. J. Q. B. 280; 54 L. T. 444 47

Oceanic Steam Navigation Co. *v.* Sutherberry, 16 Ch. D. 236; 29 W. R. 113; 50 L. J. Ch. 308; 43 L. T. 743 46
Ord *v.* Noel, 5 Mad. 438 45

Paget's Settled Estates, *Re*, 30 Ch. D. 161; 33 W. R. 898; 55 L. J. Ch. 42; 53 L. T. 90 . . . . 150, 163
Parker *v.* Taswell, 2 De G. & J. 559; 6 W. R. 608; 4 Jur. N. S. 183 . 65
—— *v.* Whyte, 1 H. & M. 167; 11 W. R. 683; 32 L. J. Ch. 520; 8 L. T. 446; 2 N. R. 157 47
Parry, *Re*, W. N. 1884, 43 . . . . . . 163, 203
Pfleger, *Re*, L. R. 6 Eq. 426 123
Phillips' Trusts, *Re*, L. R. 6 Eq. 250. 123
Pollock *v.* Lands Improvement Co., 37 Ch. D. 661; 36 W. R. 617; 57 L. J. Ch. 853; 58 L. T. 374 118
Poole *v.* Shergold, 1 Bro. C. C. 118 70
Poole's Settled Estates, *Re*, 32 W. R. 956; 50 L. T. 585 . . 22, 156
Potter, *Re*, W. N. 1889, 69 131
Poulett (Earl) *v.* Hood, L. R. 5 Eq. 115; 16 W. R. 323; 37 L. J. Ch. 224; 17 L. T. 486 83
Powell, *Re*, W. N. 1884, 67 . . . . . . 168, 177
Powys *v.* Blagrave, 4 De G. M. & G. 448; 2 W. R. 700; 18 Jur. 462; 2 Eq. Rep. 395 108
Price, *Re*, 27 Ch. D. 552; 32 W. R. 1009; 51 L. T. 497 . . 168, 206

Radnor's (Earl of), Will Trusts, 45 Ch. D. 402; 59 L. J. Ch. 782; 63 L. T. 191; 6 T. L. R. 480 129
Ranelagh's (Lord) Will, *Re*, 26 Ch. D. 590; 32 W. R. 714; 53 L. J. Ch. 689; 51 L. T. 87 123
Rawlin's Settled Estates, *Re*, L. R. 1 Eq. 286; 14 W. R. 218; 13 L. T. 626   53
Ray's Settled Estates, *Re*, 25 Ch. D. 464; 32 W. R. 458; 53 L. J. Ch. 205; 50 L. T. 80 . . . . 139, 172

TABLE OF CASES.

	PAGE
Read v. Shaw, Sug. on Powers, 953	46
Rede v. Oakes, 4 De G. J. & S. 505; 13 W. R. 303; 34 L. J. Ch. 145; 11 L. T. 549; 10 Jur. N. S. 1246	46
Ren v. Bulkeley, Dougl. 292	148
Renals v. Cowlishaw, 11 Ch. D. 866; 28 W. R. 9; 48 L. J. Ch. 830; 41 L. T. 116	48
Reveley, *Re*, 11 W. R. 744; 32 L. J. Ch. 812; 8 L. T. 450	59
Rex v. Knollys, 1 Lord Raym. 10	127
Reynolds, *Re*, 3 Ch. D. 61; 24 W. R. 991	90
Rich v. Cullen, Strange, 1142	36
Ricketts v. Bell, 1 De G. & S. 335; 11 Jur. 918	117
Ridge, *Re*, 31 Ch. D. 504; 34 W. R. 159; 55 L. J. Ch. 265; 54 L. T. 549	61, 62, 176, 177
Rivett-Carnac's Will, *Re*, 30 Ch. D. 136; 33 W. R. 837; 54 L. J. Ch. 1074; 53 L. T. 81	5, 36, 126, 127, 161
Roe v. Davis, 7 East, 363	53
— v. York (Archbishop of), 6 East, 86	52
Round v. Turner, 60 L. T. 379	91
Row, *Re*, L. R. 17 Eq. 30; 43 L. J. Ch. 347; 19 L. T. 824	90
Rowbotham v. Wilson, 8 H. L. Cas. 348; 8 El. and B. 123; 30 L. J. Q. B. 49; 2 L. T. 642	75
Rudd, *Re*, W. N. 1887, 251	90, 142
Rutland's (Duke of) Settlement, *Re*, 31 W. R. 947; 49 L. T. 196	118
Sabin's Settled Estates, *Re*, 30 S. J. 62	55
St. Katharine (Hospital of), *Re*, 17 Ch. D. 378; 29 W. R. 495; 44 L. T. 52	120
Salaman v. Glover, L. R. 20 Eq. 444; 23 W. R. 772; 44 L. J. Ch. 551; 32 L. T. 792	117
Scarth, *Re*, 10 Ch. D. 499; 27 W. R. 499; 40 L. T. 184	62
Seagram v. Knight, L. R. 2 Ch. 628; 15 W. R. 1152; 36 L. J. Ch. 918; 17 L. T. 47	109, 124
Searle v. Cooke, 43 Ch. D. 519; 37 W. R. 730; 59 L. J. Ch. 259; 62 L. T. 211	195
Sebright v. Thornton, 29 S. J. 682	153
Sebright's Settled Estates, *Re*, 33 Ch. D. 429; 35 W. R. 49; 56 L. J. Ch. 169; 55 L. T. 570	18, 33, 70, 81, 148
Selwyn v. Garfit, 38 Ch. D. 273; 36 W. R. 513; 57 L. J. Ch. 609; 59 L. T. 233	51
Seymour v. Vernon, 16 Jur. 189	109
Shannon v. Bradstreet, 1 Sch. & Lef. 52	117
Shipton (Rector of), *Ex parte*, 19 W. R. 549	120
Shipway v. Ball, 16 Ch. D. 376; 29 W. R. 302; 50 L. J. Ch. 263; 44 L. T. 49	170
Shrewsbury v. Shrewsbury, 18 Jur. 397	116
Simpson v. Bathurst, L. R. 5 Ch. 193; 18 W. R. 772; 23 L. T. 29	148
Skingley, *Re*, 3 M. & G. 221; 15 Jur. 958	108
Smith, *Re*, 40 Ch. D. 386; 37 W. R. 199; 58 L. J. Ch. 108; 60 L. T. 77	90, 118

Speight v. Gaunt, 9 App. Cas. 1 ; 32 W. R. 435 ; 53 L. J. Ch. 419 ; 50 L. T. 330	135
Spencer v. Scurr, 31 Beav. 334 ; 10 W. R. 878 ; 31 L. J. Ch. 808	61
Spicer v. Martin, 14 App. Cas. 12 ; 37 W. R. 689 ; 58 L. J. Ch. 309 ; 60 L. T. 546	47
Stafford's Charity, *Re*, 57 L. T. 846	120
Stamford's (Lord) Estate, *Re*, 56 L. T. 484	93, 121, 152
—— (Lord) Settled Estates, *Re*, 43 Ch. D. 84 ; 38 W. R. 317 ; 58 L. J. Ch. 849 ; 61 L. T. 504 . 30, 39, 48, 80, 89, 91, 97, 137, 142, 152	
Stanford v. Roberts, L. R. 6 Ch. 307 ; 19 W. R. 552	82
—— v. ——, 52 L. J. Ch. 50	126
Stiles v. Cowper, 3 Atk. 692	117
Stoneley's Will, *Re*, 27 S. J. 554	131
Strangways, *Re*, 34 Ch. D. 423 ; 35 W. R. 83 ; 56 L. J. Ch. 195 ; 55 L. T. 714	33, 142, 152, 163
Stranks v. St. John, L. R. 2 C. P. 376 ; 15 W. R. 678 ; 36 L. J. C. P. 118 ; 18 L. T. 283	65
Strelley v. Pearson, 15 Ch. D. 113 ; 28 W. R. 752 ; 49 L. J. Ch. 406 ; 43 L. T. 155	58
Styant v. Staker, 2 Vern. 250	48
Sudeley's (Lord) Settled Estates, *Re*, 37 Ch. D. 123 ; 36 W. R. 162 ; 57 L. J. Ch. 182 ; 58 L. T. 7	87, 109, 137, 188
Sutton v. Sutton, 22 Ch. D. 511 ; 31 W. R. 369 ; 52 L. J. Ch. 333 ; 48 L. T. 95	121
Swain v. Ayres, 21 Q. B. D. 289 ; 36 W. R. 798 ; 57 L. J. Q. B. 428	52, 116
Taylor, *Re*, 31 W. R. 596	131, 140, 172, 204
—— v. Poncia, 25 Ch. D. 646 ; 32 W. R. 335 ; 53 L. J. Ch. 409 ; 50 L. T. 20	157, 175, 176, 183
—— v. Sparrow, 4 Giff. 703 ; 9 L. T. 438 ; 7 Jur. N. S. 1226	82
—— v. Stibbert, 2 Ves. jun. 437	65
Tempest v. Lord Camoys, 21 Ch. D. 571 ; 31 W. R. 326 ; 51 L. J. Ch. 785 ; 48 L. T. 13	39, 121
Tennant, *Re*, 40 Ch. D. 594 ; 37 W. R. 542 ; 58 L. J. Ch. 457 ; 60 L. T. 488	29, 122
Thomas v. Sylvester, L. R. 8 Q. B. 368 ; 29 L. T. 290	195
—— v. Williams, 24 Ch. D. 558 ; 31 W. R. 943 ; 52 L. J. Ch. 603 ; 49 L. T. 111	40, 152
Thompson's Will, *Re*, 21 L. R. Ir. 109	70, 71, 150
Thomson v. Eastwood, 2 App. Cas. 215	154
Tolson v. Sheard, 5 Ch. D. 19 ; 25 W. R. 667 ; 46 L. J. Ch. 815 ; 36 L. T. 756	46, 77
Tooker v. Annesley, 5 Sim. 235	124
Townley v. Bedwell, 6 Ves. 194	73
Truscott v. Diamond Rock Boring Co., 20 Ch. D. 251 ; 30 W. R. 277 ; 51 L. J. Ch. 259 ; 46 L. T. 7	55
Tucker v. Linger, 8 App. Cas. 508 ; 32 W. R. 40 ; 52 L. J. Ch. 941 ; 49 L. T. 373	37
Tulk v. Moxhay, 2 Ph. 774 ; 18 L. J. Ch. 83 ; 13 Jur. 89	74

	PAGE
Twyford Abbey Settled Estates, *Re*, 30 W. R. 268. Sub nom. *Re* Willan's Settled Estates, 45 L. T. 745	126
VERSCHOYLE, *Ex parte*, 15 L. R. Ir. 576	118, 120
Versturme *v.* Gardiner, 17 Beav. 338	155
Viner *v.* Vaughan, 2 Beav. 466	37, 61
WADE *v.* Wilson, 33 W. R. 610; 54 L. J. Ch. 782	140, 170
Waldo *v.* Waldo, 12 Sim. 107	124
Walker's Trusts, *Re*, 31 W. R. 716; 48 L. T. 632	131
Walsh *v.* Lonsdale, 21 Ch. D. 9; 31 W. R. 106; 52 L. J. Ch. 2; 47 L. T. 379	52, 116
Warburton *v.* Farn, 16 Sim. 625	148
Warner's Settled Estates, *Re*, 17 Ch. D. 711; 29 W. R. 726; 50 L. J. Ch. 542; 45 L. T. 37	82
Warwicker *v.* Bretnall, 23 Ch. D. 188; 31 W. R. 520	109
Weld, *Re*, 28 Ch. D. 514; 33 W. R. 845; 52 L. T. 703	77
Wells, *Re*, 31 W. R. 764; 48 L. T. 859	36, 166
West *v.* Berney, 1 R. & My. 431	148
Western *v.* Macdermott, L. R. 2 Ch. 72; 15 W. R. 265; 36 L. J. Ch. 76; 15 L. T. 641	47
Wheelwright *v.* Walker, 23 Ch. D. 752; 31 W. R. 363; 52 L. J. Ch. 274; 48 L. T. 70	28, 34, 39, 40, 131
Whistler, *Re*, 35 Ch. D. 561; 35 W. R. 662; 56 L. J. Ch. 827; 57 L. T. 77	157
Whitfield *v.* Bewit, 2 P. Wms. 242	61
Whitham *v.* Kershaw, 16 Q. B. D. 613; 34 W. R. 340; 54 L. T. 124	111
Wilcock, *Re*, 34 Ch. D. 508; 35 W. R. 450; 56 L. J. Ch. 757; 56 L. T. 629	130
Wilke's Estate, *Re*, 16 Ch. D. 597; 50 L. J. Ch. 199	123
Wilkinson, *Ex parte*, 3 De G. & Sm. 633; 19 L. J. Ch. 257; 14 Jur. 301	123
Williams *v.* Williams, 9 W. R. 888	163
Wilson, *Re*, 34 W. R. 512; 54 L. T. 600	157
—— *v.* Hart, L. R. 1 Ch. 463; 14 W. R. 748; 35 L. J. Ch. 569; 14 L. T. 499; 12 Jur. N. S. 460	47
Wilson's Estate, *Re*, 11 W. R. 712; 8 L. T. 413	120
Wood's Estate, *Re*, L. R. 10 Eq. 572; 19 W. R. 59; 40 L. J. Ch. 59; 23 L. T. 430	123
Woodhouse *v.* Walker, 5 Q. B. D. 404; 28 W. R. 765; 49 L. J. Q. B. 609; 42 L. T. 770	108, 111
Wootton's Estate, *Re*, L. R. 1 Eq. 589; 14 W. R. 469; 35 L. J. Ch. 305; 14 L. T. 125	123
Wortham *v.* Mackinnon, 4 Sim. 485; 8 Bing. 564	96
Wright *v.* Robotham, 33 Ch. D. 106; 34 W. R. 668; 55 L. J. Ch. 791; 55 L. T. 241	82
—— *v.* Smith, 5 Esp. 203	52, 68
Wright's Trusts, *Re*, 24 Ch. D. 662; 53 L. J. Ch. 139	90, 118
YELLOWLY *v.* Gower, 11 Exch. 274; 24 L. J. Ex. 289	193

TABLE OF STATUTES.

	PAGE
34 & 35 Hen. VIII. c. 20 (Crown lands)	161
3 & 4 Anne, c. 6 (Marlborough Estates)	161
5 Anne, c. 3 (Marlborough Estates)	161
20 Geo. II. c. 42 (England and Wales)	48, 94
42 Geo. III. c. 116, s. 22 (Redemption of Land Tax)	88
46 Geo. III. c. 146 (Nelson Estates)	161
53 Geo. III. c. 134 (Nelson Estates)	161
55 Geo. III. c. 96 (Nelson Estates)	161
c. 186 (Wellington Estates)	161
11 Geo. IV. & 1 Will. IV. c. 65 (Leases of Infants' Land)	65
3 & 4 Will. IV. c. 42, ss. 2, 3 (Action against Executors for injury to property)	111
c. 74, s. 1 (Fines and Recoveries Act)	162
ss. 15, 41	50, 161
s. 18	161
ss. 19, 35	162
s. 34	162
ss. 40, 47	117
4 & 5 Will. IV. c. 92, s. 16 (Fines and Recoveries, Ireland)	162
6 & 7 Will. IV. c. 71 (Tithe rent-charge)	88
2 & 3 Vict. c. 4 (Wellington Estates)	161
c. 11, s. 7 (Lis pendens)	185
8 Vict. c. 18 (Land Clauses Consol. Act)	118
s. 74	122
s. 80	120
8 & 9 Vict. c. 106, s. 9 (Amendment of the Law of Real Property)	67
9 & 10 Vict. c. 73 (Tithe rent-charge)	88
c. 101 (Public Money Drainage Act)	86
12 & 13 Vict. c. 26 (Defective Leases)	52, 65, 66
13 & 14 Vict. c. 17 (Defective Leases)	52, 66
15 & 16 Vict. c. 51, s. 31 (Copyholds)	76
16 & 17 Vict. c. 117, s. 1 (Redemption of Land Tax)	88
18 & 19 Vict. c. 15, s. 3 (Lis pendens)	186
c. 43 (Infants' Settlements)	168
22 & 23 Vict. c. 35, ss. 14, 16 (Lord St. Leonards' Act)	157
s. 30	158
s. 31	134
23 & 24 Vict. c. 83 (Infants' Settlements, Ireland)	168
c. 93 (Tithe rent-charge)	88

TABLE OF STATUTES.

	PAGE
23 & 24 Vict. c. 106 (Lands Clauses Act)	118
c. 145 (Lord Cranworth's Act)	178, 181
s. 2	154
s. 4	97
ss. 8, 9	178
25 & 26 Vict. c. 108 (Confirmation of Sales Act)	74
27 & 28 Vict. c. 114 (Improvement of Land Act)	86, 112, 145, 178, 181
ss. 8, 9, 11, 15, 49, 51, 53	113
s. 9	100, 106
s. 12	100
s. 25	106
s. 34	112
ss. 72—76	109
s. 75	110
32 & 33 Vict. c. 18 (Lands Clauses Act)	118
33 & 34 Vict. c. 44 (Stamps on Leases)	56
c. 56 (Limited Owners' Residences)	102, 113
c. 97, s. 94 (Stamp Act)	43
s. 98	56, 67
34 & 35 Vict. c. 84 (Limited Owners' Residences)	102, 113
38 & 39 Vict. c. 55, s. 31 (Public Health Act)	114
c. 77, s. 10 (Judicature Act, 1875)	110
c. 83, s. 27 (Local Loans)	86
40 & 41 Vict. c. 18 (Settled Estates Act)	21, 118
s. 2	28
s. 4	21, 50, 60, 61
s. 7	67
s. 9	68
s. 17	21, 125, 178, 181
s. 20	72
s. 21	21
s. 23	149
s. 37	122
s. 40	21
s. 46	21, 50, 170
s. 55	161
c. 31 (Waterworks)	114
c. 56 (County Officers and Courts Act, Ireland)	179
c. 57 (Judicature Act, Ireland)	179
41 & 42 Vict. c. 42 (Tithe rent-charge)	88
44 & 45 Vict. c. 41, s. 3 (Conveyancing Act, 1881)	54, 63
s. 5	17
s. 9	82
s. 10	62
s. 12	67
s. 18	50, 159
s. 31	130, 200
s. 32	132
s. 41	166
s. 42	97

			PAGE
44 & 45 Vict. c. 41, s. 44			60, 63, 194
	s. 45		88
	s. 52		148
	s. 62		80
	c. 49 (Land Law, Ireland)		179
45 & 46 Vict. c. 39, s. 4 (Conveyancing Act, 1882)			117
	s. 7		171
	c. 75 (Married Women's Property)		170
46 & 47 Vict. c. 52, s. 44 (Bankruptcy)			148
	c. 61, s. 29 (Agricultural Holdings)		89, 101
	s. 43		53
48 & 49 Vict. c. 72, s. 11 (Housing of Working Classes)			102, 201
	c. 73, ss. 5, 6 (Purchase of Land, Ireland)		180
50 & 51 Vict. c. 33, s. 14 (Land Law, Ireland)			180
51 & 52 Vict. c. 20, s. 8 (Glebe Lands)			41
	c. 42, s. 6 (Mortmain and Charitable Uses)		73
	c. 43, s. 56 (County Courts)		110
	s. 67		142
	s. 68		143
	s. 116		111
	c. 51 (Land Charges and Registration)		202
	c. 59, s. 2 (Trustee Act, 1888)		135
	s. 8		153
	ss. 10, 11		178
52 & 53 Vict. c. 30 (Board of Agriculture)			12, 88, 104, 107, 146
	c. 32, s. 3 (Trust Investment)		15, 85, 86
	c. 47, s. 10 (Durham)		11, 38, 142
53 & 54 Vict. c. 5, s. 116 (Lunacy Act, 1890)			171
	s. 120		65, 77, 171
	s. 128		172
	s. 341		77
	c. 44, s. 5 (Judicature Act, 1890)		120
	c. 70, s. 74 (Housing of Working Classes)		46, 53, 102, 201

THE LAW AND PRACTICE

UNDER THE

SETTLED LAND ACTS, 1882 TO 1890.

INTRODUCTORY CHAPTER.

1. Scheme of the Acts.
2. Settled Land.
3. Powers of Tenant for Life.
4. Checks for security of Remainderman.
5. Trustees of the Settlement.
6. The Court.
7. The Board of Agriculture.
8. Capital money arising under the Act.
9. Investment and application of Capital money.
10. Position of a Purchaser under the Act.
11. Incumbrances.
12. Limited Owners who may exercise the powers.
13. Effect upon existing Settlements.
14. Effect upon the Settled Estates Act.
15. Exclusion of the Act.

1.—*Scheme of the Acts.*

THE general scheme of the Settled Land Act, 1882, which came into operation on the 1st January, 1883, may be briefly described as follows :— *General scheme of Act of 1882.*

Whenever any estate or interest in land forms the subject of a Settlement (s. 2), the tenant for life or other limited owner entitled in possession (s. 58), may exercise the powers of sale, leasing, &c., conferred by the Act. These powers are made an incident of his estate, and cannot be assigned or released; any contract not to exercise them is declared to be void; and he is elaborately protected against any provision in the settlement inconsistent with the full and free exercise of the statutory powers (ss. 50—52).

While the tenant for life is thus endowed with the widest discretion as to the disposition of the property, he cannot (except by collusion with the trustees, or a purchaser) reap any personal benefit to the prejudice of the remaindermen. For the tenant for life is bound to give notice to the trustees of the settlement of any intended exercise by him of his statutory powers (s. 45), and whenever capital money arises under the Act, it must be paid either to the trustees, or into court (s. 22). This constitutes an effective check upon actual misappropriation, and it will be found that precautions are also taken to guard against improvident investment.

The capital money may be invested or applied, according to the direction of the tenant for life, in any of the modes of investment authorized by s. 21; and if the trustees disapprove of the investment, they may apply to the Court for directions under s. 44.

A novel feature in this Act is the application of capital money for the improvement of the estate (s. 25); and adequate provision is made to prevent an expenditure upon unsuitable or unprofitable works, and also to secure their proper execution (s. 26), as well as their maintenance, repair and insurance (s. 28).

Principle of the measure.

The principle which underlies the measure, and furnishes the key to its provisions is, that the tenant for life is to be regarded as the person most interested in the welfare of the estate; and that, subject to the necessary restrictions, he is to be trusted with the powers of an absolute owner.

It is, in fact, the most emphatic contradiction of the following statement, which occurs in Lord Eldon's judgment in *Mortlock* v. *Buller*, 10 Ves. 292. "The most improvident course that can be adopted is to intrust the tenant for life with the execution of such a power as this (*i.e.*, a power of sale); for it is generally the interest of the tenant for life to convert the estate absolutely into money, either with a view to sell another estate to his family, or for the ordinary purpose of getting a better income during his life." At p. 308.

The Principal Act has been amended by no less than Amendments.
four subsequent Acts, but the amendments deal rather
with points of detail than matters of principle. The Act
of 1884 (47 & 48 Vict. c. 18), made the notice required by
s. 45 of the Principal Act less burthensome to the tenant
for life by enacting that it might be "notice of a general
intention," and that the trustees might waive it if they
pleased; and this Act also modified the provisions of s. 63
as to lands settled upon trust for sale by requiring that the
tenant for life should obtain the leave of the Court before
exercising the powers conferred by the Act. The Act of
1887 (50 & 51 Vict. c. 30), was merely the legislative reversal of *Re Knatchbull's Settled Estates* (29 Ch. D. 588),
and sanctioned the expenditure of capital money in the
redemption of a terminable rentcharge created for the purpose of paying for an authorized improvement. The Act
of 1889 (52 & 53 Vict. c. 36), enacted that an option of
purchase, subject to certain limitations, might be conferred
by a building lease, and the Act of 1890 (53 & 54 Vict.
c. 69), introduced a large number of minor amendments, the
most important of which probably is that which enables
the tenant for life to raise money by mortgage in order to
pay off incumbrances (s. 11). The extension given by this
Act to the meaning of "trustees of the settlement," so
as to include trustees with a future power of sale (s. 16),
and the express application of the powers of appointing
new trustees contained in the Conveyancing and Law of
Property Act, 1881, to the case of "trustees of the settlement" (s. 17), are also enactments of very general application.

2.—*Settled Land.*

The "settled land," an expression which occurs Settled
repeatedly throughout the Act, is the land or the estate or land.
interest therein which is the subject of a settlement; and
"settlement" is defined in the most comprehensive manner
as including "any deed, will, agreement for a settlement
or other agreement, covenant to surrender, copy of Court

Roll, Act of Parliament, or other instrument, or any number of instruments" under or by virtue of which any land, or any estate or interest in land, stands for the time being limited to or in trust for any persons by way of succession.

Settlement. In the vast majority of cases the settlement is effected either by deed on the occasion of a marriage or by will. Marriage settlements of land are broadly divisible into two classes, differing not only in form, but also in the objects which they subserve.

Strict settlement. The "real" or "strict" settlement is employed only in the case of large estates, which are intended to be preserved intact from generation to generation; and in this form the limitations are legal remainders, whereby the estates go successively to the father for life, with remainder to his first and other sons in tail male; the younger children being provided with portions, which ultimately become a charge upon the estates.

Settlement by trust for sale. In the other form of settlement, which is that adopted in ordinary cases, the land is vested in trustees upon trust for sale, and the actual trusts of the settlement are declared, not of the land, but of the personal fund produced by the sale; the rents and profits in the meantime being payable to the same persons, and in the same manner as if they were income produced by that fund. All the children of the marriage, moreover, who attain twenty-one, or marry, take in equal shares, instead of the estate going as a whole to the eldest son of the marriage, as in a strict settlement. The trust for sale, it should be observed, is only introduced for facility of ultimate distribution, and to enable the draftsman to adopt the more convenient form of a "personal" settlement.

It will be found that the language of "The Settled Land Act" is pointed for the most part to strict settlements, and large estates; but express provision is made by s. 63 (a clause which was introduced at a late stage of the Bill), for the second class of settlements to which we have referred, *i.e.*, those made by way of trust for sale.

The settlements of land by will are more varied in their forms than those which are effected on marriage, depending as they do, not on any particular object to be subserved, but on the individual caprices of testators. Still, whatever may be the form, if the essential feature is present that the land is limited to or in trust for any persons by way of succession, there will be a "settlement" within the meaning of this Act.

Will.

The state of facts and the limitations of the settlement at the time of the settlement taking effect, viz. the date of the deed or the death of the testator, determine whether the land is "settled land" or not (s. 2 (4)). Derivative settlements of undivided shares are accordingly not grafted on the original settlement so as to make with it one settlement for the purposes of the Act.

Time of settlement taking effect.

"Land" is by the definition clause extended beyond its primary signification, so as to comprehend "incorporeal hereditaments, and also an undivided share in land;" and the "settled land" may thus consist not only of an estate in fee simple, but of such interests as a lease for years, a remainder or reversion, a rentcharge, or an advowson. Indeed according to one striking decision a baronetcy is "land" within the meaning of the Act. *Re Sir J. Rivett Carnac's Will*, 30 Ch. D. 136. It should, however, be observed that the greater number of the provisions of the Act are applicable solely to corporeal hereditaments.

Land.

Whenever there is a "settlement," *i.e.*, limitations "by way of succession," then the powers conferred by the Act are capable of being exercised; but the subject-matter affected by these powers is in all cases confined to the estate or interest which is actually comprised in the settlement.

For a more detailed examination of the meaning of the expressions "settlement" and "settled land," the reader is referred to the notes on s. 2, *post*, pp. 27, 29.

3.—*Powers of Tenant for Life.*

Powers of tenant for life.

The various powers of the tenant for life may be most conveniently presented in the form of a table, as follows :—

(1.) To sell, enfranchise, exchange, and make partition (s. 3).
(2.) To transfer an incumbrance from one part of the settled land to another (s. 5).
(3.) To grant building, mining, and other leases (ss. 6, 12).
(4.) To accept surrenders of leases (s. 13).
(5.) To grant licences to copyholders (s. 14).
(6.) To appropriate land for streets and open spaces (s. 16).
(7.) To raise money by mortgage for enfranchisement or for equality (s. 18), or for discharge of incumbrances (Act of 1890, s. 11).
(8.) To convey the settled land in order to complete the exercise of the powers (s. 20).
(9.) To direct the form of investment (s. 22).
(10.) To execute improvements (s. 29).
(11.) To enter into binding contracts (s. 31).
(12.) To cut timber with consent of the trustees, or under an order of the Court, even when impeachable for waste (s. 35).
(13.) To sell heirlooms under an order of the Court (s. 37).
(14.) To execute deeds and other instruments (s. 55).
(15.) To complete contracts made by a predecessor in title (Act of 1890, s. 6).

Former practice as to powers.

The greater number of these powers were formerly, as a general rule, conferred by the settlement not upon the tenant for life but upon *the trustees*, to be exercised by them with his consent; and it should be mentioned that where such powers exist, they are not affected by this Act; except that in no case can they be exercised without the consent of the tenant for life (s. 56). Several sets of powers may therefore subsist concurrently for effecting the same objects.

The tenant for life is defined by the Act as the person who is for the time being under a settlement beneficially entitled to possession of settled land for his life; and if two or more persons are so entitled concurrently, they together constitute the tenant for life. A person being tenant for life within the foregoing definitions, is to be deemed to be such notwithstanding that the settled land, or his estate or interest therein is incumbered or charged in any manner or to any extent (s. 2 (5), (6) and (7).) To the last mentioned provision is due the instructive paradox that a person may be *beneficially entitled* to settled land, though he does not, and possibly never may, reap any benefit therefrom! *Re Jones*, 26 Ch. D. 736. See further as to the tenant for life the note to s. 2, *post*, p. 30; and as to the persons entitled to exercise the powers of a tenant for life, s. 58.

4.—*Checks for Security of Remaindermen.*

Reference must now be made to the various checks which are imposed in the interest of the remaindermen upon the exercise of the foregoing powers; and they may be conveniently considered under the three heads: {Checks upon the tenant for life.}

(1.) Amount of consideration received.
(2.) Preservation of substituted property.
(3.) Special protection to particular kinds of property.

To guard against an improvident exercise of the powers, it is enacted that the best price, rent, or other consideration must be obtained on every sale, exchange, partition, or lease (ss. 4, 7). The tenant for life, moreover, is declared to be in the position, and to have the duties and liabilities of a trustee for all parties entitled under the settlement (s. 53). Notice of the intended exercise of the powers, except in the case of a lease for a term not exceeding twenty-one years (Act of 1890, s. 7), must be sent to the trustees and their solicitors (s. 45), who may apply to the Court if they are dissatisfied with the proposed action of the tenant for life (s. 44). The tenant for life is also bound, on the request of the trustees, to furnish them with all reasonable particulars and information with reference to sales, exchanges, partitions or leases effected or in progress or immediately intended (Act of 1884, s. 5 (2)). The remainderman may, if the tenant for life fails in his duty, make him or his estate liable under s. 53, as for {i. Amount of consideration.}

a breach of trust; and if he has colluded with the purchaser or lessee, the sale or lease may be set aside as fraudulent, under the general law applicable to such transactions.

ii. Preservation of property. The most effectual check imposed by the Act is, that capital money cannot be received by the tenant for life, but must always be paid either to the trustees or into Court (s. 22): and by the same section investments are to be made in the names, or under the control of the trustees. If the capital money is re-invested in land it must be made subject to the settlement in the manner provided by s. 24; and if applied in payment for "authorized improvements" (s. 25), the propriety of the application is secured by requiring a "scheme" to be approved either by the trustees, or by the Court, while the actual expenditure of the money is guaranteed by the certificate of the Board of Agriculture, which now has taken the place of the Land Commissioners, or an approved engineer or surveyor. Lastly, an obligation is imposed upon the tenant for life to maintain, repair, and insure the "improvements," during such time, and for such a sum as the Board of Agriculture shall prescribe.

iii. Special protection. The principal mansion-house, and the pleasure grounds and park and lands usually occupied therewith, cannot be sold, exchanged or leased without the consent of the trustees, or an order of the Court (Act of 1890, s. 10); and the power of the tenant for life impeachable for waste to cut and sell timber is similarly restricted (s. 35); while, to enable him to sell heirlooms, an order of the Court must in all cases be obtained (s. 37).

5.—*Trustees of the Settlement.*

Trustees of the settlement. The powers and duties of the "trustees of the settlement" form an important part of this Act, and it should be carefully borne in mind that the expression is specially defined by s. 2 (8); and that, unless the trustees fall within the terms of the definition, they are not "trustees of the settlement" within the meaning of this Act, and cannot exercise any of its powers.

The following persons are comprised in the definition:—
(1.) Trustees with a power of sale of settled land.
(2.) Trustees with a power of consent to, or approval of the exercise of such a power of sale.
(3.) The persons *declared by the settlement* to be trustees thereof for purposes of this Act.

The Act of 1890 has (s. 16) added to this list the following persons:—
(4.) The persons (if any) who are for the time being under the settlement trustees with power of or upon trust for sale of any other land comprised in the settlement and subject to the same limitations as the land to be sold, or with power of consent to or approval of the exercise of such a power of sale.
(5.) The persons (if any) who are for the time being under the settlement trustees with future power of sale, or under a future trust for sale of the land to be sold, or with power of consent to or approval of the exercise of such a future power of sale, and whether the power or trust takes effect in all events or not.

It will be observed that there may be trustees who would be commonly spoken of as "trustees of the settlement," yet who are not comprised in these definitions. The receipt of such trustees for capital money paid to them would be waste paper, and their sanction of the acts of the tenant for life completely inoperative. If moneys were invested in their names, a breach of trust would be committed, as serious in its possible consequences, as if they were strangers to the trust; and the tenant for life might, in case of loss, be called upon to refund the money. "The trustees of the settlement" are, it must be remembered, a body created by the statute, and in this respect are analogous to the protectors of a settlement under the Fines and Recoveries Act.

No step can be taken in the exercise of the powers, except in the case of leases for terms not exceeding twenty-one years (Act of 1890, s. 7), without properly constituted "trustees of the settlement." See note to s. 45, *post*.

Appointment of trustees.

If, therefore, there are no trustees of the settlement within the foregoing definitions, the first step to be taken is to apply to the Court under s. 38, for the appointment of trustees. And when appointed those trustees are "trustees of the settlement" for all purposes as if they had been included in the definition thereof in s. 2. See *Re Countess of Dudley's Contract*, 35 Ch. D. 338.

The Act of 1890, s. 17, has declared that the powers of the Conveyancing Act, 1881, with reference to the appointment of new trustees, and the discharge and retirement of trustees, are to apply to trustees for the purposes of the Settled Land Acts, 1882 to 1890, whether appointed by the Court or by the settlement, or under provisions contained in the settlement. This section is expressly retrospective without prejudice to the appointment, discharge or retirement of trustees otherwise effected.

Duties of the trustees.

The duties of the trustees of the settlement are, to exercise a general supervision over the acts of the tenant for life, and to appeal to the Court if a difference arises between him and them (s. 44); to receive capital moneys (s. 22) and invest them in their own names (s. 21), or apply them according to the direction of the tenant for life, and to see that purchased land is made properly subject to the trusts of the settlement (s. 24).

Protection of trustees.

It should be noticed that clauses are introduced to protect each individual trustee from the consequences of signing receipts for conformity, and from losses not happening through his own wilful default (s. 41); and also to indemnify the trustees as a body in respect both of what they do, and what they leave undone (s. 42). But it is difficult to say how far, in particular cases of negligence, these protecting clauses will be practically effective.

Powers of trustees.

The special powers of the trustees are:

(1.) To approve of a scheme for the execution of improvements, and to nominate a surveyor or engineer to inspect them (s. 26).
(2.) To consent to the cutting and sale of timber (s. 35), and to the alienation of the principal mansion-house and park (Act of 1890, s. 10).
(3.) To apportion, between tenant for life and remainderman, purchase money paid for a lease or reversion (s. 34).
(4.) To give receipts for capital money (s. 40).
(5.) To exercise on behalf of an infant all the powers of a tenant for life (ss. 59, 60).
(6.) To reimburse themselves, or pay and discharge out of the trust property, all expenses properly incurred (s. 43).
(7.) To exercise the powers of the tenant for life in transactions where his interest is inconsistent with the personal exercise of those powers (Act of 1890, s. 12).

6.—*The Court.*

One of the main objects of the present Act is to supersede the necessity of applying to the Court under the Settled Estates Act; yet applications to the Court form a conspicuous feature in the scheme of the present Act. These applications may be made either by petition or summons at chambers (s. 46 (3)), but by the Settled Land Act Rules, 1882 (r. 2), it is provided that if in any case a petition shall be presented without the direction of the judge no further costs shall be allowed than would be allowed upon a summons. These rules also give directions as to the persons who are to be served with notice of applications to the Court (rr. 4, 5, 6), as to the evidence to be adduced (r. 7), as to the manner in which any sale authorized or directed by the Court is to be carried into effect (r. 8); and as to the proceedings on payment of money into Court (rr. 10 to 14). Forms for use under the Act are supplied in an Appendix to the Rules.

It should be premised, that by "the Court" is meant the Chancery Division of the High Court (ss. 2, 46), and that its powers may be exercised, as to land in Lancashire and Durham respectively, by the Palatine Courts of those counties (s. 46 (8), 52 & 53 Vict. c. 47, s. 10), and to a

Interference of the Court.

limited extent by the County Courts, within their several jurisdictions, s. 46 (10).

The purposes for which application may be made to the Court are :—

<small>Applications to the Court.</small>

(1.) The variation of a building or mining lease, to suit the circumstances of the district (s. 10).
(2.) For directions as to investment of moneys in Court (ss. 22, 32).
(3.) To approve a scheme of improvement, and order payment therefor (s. 26, and Act of 1890, s. 15).
(4.) For directions as to enforcing contracts (s. 31).
(5.) As to the application of money paid for a lease or reversion (s. 34).
(6.) To sanction the cutting and sale of timber (s. 35).
(7.) To approve proceedings for protection or recovery of settled land (s. 36).
(8.) To sanction sale of heirlooms (s. 37).
(9.) For the appointment of trustees of the settlement (s. 38), or of persons to exercise powers on behalf of infant (s. 60).
(10.) To determine differences between tenant for life and trustees (s. 44), or settle questions as to conflict of powers (s. 56).
(11.) For the raising of costs, charges, and expenses (ss. 46, 47).
(12.) For leave to exercise the powers conferred by s. 63 (Act of 1884, s. 7).
(13.) To sanction the alienation of the principal mansion-house or the park or lands usually occupied therewith (Act of 1890, s. 10).
(14.) For payment out of Court of capital money to the trustees of the Settlement (Act of 1890, s. 14).
(15.) To direct or authorise payment for improvements executed without a preliminary scheme (Act of 1890, s. 15).

7.—*The Board of Agriculture.*

The Inclosure, Copyhold, and Tithe Commissioners received by this Act the new style of "the Land Commissioners," and a common seal (s. 48). The same individuals were previously commissioners for the three purposes, and used different styles and seals, according to the jurisdiction which, at the moment, they happened to be exercising. Now by 52 & 53 Vict. c. 30, a Board of Agriculture has been established, and the powers and duties of the Land

Commissioners under this and other Acts have devolved upon the new Board.

The functions which the Board may be called on to perform, for its interference is not indispensable, are—

(1.) *After* the works have been executed wholly or in part, to make a certificate as to the execution thereof, specifying the *amount* which is properly payable in respect thereof, or to approve of an engineer or surveyor to make the like certificate.

(2.) To prescribe by certificate the period during which the tenant for life is to maintain and repair the works, and the amount in which he is to insure such of them as are of an insurable nature.

(3.) To receive reports from the tenant for life, which he may be required to make, as to the state of the improvements, executed under the Act.

8.—*Capital Money arising under the Act.*

The exercise of the powers of the Act causes, in a variety of ways to be presently noticed, capital money to be substituted for the settled land, or some part thereof; and it is this facility of conversion, more than anything else, which confers upon this Act a distinctive character. Second only in importance to the large powers of the tenant for life, are the provisions relating to the capital money which takes the place of the settled land. It may be mentioned that it can never be received by the tenant for life, but must in every instance be paid to the trustees of the settlement, or into Court (s. 22), in order that it may be invested or applied in the prescribed manner. This is, as has been already stated, the chief guarantee against the abuse of the powers conferred by the Act; and it would seem in most cases to be amply sufficient for the purpose. The application of the capital money will be dealt with in the next article of this chapter; at present it

Capital money.

will be sufficient to enumerate the various sources whence capital money may arise.

The following table will be found convenient by the reader, since the provisions of the Act relating to this subject are scattered at wide intervals through a number of sections. Capital money arises under the Act in the following cases :—

Sources whence capital money arises.

(1.) Sale of the settled land or part thereof (s. 3).
(2.) Enfranchisement (s. 3).
(3.) Money paid for equality of exchange or partition (s. 3).
(4.) Fine taken on the grant of a lease (s. 7 (2), Act of 1884, s. 4).
(5.) Proportion of rent set aside under a mining lease (s. 11).
(6.) Consideration paid on surrender of lease (s. 13).
(7.) Money raised by mortgage for enfranchisement or equality of exchange on partition (s.18).
(8.) Conversion of securities in which capital money has been invested (s. 22).
(9.) Consideration paid on variation or rescission of contract (s. 31) (1) ii.
(10.) Proportion of proceeds of sale of timber set aside, where tenant for life is impeachable for waste (s. 35).
(11.) Sale of heirlooms (s. 37).
(12.) Money received under option of purchase in building lease (Act of 1889, s. 3).
(13.) <u>Money raised by mortgage for discharge of incumbrances</u> (Act of 1890, s. 11).

It may also be observed that money in Court, or in the hands of trustees, which is "liable to be laid out in the purchase of land to be made subject to the settlement," may be invested or applied as "capital money arising under the Act," ss. 32, 33.

9.—*Investment and Application of Capital Money.*

Investment of capital money.

Capital money being supposed to have arisen in some of the ways which have just been mentioned, the next point to be considered is the manner in which it is to be dealt with. Here again, as in the exercise of the powers of the Act, the tenant for life is placed in a position of authority, so far, at least, as is consistent with the interests of the remaindermen. If the money is in the hands of trustees he may direct the mode in which it is to be invested or applied. If it has been paid into Court, it can of course be dealt with only under an order, which may be obtained on the application either of the tenant for life or the trustees; but it is presumed, that in the absence of special circumstances, the Court will have regard to the wishes of the tenant for life as to the selection of authorized investments. See *Clarke* v. *Thornton*, 35 Ch. D. 307.

The twenty-first section prescribes the various modes in which capital money may be invested or applied; and these seem for the most part to fall under the three heads:— (1.) Investment in specified securities; (2.) Re-investment in land or some estate or interest in land; and (3.) Payment for authorized improvements. It may also be paid to a person absolutely entitled, or applied in payment of costs, charges, and expenses, or in any other mode specially authorized by the settlement; but the three heads above mentioned are those to which it is important to direct attention.

i. Investment.

The capital money may be invested on Government or any other securities authorized by the settlement, or by law (as to which see note to s. 21, *post*); or, railway bonds, mortgages, debentures, or debenture stock, where a dividend has, for ten years before the date of investment, been paid on the ordinary stock or shares of the company. An amendment moved in the House of Commons by Mr. Shaw Lefevre to add to this clause, the words, "or in any debentures or debenture stock, issued under the Local Loans Act, 1875," was lost on a division, and it may be incidentally mentioned that this was the only division ever taken upon the measure. "The Trust Investment Act, 1889" (52 & 53 Vict. c. 32), s. 3, specifies a large number of securities on which trustees are now authorized to invest trust moneys unless expressly forbidden to do so by the instrument creating the trust, including the nominal or inscribed stock issued by any municipal borough whose population exceeds 50,000, or by any County Council under

into Court to satisfy the charges on the land sold; but this manifestly only meets the cases in which the purchase-money is sufficiently large to cover all demands upon it.

Difficulty on the sale of a small part.
It more commonly occurs that a small part is sold, and then the redemption of the charges is out of the question. Under the 5th section of the present Act the tenant for life may, with the consent of the incumbrancer, charge the incumbrance on any other part of the settled land, whether already charged therewith or not, in exoneration of the part sold; but this transfer of the charge from the land intended to be sold to another part of the estates implies that the incumbrancer is *sui juris*, and satisfied with the security offered to him in substitution. If he is under disability, or if the incumbrance is the subject of a settlement, this arrangement cannot be carried out.

Substituted security.
There is a further provision in s. 24 (5) that land acquired by purchase may be made a substituted security for a charge from which the land sold was released "on the occasion and in order to the completion of a sale, &c." Here, also, it is clear that the owner of the charge must be able and willing to release the land. In the majority of cases the procedure indicated in s. 20 will have to be followed, viz., the conveyance must be made subject to (1) all estates, interests, and charges having priority to the settlement, and (2) all such other, if any, estates, interests, and charges, as have been conveyed or created for securing money actually raised at the date of the deed.

There is now power under the Act of 1890, s. 11, to raise money by mortgage of the settled land for the discharge of incumbrances.

Incumbrances on the life estate.
The fact that the tenant for life has assigned or incumbered his life estate does not prevent him from exercising the powers conferred by the Act (s. 50), but this section contains special provisions for the security of such assignees for value, and without their consent (except as to leases when they have not taken possession), the tenant for life cannot practically exercise the powers of the Act. See *Re Sebright's Settled Estates*, 33 Ch. D. 429.

12.—*Limited owners who may exercise the powers.*

The great body of the Act is concerned only with tenants for life, upon whom it confers, as we have already seen, extensive powers of disposition and management. These powers, however, are by s. 58 vested in other "limited owners," when their estate or interest is "in possession." It is unnecessary here to recapitulate the full list of such "persons who have the powers of a tenant for life," but it may be mentioned that it includes tenants in tail, tenants in fee simple subject to an executory limitation over, defeating their estate *in any event*, tenants for years determinable on life, tenants *pur autre vie*, and persons entitled under a trust or direction for payment of the income of land to them for certain limited periods therein mentioned. Provision is made by ss. 59—62 for the disabilities of infancy, coverture, and lunacy, and a general idea of their provisions may be gathered from the following summary.

<small>Other limited owners.</small>

Whenever an infant is entitled to land, either in fee simple or for a limited estate, the powers of the Act may be exercised on his behalf by the trustees of the settlement, or, if there are none, by persons specially appointed for the purpose by the Court.

<small>i. Infants.</small>

If a married woman is entitled for her separate use, or as her separate property, either to a life estate or to any other limited interest within the meaning of s. 58, she may, without her husband, exercise all the powers conferred by the Act. But if she is not entitled for her separate use the concurrence of her husband is requisite. It is not necessary, however, that she should acknowledge the deed by which she exercises her statutory powers.

<small>ii. Married women.</small>

Where a tenant for life or other limited owner is a lunatic so found by inquisition, the committee of his estate may, in his name and on his behalf, on obtaining an order in lunacy, exercise the powers of a tenant for life under the Act.

<small>iii. Lunatics.</small>

It must also be mentioned that when a settlement is

made by way of trust for sale, *i.e.*, where the land is vested in trustees upon trust to sell, and the trusts are declared of the proceeds of sale, the person entitled for his life, or any other limited period, to the income of the land until sale, is placed, by s. 63, in the position of a tenant for life, a position, however, which has been considerably modified by the Act of 1884, which enacts that the powers conferred by s. 63 are not to be exercised without the leave of the Court. If the quasi tenant for life obtains an order authorising him to exercise the powers, the trustees cannot thenceforward execute their trust for sale, but purchasers from them are protected unless the order has been registered as a *lis pendens.* Act of 1884, s. 7.

13.—*Effect upon existing Settlements.*

Existing settlements.

The Act applies to previously existing as well as to future settlements, and there are several points of practical importance which require special notice in connection with the former.

i. Position of trustees.

In the first place, it must be carefully observed that "the trustees of the settlement" are an artificial body created by this Act, and that the actual trustees under an existing settlement, where there is not a power of sale, are not "the trustees of the settlement," and are incapable of exercising any of its powers.

ii. Powers.

Secondly, it should be remembered, that not only are new powers conferred by this Act, but also existing powers are in some respects paralyzed. No power or trust for sale can after 1882 be exercised without the consent of the tenant for life (s. 56), unless indeed he happens to be an infant (ss. 59, 60); but if the powers of the settlement prescribe any further consents or additional conditions, they must in the exercise of those powers be strictly observed. The powers of the Act are cumulative, and the existing powers may still be exercised subject to the one limitation that the tenant for life must give his consent.

14.—*Effect upon the Settled Estates Act.*

Although the tenant for life can now do almost all that the Court could order under the Settled Estates Act (40 & 41 Vict. c. 18), yet that Act has not been repealed, except as to s. 17, which relates to proceedings being sanctioned for the protection of the estate, and which is replaced by a more extensive enactment in the present measure (s. 36).

Settled Estates Act.

There are indeed some circumstances in which it may be still desirable to apply for an order under its provisions, as for example in the following cases:

(1.) When the assignee of the tenant for life desires that the powers of the Settled Estates Act may be exercised, he may apply by petition under s. 23 of that Act. He is powerless under the present Act.

Cases in which the Settled Estates Act may still be made use of.

(2.) When a tenant for life impeachable for waste wishes to grant mining leases of *open* mines. For in such a case, under the Settled Estates Act, s. 4, only one-fourth of the rent need be set aside as capital, instead of three-fourths, as directed by s. 11 of the present Act.

(3.) If, on the dedication of part of the estate for streets, roads, squares, gardens, &c., it is desirable to raise the expenses of doing so by mortgage, application must be made to the Court under s. 21 of the Settled Estates Act, no similar power being here conferred.

(4.) Leases by a husband of his wife's fee simple estate, not settled to her separate use, and by a tenant in dower, may still require to be made under s. 46.

Lastly. It is to be remembered that by the combined effect of the Settled Estates Act, s. 40, and the Conveyancing Act, 1881, s. 70, a purchaser acquires a more perfect title than under this Act. See *Re Hall Dare's Contract*, 21 Ch. D. 41.

If an order has been obtained under the Settled Estates

Act, and it is desired to exercise the powers of this Act for any purpose included in the order, proceedings should be stayed by an order obtained on petition under the former Act: *Re Barrs-Haden's Settled Estates*, 32 W. R. 194; *Re Poole's Settled Estates*, 32 W. R. 956.

15.—*Exclusion of the Act.*

<small>Exclusion of the Act.</small>

This chapter may be concluded by a brief reference to the precautions taken for the purpose of preventing the exclusion or evasion of the Act.

<small>Two classes of restrictive provisions.</small>

The restrictive provisions which are contained in ss. 50, 51, and 52 may be divided into two classes, *i.e.*, those which prevent the tenant for life from divesting himself of his powers, and those which render abortive any attempt on the part of the settlor to exclude the Act. Under the former head are included the following provisions:

(1.) The powers are expressly declared to be incapable of assignment or release.

(2.) They do not pass to an assignee of a tenant for life by an assignment of his estate or interest under the settlement.

(3.) A contract by a tenant for life not to exercise the powers is void.

Notwithstanding any assignment or contract, the tenant for life may continue to exercise his powers, but in doing so, the assignee's rights are not to be affected without his consent. The practical result of which will be that, in every case (except the grant of leases), the assignee must concur with the tenant for life in executing the provisions of the Act.

In the second class of restrictive provisions, viz., those which control the caprices of settlors and testators, we find that

(1.) Any direct prohibition "by way of direction, declaration, or otherwise;"

(2.) Any limitation, gift, or disposition over of the settled land;

(3.) Any limitation, gift, or disposition of other property; and

(4.) The imposition of any condition or of any clause of forfeiture,

are declared to be void " so far as they purport or attempt, or tend, or are intended to have, or would or might have, the effect of prohibiting or preventing the tenant for life from exercising, or of inducing him to abstain from exercising, or of putting him in a position inconsistent with his exercising any power under the Act."

These provisions seem to have carried out effectively the object with which they were framed.

THE SETTLED LAND ACT, 1882.

CHAPTER XXXVIII.

An Act for facilitating Sales, Leases, and other dispositions of Settled Land, and for promoting the execution of Improvements thereon. [10th August, 1882.]

BE it enacted by the Queen's most Excellent Majesty, by and with the advice and consent of the Lords Spiritual and Temporal, and Commons, in this present Parliament assembled, and by the authority of the same, as follows:

I.—PRELIMINARY.

§ 1.
Short title; commencement; extent.

1.—(1.) This Act may be cited as the Settled Land Act, 1882.

(2.) This Act, except where it is otherwise expressed, shall commence and take effect from and immediately after the thirty-first day of December one thousand eight hundred and eighty-two, which time is in this Act referred to as the commencement of this Act.

(3.) This Act does not extend to Scotland.

II.—DEFINITIONS.

§ 2.
Definition of settlement, tenant for life, &c.

2.—(1.) Any deed, will, agreement for a settlement, or other agreement, covenant to surrender, copy of court roll, Act of Parliament, or other instrument, or any number of instruments, whether made or passed before or after, or partly before and partly after, the commencement of this Act, under or by virtue of which instrument or instruments any land, or any estate or interest in land, stands for the time being limited to or in trust for any persons by way of succession, creates or is for purposes of this Act a settlement, and is in this Act referred to as a settlement, or as the settlement, as the case requires.

(2.) An estate or interest in remainder or reversion not disposed of by a settlement, and reverting to the settlor or descending to the testator's heir, is for purposes of this Act an estate or interest coming to the settlor or heir under or by virtue of the settlement, and comprised in the subject of the settlement.

(3.) Land, and any estate or interest therein, which is the subject of a settlement, is for purposes of this Act settled land, and is, in relation to the settlement, referred to in this Act as the settled land.

(4.) The determination of the question whether land is settled land, for purposes of this Act, or not, is governed by the state of facts, and the limitations of the settlement, at the time of the settlement taking effect.

(5.) The person who is for the time being, under a settlement, beneficially entitled to possession of settled land, for his life, is for purposes of this Act the tenant for life of that land, and the tenant for life under that settlement.

(6.) If, in any case, there are two or more persons so entitled as tenants in common, or as joint tenants, or for other concurrent estates or interests, they together constitute the tenant for life for purposes of this Act.

(7.) A person being tenant for life within the foregoing definitions shall be deemed to be such notwithstanding that, under the settlement or otherwise, the settled land, or his estate or interest therein, is incumbered or charged in any manner or to any extent.

(8.) The persons, if any, who are for the time being, under a settlement, trustees with power of sale of settled land, or with power of consent to or approval of the exercise of such a power of sale, or if under a settlement there are no such trustees, then the persons, if any, for the time

§ 2.   being, who are by the settlement declared to be trustees thereof for purposes of this Act, are for purposes of this Act trustees of the settlement.

(9.) Capital money arising under this Act, and receivable for the trusts and purposes of the settlement, is in this Act referred to as capital money arising under this Act.

(10.) In this Act—

(i.) Land includes incorporeal hereditaments, also an undivided share in land; income includes rents and profits; and possession includes receipt of income:

(ii.) Rent includes yearly or other rent, and toll, duty, royalty, or other reservation, by the acre, or the ton, or otherwise; and, in relation to rent, payment includes delivery; and fine includes premium or fore-gift, and any payment, consideration, or benefit in the nature of a fine, premium, or fore-gift:

(iii.) Building purposes include the erecting and the improving of, and the adding to, and the repairing of buildings; and a building lease is a lease for any building purposes or purposes connected therewith:

(iv.) Mines and minerals mean mines and minerals whether already opened or in work or not, and include all minerals and substances in, on, or under the land, obtainable by underground or by surface working; and mining purposes include the sinking and searching for, winning, working, getting, making merchantable, smelting or otherwise converting or working for the purposes of any manufacture, carrying away, and disposing of mines and minerals, in or under the settled land, or any other land, and the erection of buildings, and the execution of engineering and other works, suitable for those purposes; and a mining lease is a lease for any mining purposes or purposes connected therewith, and includes a grant or licence for any mining purposes:

(v.) Manor includes lordship, and reputed manor or lordship:

(vi.) Steward includes deputy steward, or other proper officer, of a manor:

(vii.) Will includes codicil, and other testamentary instrument, and a writing in the nature of a will:

(viii.) Securities include stocks, funds, and shares:

(ix.) Her Majesty's High Court of Justice is referred to as the Court:

(x.) The Land Commissioners for England as constituted by this Act are referred to as the Land Commissioners:

(xi.) Person includes corporation.

§ 2.

The definitions in this section of "settlement," "settled land," "tenant for life," and "trustees of the settlement," are of more than ordinary importance, since the whole scope and operation of the Act hinge upon the meanings given to these expressions.

Sect. 2. Definitions.

The tenant for life, who is the donee of the very extensive statutory powers, is defined by reference to the "settled land," which is again itself defined as the subject of a "settlement." It becomes, then, extremely important to ascertain what settlements are comprised in this definition.

SETTLEMENT.

The definition of "Settlement" contained in this section has been amended by s. 4 of the Act of 1890, which is in the following terms:—

Sub-s. 1. "Settlement."

4.—(1.) Every instrument whereby a tenant for life, in consideration of marriage or as part or by way of any family arrangement, not being a security for payment of money advanced, makes an assignment of or creates a charge upon his estate or interest under the settlement, is to be deemed one of the instruments creating the settlement, and not an instrument vesting in any person any right as assignee for value within the meaning or operation of section fifty of the Act of 1882.

Instrument in consideration of marriage, &c., to be part of the settlement.

(2.) This section is to apply and have effect with respect to every

45 & 46 Vict. c. 38.

§ 2.

Derivative settlement.

disposition before as well as after the passing of this Act, unless inconsistent with the nature or terms of the disposition.

A derivative settlement of a reversionary interest expectant on the death of the tenant for life under the original settlement is not part of the settlement under the Act: *Re Knowles' Settled Estates*, 27 Ch. D. 707. See, however, *Wheelwright* v. *Walker*, 23 Ch. D. 752, at p. 759.

An estate was settled by deed to the use of A. for life, with remainder to the use of his eldest son for life, with divers remainders over. A., by his will, devised real estate to the trustees of the settlement to the uses thereby declared, and he bequeathed the residue of his personal estate to his executors upon trust to invest the same in the purchase of real estate, and directed them to settle such real estate to the uses therein declared concerning his real estate thereinbefore devised. North, J., felt great doubt as to whether, as regards the personal estate, the settlement and will constituted only one settlement, and directed that the opinion of the Court of Appeal should be taken on the point: *Re Mundy's Settled Estates*, 63 L. T. 311 (*a*).

It will be found that, setting aside verbal differences, the definition of "settlement" here given differs from that in the Settled Estates Act, 1877 (40 & 41 Vict. c. 18), s. 2, in the following particulars:—

(1.) The words "for the time being" do not occur in the definition in the Settled Estates Act.

(2.) The concluding words of that definition, "including any such instruments affecting the estates of any one or more of such persons exclusively," are here omitted, presumably with reference to the provisions of s. 50, *post*, p. 146.

The words "limited to or in trust for any person by way of succession" are common to both definitions, and, accordingly, the cases which have been decided upon these words in the Settled Estates Act, throw some light upon the construction of the same words occurring in this Act.

What is a succession.

Alternative gifts in fee do not satisfy the words "by way of succession:" *Re Clark*, L. R. 1 Ch. 292; but it is probable that s. 58, sub-s. (1), ii., *post*, would be held to apply to such a case. If the estate in possession belongs to an infant the powers of the Act may be exercised whether the land is "settled" or not: see ss. 59 and 60, *post*, p. 166. A devise to a class, with benefit of survivorship, seems to be sufficient to create a "succession:" *Re Goodwin's S. E.*, 3 Giff. 620; *Re Horn's S. E.*, 29 L. T. Rep. 830; *Collett* v. *Collett*, L. R. 2 Eq. 203. See, however, *Re Burden's Will*, 5 Jur. N. S. 1378.

There may be a "succession" although the successor is an unascertained person, as for example the heir-at-law of the tenant for life: *Beioley* v. *Carter*, L. R. 4 Ch. 230.

(*a*) Since reported on Appeal, 35 S. J. 191.

The words "for the time being" occurring in this definition show that the settlement must be a subsisting one at the date of the exercise of the powers. Where, however, a sum of money was bequeathed to trustees upon trust to lay it out in the purchase of land to be settled in strict settlement, it was held that the trustees might, before any land had been purchased, invest the money in debenture stock, in pursuance of the powers conferred by the Act : *Re Mackenzie's Trusts*, 23 Ch. D. 750. This decision, which was followed by North, J., in *Re Tennant*, 40 Ch. D. 594, proceeded on the ground that "it is absurd to suppose that that could not be done at once which a tenant for life could without question do after an estate had been purchased, by selling the estate and investing the moneys arising from the sale as asked for by the petition." The correctness of these decisions has since been questioned by North, J., and trustees should therefore—pending the decision of the Court of Appeal—decline to act upon them without the express sanction of the Court in the particular case. See *Re Mundy's Settled Estates*, 63 L. T. 311 (*b*).

§ 2. "For the time being."

This sub-section seems to be intended to meet the case of remote outstanding interests, and has no application where there is no settlement, *i.e.*, a limitation by way of succession, independently of the remainder or reversion. To put a simple case, a testator devises an estate to A. for life, and dies intestate as to the reversion in fee. After the death of the testator this is not a settled estate, and A. cannot exercise the powers of the Act, because the will did not limit the estate to any persons by way of succession, and was not therefore a "settlement" which failed to dispose of the reversion. It may, however, be urged that, although not strictly included in the words of the clause, the case which has been supposed is so manifestly within the purview of the Act, that the "general intention" ought to be allowed to prevail.

Sub-s. 2. Remainder or reversion.

SETTLED LAND.

"Settled land" is an expression which constantly occurs throughout the Act, and it is of paramount importance to understand its precise meaning. If the fee simple is settled, the "settled land" comprises the fee; but if only a partial interest, as a term of years, or a mortgage, is comprised in the settlement, then only that particular interest will be included in the expression.

Sub-s. 3. Settled land.

Two or more estates settled by the same instrument constitute together the "settled land," if the limitations are identical; and money arising from the sale of one of such estates may be expended in authorised "improvements" upon any of the others. The limi-

---

(*b*) Since the above was written the Court of Appeal has held that the earlier cases were correctly decided. 35 S. J. 191.

§ 2.

**Sub-s. 4.
Determination of what is settled land.**

**Sub-s. 5.
Tenant for life.**

tations will for this purpose be treated as identical, even if one of the estates is by the settlement subjected to a charge from which the others are exempt, and a term of years for the purpose of securing it is interposed in the limitations immediately after the first estate for life: *Re Lord Stamford's Settled Estates*, 43 Ch. D. 84. In *Re Houghton Estate*, 30 Ch. D. 102, an order was made that the proceeds of sale of one estate should be applied in improving another, although they were settled by different instruments, and one estate was vested in trustees upon trust for sale, while the other was the subject of legal limitations.

Although the question whether land is "settled land" for the purposes of the Act is by sub-s. 4 to be determined at the time when the settlement takes effect, yet it is clear that the land must also be settled at the time when the powers are exercised.

In order that two estates may be considered as the "settled land," the subject of a single settlement, the limitations must be identical when the settlement takes effect. It not unfrequently happens that, by the failure of the earlier limitations of one estate it becomes subject to the same uses as another estate devised by the same will. In such a case, however, there would seem to be no power to expend the proceeds of sale of one estate in the improvement of the other. See *Re Lord Stamford's Settled Estates*, 43 Ch. D. 84, 90.

If land is devised so that it comes to be held in undivided shares, each share being settled upon a tenant for life and remainderman, and some of the shares come by subsequent events to be held absolutely, the tenants for life of the shares remaining in settlement cannot sell those shares except by concurring in a sale of the entirety with the absolute owners of the other shares : *Re Collinge's Settled Estates*, 36 Ch. D. 516, more fully reported 36 W. R. 264.

TENANT FOR LIFE.

The extensive powers of the Act are conferred upon the tenant for life, who is here defined as "the person for the time being under a settlement beneficially entitled to possession of settled land for his life."

This definition includes both a legal tenant for life, and a person entitled to the equitable interest where, according to the doctrines of Courts of Equity, he would be entitled to be placed in the actual possession or receipt of the rents and profits of the settled land. See the definition of "possession" in sub-s. 10, i, *ante*, p. 26.

If the trustees are entitled to the actual possession of the land with powers of management, the question has been raised, but left undecided, whether the person who receives during his life the net income from the trustees is a "tenant for life" within the meaning of this definition. Nor is it necessary to decide the point ; for, if he is not a tenant for life, he has the powers of a tenant for life under s. 58 (1) (ix): *Re Jones*, 26 Ch. D. 736, when Cotton, L. J., said, "I think that s. 58 (1) (ix) was introduced to meet the very case which exists here of trustees who are not simply trustees in whom the legal estate is vested (in which case the equitable tenant for life would be entitled to possession or to receipt of the rents from the tenants) but have powers of management which necessitate their remaining in possession, that is to say, managing the estates and receiving the rents from the tenants." See also *Re Clitheroe Estate*, 31 Ch. D. 135.

§ 2.

Where land is vested in trustees upon trust to pay and apply the net rents for the benefit of A., his wife and children, or for the benefit of any one or more of such objects, A. and his wife (there being no children in existence) do not together constitute a tenant for life under this act: *Re Atkinson*, 31 Ch. D. 577.

The question whether a person is tenant for life or has the powers of a tenant for life may be determined on a summons taken out to obtain the opinion and direction of the Court under s. 56, *post*, or it may be raised on a Vendor and Purchaser Summons as in the following instructive case: Under a settlement made between a father, his two sons and trustees, an estate was conveyed to the use of the father for life, with remainder to the use of the trustees during the life of the first son, with remainder to the use of his sons successively in tail, with remainder to the use of the trustees during the life of the second son with remainders over; and it was thereby declared that the appointments of the reversionary life estates to the trustees were made upon trust to sell and pay the net proceeds to the two sons in equal shares as tenants in common. The sons also covenanted with their father and also with the trustees that they would not claim their life estates *in specie*, it being the intention of the parties that the trust for sale should be absolute and irrevocable. It was held that the two sons were after the death of their father tenants in common for life, and that they could, notwithstanding their covenants, sell the estate under the Settled Land Act: *Re Hale and Clark*, 34 W. R. 624.

This sub-section provides for the case of several persons being concurrently entitled, and consolidates them into a tenant for life for the purposes of the Act. If one of several tenants for life refuses to concur in the exercise of the powers conferred by the Act, his co-owners have no means of compelling him to join, however unreasonable his refusal may be. See *Camden v. Murray*, 16 Ch. D. 161.

Sub-s. 6. Persons jointly entitled as tenants for life.

And the tenant for life of an undivided moiety cannot sell such moiety independently of the owner of the other undivided moiety: *Re Collinge's Settled Estate*, 36 Ch. D. 516; unless, it is presumed, his moiety was alone the subject-matter of the original settlement.

§ 2. Although all the co-tenants for life must concur in the exercise of the powers conferred by the Act, the consent of one only has been by the Settled Land Act, 1884, s. 6, made sufficient to satisfy the requirements of s. 56, sub-s. (2), *post*, p. 155.

The words "so entitled" in this sub-section mean entitled as in the preceding sub-section, namely for life : *Re Atkinson*, 31 Ch. D. 577.

Sub-s. 7.
Incumbrances.

This sub-section enables the tenant for life to exercise the powers of the Act notwithstanding charges or incumbrances either on the corpus of the settled land, or on the estate of the tenant for life, and whether the latter are created by the settlement or by the tenant for life himself. Even if the incumbrances are so heavy as to exhaust the whole income of the estate, the person who according to the limitations of the settlement is entitled to the income of the land for his life is a tenant for life, or a person having the powers of a tenant for life within the meaning of the Act : *Re Jones*, 26 Ch. D. 736. In this case a testator having an estate incumbered to the extent of between £80,000 and £90,000, and producing an annual income of between £4,000 and £5,000 per annum, devised it to trustees for 2,000 years upon trust to raise two sums of £30,000 and £15,000, and subject thereto he devised the estate to the use of a second set of trustees during the life of Colonel Grey upon the trusts therein mentioned and after the death of Colonel Grey to the use of his sons successively for life with divers remainders over. The trustees of the life estate were to enter into possession and manage the property, and after paying interest on the incumbrances were to pay a certain annuity of £400 per annum, and to pay the surplus rents to Colonel Grey for life. The rents were insufficient, after payment of interest on the incumbrances, to pay the annuity of £400 per annum. There was no income, therefore, for Colonel Grey to receive, and would probably be none for many years to come. In these circumstances it was held by the Court of Appeal that Colonel Grey was a person "entitled to the income of the land" although there was no income to receive. A startling paradox which Lord Justice Lindley answered by saying that "You must not look at the rent-roll or the charges, to do which would I think be entirely contrary to the whole scope of the Act of Parliament, but you must look at the settlement which gives him his title." In the course of his judgment Lord Justice Lindley also said that "A term of years, when it is merely a security for charges, is not such an interest as prevents the person entitled to the income subject to that charge from being in possession within the meaning of s. 58." To the same effect as *Re Jones* are the subsequent cases of *Re Cooke's Settled Estates*, W. N. 1885, 177, and *Re Clitheroe Estate*, 31 Ch. D. 135.

Where, however, land was devised to trustees upon trust during a term of twenty years to accumulate the net rents and invest them in the purchase of land, and after the determination of the term of twenty years to settle the land (including what might be purchased by the trustees) to certain uses, it was held that the first tenant for life under those uses could not exercise the powers of a tenant for life, as his estate was not in possession : *Re Strangways*, 34 Ch. D. 423. Lord Justice Cotton, in the course of his judgment, distinguished the case from those which have been cited above, on the ground that there was "a disposition of the entire rent for a given period, and a postponement until the expiration of that period of any interest whatever in the tenant for life. Here," observed the Lord Justice, "treating him in popular language as future tenant for life, what could he do during twenty years? He could not say, 'Hand over the rents to me, and I will provide for the direction to accumulate.' No; there is a direction to take all the rents and apply them for a particular purpose for twenty years. His interest, therefore, is not to arise till after the twenty years, and he has no right whatever to interfere with the present income or rent of the lands."

§ 2.

As to incumbrances on the life estate, see *Re Sebright's Settled Estates*, 33 Ch. D. 429.

The Trustees of the Settlement.

The trustees of the settlement are intended to act as a check upon the tenant for life, in the exercise of those powers which more materially affect the inheritance of the estate. With the powers of leasing (ss. 6—9), accepting surrenders (s. 13), and granting licences to copyholders (s. 14), they have, in general, nothing to do beyond receiving formal notice under s. 45. The tenant for life may, in like manner, without their concurrence, transfer an incumbrance from one part of the estate to another (s. 5), and dedicate part of the settled land for streets and open spaces (s. 16). But when capital money "arises under the Act" (as to which see *ante*, p. 14), it must, if not paid into Court, be received by the trustees for the purpose of investment in accordance with the provisions of the Act (ss. 21—24). Thus, for example, when it is intended to exercise the power of sale conferred by s. 3, the trustees of the settlement are, in general, necessary parties to the transaction ; and also where money is raised for enfranchisement, or for equality of exchange or partition (s. 18), or for the discharge of incumbrances (Act of 1890, s. 11). They must also, unless their office in this particular is assumed by the Court, be consenting parties to any alienation of the principal mansion house (Act of 1890, s. 10, which repeals s. 15 of the

Sub-s. 8. Trustees of the settlement.

§ 2. principal Act), and to the sale of timber by a tenant for life impeachable for waste (s. 35).

In one of the first cases which arose under the Act, it was held that trustees who had only a power of sale on the death of the tenant for life were not trustees of the settlement within the meaning of this definition: *Wheelwright* v. *Walker*, 23 Ch. D. 752; but the Act of 1890 (53 & 54 Vict. c. 69) has altered the law as laid down in that case, and has considerably extended the comprehension of the expression "the trustees of the settlement" by the following enactment :—

Trustees for the purposes of the Act.

16. Where there are for the time being no trustees of the settlement within the meaning and for the purposes of the Act of 1882, then the following persons shall, for the purposes of the Settled Land Acts, 1882 to 1890, be trustees of the settlement; namely,

(i.) The persons (if any) who are for the time being under the settlement trustees, with power of or upon trust for sale of any other land comprised in the settlement and subject to the same limitations as the land to be sold, or with power of consent to or approval of the exercise of such a power of sale, or, if there be no such persons, then

(ii.) The persons (if any) who are for the time being under the settlement trustees with future power of sale, or under a future trust for sale of the land to be sold, or with power of consent to or approval of the exercise of such a future power of sale, and whether the power or trust takes effect in all events or not.

Trustees having a power of sale, but only with the consent of the tenant for life, are "Trustees of the Settlement" for the purposes of the Settled Land Acts (*Constable* v. *Constable*, 32 Ch. D. 233; *Re Johnstone*, 17 L. R. Ir. 172), for the Act itself by s. 56 imposes this restriction in all cases on the exercise of such a power by trustees (*Re Duke of Newcastle's Estates*, 24 Ch. D. 129), and therefore the condition expressed in the settlement does not in reality fetter the exercise of the power.

By the marriage settlements of two sisters personal property was vested in the respective trustees upon trust (in the one case expressed, in the other implied) to sell and re-invest the proceeds; and each settlement contained a covenant for the settlement of after-acquired property of the wife. Real estate subsequently descended upon the two sisters during coverture as co-heiresses in undivided moieties, and it was held that the covenant to settle after-acquired property placed the descended realty in exactly the same position as the original capital, and that the trustees were trustees of the settlement within the meaning of the Act: *Re Garnett Orme and Hargreave's Contract*, 25 Ch. D. 595.

See further as to the powers and duties of the trustees of the settlement, *ante*, p. 8; and as to the appointment of such trustees, s. 38, *post*, p. 129, and the Act of 1890, s. 17, *post*, p. 200.

It is important to remember that the ordinary trustees under a will, even if they take the legal estate, and are charged with active duties, do not, in the absence of a power of sale, possess any powers under the Act, not being "trustees of the settlement" within the meaning of this definition.

CAPITAL MONEY.

On the subject of "Capital money arising under this Act" the following references may be found convenient:— *Sub-s. 9. Capital money arising under the Act.*

(1.) Capital money may arise from a sale, enfranchisement, exchange, or partition (s. 3); from a lease where a fine is taken (s. 7, and Act of 1884, s. 4); or an option of purchase is conferred by a building lease (Act of 1889, s. 3); from a mining lease (s. 11); from the surrender of a lease (s. 13); from a mortgage to raise money for enfranchisement or for equality of exchange or partition (s. 18); or for the discharge of incumbrances (Act of 1890, s. 11); from the variation or rescission of a contract (s. 31 (1) ii.); from the sale of timber (s. 35); or of heirlooms (s. 37).

(2.) The investment and application of capital money are governed by ss. 21, 22, 23, 25, 63 (2) ii.; Act of 1887, s. 1, Act of 1890, s. 13.

(3.) Payment to the trustees or into Court is required by s. 22, and Act of 1890, s. 14.

(4.) Receipt of capital money by the trustees: see ss. 39 and 40, and

(5.) As to payment of costs thereout see s. 47.

Money in Court under the Lands Clauses Consolidation Act or other Acts of Parliament (s. 32), and money in the hands of trustees liable to be laid out in the purchase of land to be made subject to the settlement may also be invested or applied as capital money arising under the Act.

INTERPRETATION CLAUSE.

The definitions furnished by sub-s. 10 may be usefully compared with those contained in the Conveyancing Act, 1881, s. 2. *Sub-s. 10. i. Land.*

"Land," the primary meaning of which is "any ground, soil, or earth" (Co. Litt. 4 a), is here extended so as to include "incorporeal hereditaments," and an undivided share in land. Thus reversions, remainders, and other future estates, advowsons, rent-charges, ease-

§ 2.

ments, and other rights over or in relation to land, fall within the meaning of the term.

Tithes issuing out of a rectory in the City of London are incorporeal hereditaments : *Esdaile* v. *Esdaile*, 54 L. T. 637 ; and so also is a dignity which descends to the heirs general or the heirs of the body, whether the dignity does or does not concern lands or a particular place : *Re Sir J. Rivett-Carnac's Will*, 30 Ch. D. 136 ; *Re Earl of Aylesford's Settled Estates*, 32 Ch. D. 162.

The Act applies notwithstanding that the land subject to the trusts of the settlement ought to have been sold by the trustees, and has been retained by them in breach of trust : *Re Wells*, 31 W. R. 764. See *Re Durrant and Stoner*, 18 Ch. D. 106.

When an undivided share in land forms the subject of the original settlement, it constitutes the "settled land"; and the tenant for life can exercise in respect thereof all the powers conferred by the Act, either alone or concurrently with the owners of the other shares ; but if the entirety was included in the settlement and comes to be held in undivided shares, the tenant for life of one such share, the others having vested absolutely, cannot deal with his share as if it were "settled land," and is only entitled to exercise the powers expressly conferred by s. 19, *post*, p. 76 ; *Re Collinge's Settled Estates*, 36 Ch. D. 516.

ii. Rent.

"Rent," as the term is employed in this Act, is except in ss. 20 (2) ii. and 21 (ii.), the rent payable by a lessee. See as to the reservation of the "best rent" s. 7 (2), of a "peppercorn or other nominal rent" for the first five years of a building term, s. 8 (2), and as to the manner in which rent may be ascertained in a mining lease, s. 9. It is with special reference to this last case that the terms "toll, duty, and royalty" are here included in the meaning of rent ;" and they may be defined, for the purposes of this Act, in the following terms :—" Toll " is the rent payable for a way-leave, *e.g.*, a certain sum per ton for all the minerals carried over a certain road, or brought to bank from another mine through the demised premises. " Duty " is the proportion of the ore delivered to the lessor, a form of reservation not uncommon in the case of metalliferous mines. " Royalty " is a rent varying with the quantity of the minerals extracted.

iii. Building lease.
iv. Mines and minerals.

As to the meaning of "building lease," see note to s. 8, *post*, p. 55.

The actual stratum of mineral substance forms, as a general rule, part of the inheritance of the land under which it lies, *cujus est solum ejus est usque ad inferos;* but, " the mines are a distinct possession, and may be different inheritances :" *Rich* v. *Cullen*, Strange, 1142. See *Errington* v. *Metropolitan District Railway Co.*, 19 Ch. D. 559.

The importance of the distinction between mines which have been opened and those which have not, arises from the tenant for life impeachable for waste being permitted to continue the working of those which have been opened, while he commits waste by opening fresh mines, or digging new pits: *Viner* v. *Vaughan*, 2 Beav. 466, and see note to s. 11, *post*, p. 61.

§ 2.

The primary meaning of the word "mine" is an underground excavation, made for the purpose of getting minerals, but it is commonly used as including the stratum of minerals as well as the excavation made to win it: *Midland Railway Co.* v. *Haunchwood Brick and Tile Co.*, 20 Ch. D. 552. "Minerals" on the other hand, includes, as a general rule, every substance which can be got from underneath the surface of the earth for the purpose of profit: *Hext* v. *Gill*, L. R. 7 Ch. 699, where china clay was held to be included in the reservation of mines and minerals. For examples of particular substances being decided to be minerals, see *Duchess of Cleveland* v. *Meyrick*, 16 W. R. 104 (slate in a quarry): *Bell* v. *Wilson*, L. R. 1 Ch. 303 (freestone); *Midland Railway Co.* v. *Checkley*, L. R. 4 Eq. 19 ("gravel, marble, fireclay, and every species of stone, whether marble, limestone, or ironstone"); *Attorney-General* v. *Tomline*, 5 Ch. D. 750 (coprolites); *Tucker* v. *Linger*, 8 App. Cas. 508 (surface flints). *Attorney-General* v. *Welsh Granite Co.*, 35 W. R. 617 (Granite).

What are minerals.

As to the rights conferred by a mining licence, see *Carr* v. *Benson*, L. R. 3 Ch. 524.

Mining licence.

Lands and seigniories, anciently united, constitute a manor: Burton's Compendium (1023). A manor cannot exist without a Court baron, nor a Court baron without at least two free suitors: Gilbert on Tenures, vol. 2, 431. The prescriptive or customary rights, however, are not in general lost by the legal extinction of the manor, which is then said to subsist by *reputation*. A reputed manor, therefore, may arise either by the severance of the services from the demesnes, or by the right to hold a Court baron being lost: see Coke, Cop., s. 31. "Lordship" is often used as equivalent to manor, but it is more properly applied to the seigniorial rights of the lord, *i.e.*, the rents and services of the freehold tenants, without the demesnes which were formerly annexed to them. See further, Cru. Dig. vol. i. 3, 293; Scriven, p. 3, *et seq.*, 6th ed.

v. Manor, lordship.

The word "manor" occurs only in ss. 3 (ii.); 14 (1), and 20 (3).

As to the steward of a manor, who is only mentioned in ss. 14 and 20, see Scriven, p. 341, 6th ed.; and as to the deputy steward, *ibid.* p. 349.

vi. Steward.

The word "will" occurs only in the definition of "settlement," *ante*, p. 24, and in ss. 51, 63.

vii. Will.

As to "securities," see s. 21, relating to investment of capital money; s. 22 (5) under which they retain the character of land; and ss. 40, 41, as to the receipts and protection of trustees.

viii. Securities.

§ 2.

ix. The Court.

By s. 46 (8) the Court of Chancery of the County Palatine of Lancaster has concurrent jurisdiction as regards land within that county; and by s. 10 of the Palatine Court of Durham Act, 1889 (52 & 53 Vict. c. 47), the like jurisdiction is conferred upon the Palatine Court as regards lands and estates in the County Palatine of Durham. By s. 46 (10) the County Courts are likewise entrusted with a limited jurisdiction under the Act.

For the meaning of "the Court" in Ireland, see s. 65, *post*; and as to the cases in which application may or must be made to the Court, *ante*, p. 12.

x. Land Commissioners.

For the constitution of the "Land Commissioners," see s. 48, and for their powers generally under the Act, which are now vested in the Board of Agriculture, *ante*, pp. 12, 13.

III.—SALE; ENFRANCHISEMENT; EXCHANGE; PARTITION.

General Powers and Regulations.

§ 3.

Powers to tenant for life to sell, &c.

3. A tenant for life—

(i.) May sell the settled land, or any part thereof, or any easement, right, or privilege of any kind, over or in relation to the same; and

(ii.) Where the settlement comprises a manor,—may sell the seignory of any freehold land within the manor, or the freehold and inheritance of any copyhold or customary land, parcel of the manor, with or without any exception or reservation of all or any mines or minerals, or of any rights or powers relative to mining purposes, so as in every such case to effect an enfranchisement; and

(iii.) May make an exchange of the settled land, or any part thereof, for other land, including an exchange in consideration of money paid for equality of exchange; and

(iv.) Where the settlement comprises an undivided share in land, or, under the settlement, the settled land has come to be held in undivided shares,—may concur in making partition of the entirety, including a partition in consideration of money paid for equality of partition.

§ 3.

The tenant for life is placed by this section, so far as the alienation of the settled land is concerned, very nearly in the position of an absolute owner. In *Wheelwright* v. *Walker*, 23 Ch. D. 752, Pearson, J., said : " So far as I can see, there is no restriction whatever in the Act on the power of a tenant for life to sell. There is nothing that I can see in the Act to enable the Court to restrain him from selling, whether he desires to sell because he wishes to increase his income ; or whether he desires to sell from mere unwillingness to take the trouble involved in the management of landed property ; or whether he acts from worse motives, as from mere caprice or whim, or because he is desirous of doing that which he knows would be very disagreeable to those who expect to succeed him at his death. There is not so far as I can see, any power either in the Court or in trustees to interfere with his power of sale," p. 758. And again, in *Re Chaytor's Settled Estate Act*, 25 Ch. D. 651, the same learned judge said—" The Settled Land Act gives the tenant for life an absolute power to convert the settled estate into money for any purpose whatever, even for mere caprice."

Sect. 3. Power of sale.

The tenant for life, however, is in the exercise of his statutory powers placed by s. 53 in the position of a trustee for all parties entitled under the settlement, and accordingly the Court will, in this as in other cases of powers in the nature of trusts, see that the powers are not improperly or fraudulently exercised : see *Tempest* v. *Lord Camoys*, 21 Ch. D. 571 ; *Re Lord Stamford's Settled Estates*, 43 Ch. D. 84.

Tenant for life a trustee of the powers.

In *Wheelwright* v. *Walker*, *supra*, the facts were as follows :—the tenant for life was a widower upwards of seventy years of age, and the equitable reversion in fee had vested absolutely in his only child, subject only to be partially devested by the birth of other children. Before the passing of the Settled Land Act the reversioner contracted to sell her interest to the plaintiff, and very shortly after the commencement of that Act the tenant for life advertised the property for sale, whereupon the plaintiff applied for an injunction to restrain the sale. The Court, on the ground that there were no trustees of the settlement to whom notice could be given as required by the Act, granted an injunction restraining the tenant for life from selling the property or offering it for sale until proper trustees should have been appointed for the purposes of the Act, and notice given to them of the intention to sell. But in a more recent case it was held that as the purchaser had nothing whatever to do with the trustees except to pay his purchase money to them, the fact that there were no trustees at the time, or that no notice had been given to them, was not a defect of the title of the tenant for life to sell. The non-existence

§ 3. of trustees of the settlement is a defect which may be cured at any time before completion: *Hatten* v. *Russell*, 38 Ch. D. 334.

In order to induce the Court to interfere with the tenant for life in the exercise of his powers it is conceived that a case of breach of trust (having regard to s. 53) must be established against him.

Thus Bacon, V-C., refused to grant an injunction on speculative evidence of "experts" that a large increase in the value of the property might be expected owing to the construction of a railway near the property and the consequent development of its mineral wealth: *Thomas* v. *Williams*, 24 Ch. D. 558. An injunction was, however, granted in this case by the Court of Appeal pending an appeal from the judgment at the trial of the action.

The powers conferred by this Act are cumulative and are to prevail over any inconsistent provisions in the settlement (s. 56, *post*). Thus where a private estate Act gave a power of sale to the trustees, but enacted that certain specified lands should not be sold unless it should be absolutely necessary for the purposes of the Act, and in that event not until all the other settled estates had been sold, it was held that the tenant for life could make a good title to the specified lands without regard to the restrictions imposed by the Act of Parliament: *Re Chaytor's Settled Estate Act*, 25 Ch. D. 651. It is scarcely necessary to observe that a private Act which expressly limited or abrogated the powers of a tenant for life under this Act would be effectual, and would amount to a repeal of the Settled Land Act in the particular case.

Notice to trustees.

In order to impose some check on the improvident or fraudulent exercise of his powers by the tenant for life, it is provided that one month's previous notice of his intention to make a sale, exchange, partition, lease, mortgage or charge shall be given to the trustees of the settlement, and to their solicitor, if he is known to the tenant for life, s. 45, *post*, p. 138. The trustees, however, are not bound to take any action (s. 42); unless it is conceived they are cognisant of an intended fraud : see *Wheelwright* v. *Walker*, 23 Ch. D. 752, at p. 762; *Hatten* v. *Russell*, 38 Ch. D. 334. The provisions in the principal Act as to notices to the trustees seem to have been considered too stringent, and were modified by the Act of 1884 ; which enacts by s. 5 that the notice may be notice of a general intention to make a sale, exchange, partition or lease. The same section provides that the tenant for life is upon request of a trustee to furnish him with particulars and information as well in relation to past transactions as to those in progress or immediately intended. The trustee is also empowered to waive notice, or to accept less than a month's notice.

Payment of purchase money.

The most effectual safeguard provided by the Act against the abuse of its powers seems to be that capital money arising under the Act can never be received by the tenant for life, but must in all cases be paid either to the trustees of the settlement or into Court (s. 22).

§ 3.

A decree for the execution of the trusts of the settlement made before the Settled Land Act came into operation has been held to impose no restraint upon the tenant for life in the exercise of his powers: *Cardigan* v. *Curzon-Howe*, 30 Ch. D. 531, where Chitty, J., expressed an opinion that the result would have been the same if the decree had been made subsequently to the commencement of the Act. See as to the effect of an order for sale under the Settled Estates Act upon the powers of the tenant for life: *Re Barrs-Haden's Settled Estates*, 32 W. R. 194.

Incidental matters.

The power of sale may, it seems, be exercised by the tenant for life even where there is a trust to accumulate rents for the payment of incumbrances: *Norton* v. *Johnstone*, 30 Ch. D. 649. Although the result of his doing so is to give him an advantage at the expense of the remaindermen by accelerating his possession of the estate.

For the definition of "tenant for life," see s. 2 (7), and for the enumeration of other "limited owners" who may exercise the powers of a tenant for life, s. 58, *post*, p. 159.

The trustees of the settlement, or, if there are none, some person specially appointed by the Court may exercise the powers in the case of an infant's land (s. 60); and where the tenant for life or a person having the powers of a tenant for life is a lunatic so found by inquisition the Committee acting under an order in lunacy is authorised to act on his behalf (s. 62). Where the tenant for life is himself the purchaser, the trustees of the settlement are empowered by the Act of 1890 to exercise all his powers in reference to negotiating and completing the transaction (Act of 1890, s. 12).

By the "Glebe Lands Act, 1888," the incumbent of any benefice is authorised with certain restrictions to sell any glebe land, and the provisions of the Settled Land Act, 1882, are made to apply as if the incumbent were a tenant for life, 51 & 52 Vict. c. 20, s. 8.

Glebe lands.

It may be pointed out in connection with the statutory power of sale, that if trustees enter into a contract for sale, and it turns out that they have no power to sell, they cannot compel the purchaser to accept a title from the tenant for life under this Act: *Re Bryant and Barningham's Contract*, 44 Ch. D. 218; *Re Head's Trustees and Macdonald's Contract*, 45 Ch. D. 310.

See, as to the power of the tenant for life to deal with incumbrances, s. 5; to enter into preliminary contracts, s. 31; and to complete the sale by conveyance, s. 20; as to the payment of the purchase-money, s. 22; as to the appointment, receipts, and protection of trustees, ss. 38-42; and as to the investment or application by them of the money coming to their hands, ss. 21, 25, *post*, pp. 83, 98.

Matters connected with power of sale.

It will be observed that the "settled land," which the tenant for

What may be sold.

§ 3. life is hereby empowered to sell, does not necessarily include the fee simple, but is limited by s. 2 (3) to the estate or interest which is the subject of a settlement. Where a lease for years, or life, or years determinable on life, or any other estate or interest less than the fee simple, or a reversion is sold under this Act, the purchase-money may be dealt with under s. 34, *post*. Under the ordinary power of sale a tenant for life in such case accelerates his possession: Sugden on Powers, 842, 8th ed., and see *Clark* v. *Seymour*, 7 Sim. 67.

Easements. Easements are also included in the expression, "land" as defined by s. 2 (10), and a right of way or other easement appurtenant to the settled land may accordingly be sold with the land to which it is appurtenant. A distinction must be pointed out between such easements and those referred to in sub-s. 1. The case contemplated by that sub-section is the creation of an easement *de novo*, not the sale of one already in existence. The tenant for life may, for example, grant for a money consideration, a right of way over the settled land, either to an adjoining owner, or to a purchaser of some other part of the property. See s. 20, *post*, which refers to the conveyance of the land sold, and enables the tenant for life to "convey or create" easements or other rights or privileges in the manner there described.

The surface and the minerals may be sold separately (s. 17); but if the tenant for life wishes to sell the timber he must obtain the consent of the trustees or an order of the Court (s. 35). The like restriction is placed on a sale of the principal mansion house and the pleasure grounds, park and lands usually occupied therewith (Act of 1890, s. 10).

Sub-s. 2. Manor. This sub-section is intended to supply the place of the ordinary power of enfranchisement, and enables the tenant for life to act as if he were the owner of the fee simple. The enfranchisement money, however, being "capital money arising under the Act," must, as in the case of a sale under sub-s. i., be paid either to the trustees or into Court, as provided by s. 22, *post*.

It is to be observed that the power extends to the sale of the seigniory of freehold land within the manor; and, *semble*, this sale must be made to the freehold tenant, and not to a stranger, for the words "so as in every such case to effect an enfranchisement," seem to apply to this case as well as to the enfranchisement, properly so called, of copyhold or customary land.

"An enfranchisement under a power operates as an appointment of the fee of the tenement enfranchised to the copyholder, so as by the union of the freehold and copyhold interests to extinguish the latter and convert the tenure into freehold:" Dav. Conv. iii. 544, 3rd ed.

Sub-s. 3. If money has to be paid with the settled land for equality of exchange, it must be raised by mortgage under s. 18, *post;* if on the other hand the equality money is paid by the other party the transaction partakes of the nature of a sale (*Bartram* v. *Whichcote,* 6 Sim. 86), and the money received is "capital money arising under the Act." It must therefore be paid to the trustees, or into Court under s. 22.

§ 3. Power of exchange.

If the consideration given for equality exceeds in amount or value the sum of one hundred pounds, the principal or only instrument is chargeable with *ad valorem* duty as a conveyance on sale for the same consideration: and in any other case with a duty of ten shillings. See the Stamp Act, 1870 (33 & 34 Vict. c. 97), s. 94.

Stamp duty.

Incorporeal hereditaments, and an undivided share in land are, by virtue of s. 2 (10), included in this power; and, by s. 17, the "mines and minerals" may be treated as distinct from the surface beneath which they lie, and dealt with accordingly.

What may be given in exchange.

The restriction in s. 15, *post,* as to the mansion house and park, was not extended to the power of exchange, but now by s. 10 of the Act of 1890 which repeals the former enactment, the tenant for life is prohibited from exchanging the principal mansion house and the pleasure grounds and park and lands (if any) usually occupied therewith without the consent of the trustees of the settlement or an order of the Court.

It will be observed that the power is unrestricted as to the tenure of the land taken in exchange. Freeholds may, therefore, be exchanged for copyholds, or *vice versâ;* and lands held in common socage for gavelkind land (see *Minet* v. *Leman,* 20 Beav. 269; 7 D. M. & G. 340); but there is no express power to exchange freeholds for leaseholds. The power of exchange, however, must be read with the provisions of the Act as to re-investment of the proceeds of sale; for an exchange may be regarded as a sale and re-investment carried out by one transaction. By s. 21 capital money may be invested in long leaseholds, and it would be a narrow construction to place upon the words of this section, to hold that leaseholds were excluded from the power of exchange. See also s. 24, which provides for the settlement of "leasehold land" acquired by purchase, or in *exchange,* or on partition.

What may be taken in exchange.

This and the following subsection have been amended by s. 5 of the Act of 1890, which is in the following terms:—

5. On an exchange or partition any easement, right, or privilege of any kind may be reserved, or may be granted over, or in relation to the settled land or any part thereof, or other land or an easement, right, or privilege of any kind may be given or taken in exchange or on partition for land or for any other easement, right, or privilege of any kind.

Creation of easements on exchange or partition.

The power of making partition here conferred is more extensive

Sub-s. iv.

§ 3.
Partition.

than the ordinary power, which is confined to the case of an undivided share being comprised in the settlement. Here the power includes that case, and also that of land originally settled *in globo*, coming to be held in undivided shares under the provisions of the settlement itself. If, for example, there is a devise to A. for life, and after his decease for his children as tenants in common for life with remainders over, the children of A. may after his decease concur in the partition of the property.

In *Re Frith and Osborne*, 3 Ch. D. 618, it has been held, "removing the doubts of conveyancers" on the subject, that the ordinary power of sale and exchange authorizes a partition.

References to incidental provisions.

The several powers conferred by this section are affected in various ways by almost all the subsequent provisions of the Act, but the special attention of the reader may be usefully directed to the following table of references:—

1. Transfer of incumbrances, s. 5.
2. Separate dealing with surface and minerals, s. 17.
3. Raising money by mortgage for enfranchisement or equality of exchange or partition, s. 18.
4. Conveyance under the statutory power, s. 20.
5. Investment of capital money, s. 21.
6. Settlement of land acquired, s. 24.
7. Preliminary contracts, s. 31.
8. Notice to trustees, s. 45; Act of 1884, s. 5.
9. Creation of easements, Act of 1890, s. 5.

§ 4.
Regulations respecting sale, enfranchisement, exchange, and partition.

4.—(1.) Every sale shall be made at the best price that can reasonably be obtained.

(2.) Every exchange and every partition shall be made for the best consideration in land or in land and money that can reasonably be obtained.

(3.) A sale may be made in one lot or in several lots, and either by auction or by private contract.

(4.) On a sale the tenant for life may fix reserve biddings and buy in at an auction.

(5.) A sale, exchange, or partition may be made subject to any stipulations respecting title, or evidence of title, or other things.

(6.) On a sale, exchange, or partition, any restriction or reservation with respect to building on or other user of land, or with respect to mines and minerals, or with respect to or for the purpose of the more beneficial working thereof, or with respect to any other thing, may be imposed or reserved and made binding, as far as the law permits, by covenant, condition, or otherwise, on the tenant for life and the settled land, or any part thereof, or on the other party and any land sold or given in exchange or on partition to him.

§ 4.

(7.) An enfranchisement may be made with or without a re-grant of any right of common or other right, easement, or privilege theretofore appendant or appurtenant to or held or enjoyed with the land enfranchised, or reputed so to be.

(8.) Settled land in England shall not be given in exchange for land out of England.

The tenant for life being by s. 53, *post*, placed in the position of a trustee for all parties entitled under the settlement, the rules which govern sales, &c., by persons in a fiduciary position would seem to apply to the exercise of the powers under this Act, as to which, see Dart, V. & P. 58, *et seq.*, 6th ed. The most important of those rules, however, are in this section expressly enacted.

Sect. 4. Regulations respecting sale, &c.

A purchaser or other person dealing in good faith with the tenant for life is amply protected by s. 54, *post*, and is to be taken to have given the best price or consideration that could reasonably be obtained by the tenant for life, and to have complied with all the requisitions of the Act.

The "best price" depends of course on the circumstances of each particular case: but it is certain that if fiduciary vendors fail in reasonable diligence—if they contract under circumstances of haste and improvidence—if they make the sale with a view to advance the particular purposes of one party at the expense of another, the Court will not enforce specific performance of the contract: *Ord* v. *Noel*, 5 Mad. 438.

Sub-ss. 1, 2. "Best price."

Where the sale is made by the tenant for life, as under this Act, there seems to be no reason to scrutinize closely the amount of the purchase-money, since his interests are, in that respect, coincident with those of the remaindermen. Still he must "use all reasonable diligence—as if the estate were his own, to obtain a fair price; and therefore should ascertain its value, even at the expense of a valuation, where circumstances seem to render such a course expedient." Dart, V. & P. 90, 6th ed.

The price ought not to be left to the determination of valuers (*ibid.*); nor is the tenant for life in general justified in granting an option to purchase at a future time for a fixed price: *Clay* v. *Rufford*,

§ 4.

5 De G. & Sm. 768, 780; *Oceanic Steam Navigation Co.* v. *Sutherberry*, 16 Ch. D. 236. But it is provided by s. 2 of the Act of 1889 that such an option may be conferred by a building lease provided it is limited to a period of ten years.

The price should consist of a gross sum, and not a rent-charge: *Read* v. *Shaw*, Sug. on Powers, 953, 8th ed. See, however, s. 9 of the Act of 1890 which authorizes the reservation of a perpetual rent-charge on a grant for building purposes.

Housing of the Working Classes Act.

By the Housing of the Working Classes Act, 1890 (53 & 54 Vict. c. 70), s. 74, the provisions of this section as to "best price" are modified in the case of a sale, exchange, or lease, made for the purpose of the erection on the land of dwellings for the working classes. The section is in the following terms :—

"74.—(1.) The Settled Land Act, 1882, shall be amended as follows :—

"(*a.*) Any sale, exchange, or lease of land in pursuance of the said Act, when made for the purpose of the erection on such land of dwellings for the working classes, may be made at such price, or for such consideration, or for such rent, as having regard to the said purpose, and to all the circumstances of the case, is the best that can be reasonably obtained, notwithstanding that a higher price, consideration, or rent might have been obtained if the land were sold, exchanged, or leased for another purpose."

See, also, with reference to this enactment, s. 18 of the Act of 1890, which materially extends the meaning of the expression "working classes."

Interchange of settled estates.

There seems to be no reason to prevent capital money arising under one settlement from being employed in the purchase of settled land comprised in another; and it would seem that two "limited owners" may exchange parts of their respective estates.

Semble, notwithstanding *Ferrand* v. *Wilson*, 4 Hare, 344, 385, that inadequacy of price would not, under this Act, prevent the power from being legally exercised, so as to pass the legal estate under s. 20, *post*, the purchaser being protected by s. 54 if dealing in good faith.

Timber.

Even if the tenant for life is unimpeachable for waste, the timber must be sold with the land: *Cholmeley* v. *Paxton*, 3 Bing. 207; *Cockerell* v. *Cholmeley*, 1 R. & M. 418; Sugden on Powers, 864, 8th ed. Express authority is given by s. 17 in the case of an undivided share, to concur with the owners of the other shares in the sale of the property as a whole, but there is no power to sell jointly with the owner of an adjoining property: *Rede* v. *Oakes*, 4 D. J. & S. 505; *Tolson* v. *Sheard*, 5 Ch. D. 19; or with the owner of a beneficial lease, or reversion, unless such a sale is advantageous and the purchase-money is apportioned before completion: *In re Cooper and Allen's Contract*, 4 Ch. D. 802; and see as to the application of the purchase-money in the case of a lease or reversion, s. 34, *post*, p. 122.

Sub-sections 3—5, which prescribe the manner in which the sale is to be made, merely express the general law as to sales by fiduciary vendors. See s. 35 of the Conv. Act, 1881. The tenant for life under this section has a wide discretion as to the conditions of sale, which he thinks it expedient to adopt; still, having regard to s. 53, *post*, he is bound to exercise his discretion for the benefit of all persons entitled under the settlement. Being in the position of a trustee, he is liable, notwithstanding the Trustee Act, 1888 (51 & 52 Vict. c. 59), s. 3, to be restrained from employing unduly depreciatory conditions. See *Dance* v. *Goldingham*, L. R. 8 Ch. 902.

§ 4.

Sub-ss. 3—5. Manner of sale.

Sub-section 6 enables a tenant for life to enter into restrictive covenants as to any part of the settled land not disposed of, and also to sell subject to similar covenants on the part of the purchaser.

It is submitted that, having regard to the qualifying words "*as far as the law permits*," the extent to which these covenants may be made to bind an assignee, has not been altered by this section; the object being to place the tenant for life in the position of an absolute owner for the purposes of sale, exchange or partition.

In the leading case of *Tulk* v. *Moxhay*, 2 Ph. 774, it was decided, that a covenant by a purchaser to use or abstain from using the land in a particular way, will be enforced in equity against all subsequent purchasers with notice, independently of the question whether the covenant runs with the land or not; but this doctrine has been recently held not to extend to affirmative covenants: *Haywood* v. *The Brunswick Benefit B. Soc.*, 8 Q. B. D. 403; *London and South-Western Ry. Co.* v. *Gomm*, 20 Ch. D. 562: *Austerberry* v. *Corporation of Oldham*, 29 Ch. D. 750, overruling *Cooke* v. *Chilcott*, 3 Ch. D. 694.

Constructive notice of the covenant is sufficient to bind an assignee: *Parker* v. *Whyte*, 1 H. & M. 167; *Wilson* v. *Hart*, L. R. 1 Ch. 463; and if he does not get the legal estate, notice is immaterial. See *London and South-Western Ry. Co.* v. *Gomm, supra*.

Sub-s. 6. Restrictive covenants, &c.

Where land is sold on a general building scheme, the restrictive covenants of each purchaser are in the nature of a reservation by the vendor for the benefit of the other purchasers, any one of whom may accordingly enforce the obligation of the covenant: *Western* v. *Macdermott*, L. R. 2 Ch. 72; *Gaskin* v. *Balls*, 13 Ch. D. 324. See *Nottingham Brick and Tile Co.* v. *Butler*, 16 Q. B. D. 778. And the vendor himself may be restrained from violating or authorising the violation of the building scheme. *Mackenzie* v. *Childers*, 43 Ch. D. 265, and see *Spicer* v. *Martin*, 14 App. Cas. 12. But if part of the property is sold to a purchaser with a restrictive covenant, and afterwards the rest is sold without any mention of the covenant, there is

Who are entitled to benefit of covenants.

§ 4.

Mines.

Sub-s. 7.
Re-grant of commons.

Sub-s. 8.

in such a case no privity between the two purchasers, and the second has no right to enforce the covenant: *Keates* v. *Lyon*, L. R. 4 Ch. 218; *Master* v. *Hansard*, 4 Ch. D. 718; *Renals* v. *Cowlishaw*, 11 Ch. D. 866.

The restrictions or reservations with respect to mines and minerals referred to in this sub-section seem to be of a different character from the rights and easements which may be granted or reserved under s. 17. The latter are intended to enlarge the rights of the person taking the mine, the provisions of the present sub-section on the contrary are pointed to a restriction of the full rights of ownership. For example, upon the sale of mines apart from the surface, the purchaser may under this section, covenant not to work the mine so as to let down the surface, or the tenant for life may covenant to work adjacent mines so as not to interfere with those which have been sold.

"Rights of common in the waste of the manor are extinguished by enfranchisement, unless they should be specially preserved to the copyholder under terms equivalent to a re-grant:" Scriven, 283, 6th ed.; *Bradshaw* v. *Eyr*, Cro. Eliz. 570; but it is said that these rights, although legally extinguished, subsist in equity: *Styant* v. *Staker*, 2 Vern. 250; Dav. Conv., ii., pt. i. 388, 4th ed.; iii. 545, 3rd ed.

"England" includes "Wales," 20 Geo. II. c. 42, s. 3.

Special Powers.

§ 5.

Transfer of incumbrances on land sold, &c.

5. Where on a sale, exchange, or partition, there is an incumbrance affecting land sold or given in exchange or on partition, the tenant for life, with the consent of the incumbrancer, may charge that incumbrance on any other part of the settled land, whether already charged therewith or not, in exoneration of the part sold or so given, and, by conveyance of the fee simple, or other estate or interest the subject of the settlement, or by creation of a term of years in the settled land, or otherwise, make provision accordingly.

Sect. 5.
Transfer of incumbrances.

The Act contemplates, as pointed out by Mr. Justice Stirling in *Re Lord Stamford's Settled Estates*, 43 Ch. D. 84, 93, that the settled land may as to part be subject to a charge, and as to the rest free from it; and this section enables the tenant for life in such a case, with the consent of the incumbrancer, to shift the charge from one part of the land to another, for the purpose of making a title free from incumbrances. In order to ascertain the scope of this section it should be read with s. 20, *post*, which provides that the conveyance of the tenant for life under the Act shall be effectual to pass the land conveyed, discharged from estates, interests and charges subsisting or to arise under the Settlement, but subject (*inter alia*) to (i) charges having priority to the Settlement ; (2) charges created for securing money actually raised at the date of the deed ; and (3) all grants of easements, rights of common, or other rights or privileges granted or made for value in money or money's worth, or agreed so to be, before the date of the deed, if they are binding on the Successors in title of the tenant for life. It is to clear the land sold from such charges as these that the aid of the present section is required ; and it is not unreasonable to construe it as limited to the cases for which it is actually necessary. The words of the section are wide enough to enable a tenant for life, who had mortgaged his life interest in one part of the property, to sell that part free from the incumbrance, and to charge his personal debt upon the inheritance of any other part of the estate.

§ 5.

The tenant for life, however, in exercising this, as well as all other powers under the Act, is in the position of a trustee, and must have regard to the interests of all persons entitled under the settlement (s. 53) ; and he cannot therefore by transferring an incumbrance be permitted to prejudice the interests of the remainderman. It is also possible that the section may be read as not authorizing the tenant for life to alter the nature or extent of the security held by the incumbrancer before the transfer. If so the alternative given by the words—" by conveyance of the fee simple or by creation of a term of years in the Settled land, or otherwise "—must be determined by the nature of the incumbrance and not by the agreement between the tenant for life and the incumbrancer.

Tenant for life a trustee.

A question seems to arise whether, having regard to the words "in exoneration of the part sold or so given," the concurrence of the incumbrancer in the conveyance of the exonerated land is in any case necessary. It is conceived that the land is freed from the incumbrance by force of the Statute and that no conveyance by the incumbrancer is requisite in order to revest the estate.

It is presumed that the Stamp duty payable on a deed transferring an incumbrance under this section is only ten shillings.

Stamp duty.

IV.—LEASES.

General Powers and Regulations.

6. A tenant for life may lease the settled land or any part thereof, or any easement, right, or privilege of any

§ 6.

Power for tenant for

C.S.L.A.   E

§ 6.
life to
lease for
ordinary
or building
or mining
purposes.

kind, over or in relation to the same, for any purpose whatever, whether involving waste or not, for any term not exceeding—

(i.) In case of a building lease, ninety-nine years:
(ii.) In case of a mining lease, sixty years:
(iii.) In case of any other lease, twenty-one years.

Sect. 6.
Powers of
leasing.

The manner in which the powers by this section conferred in general terms are to be exercised is regulated by s. 7; and further provisions are contained as to building and mining leases in ss. 8—11. The tenant for life under this section takes more extensive powers of granting leases than those conferred upon the Court by the Settled Estates Act, 1877 (40 & 41 Vict. c. 18), s. 4.

The powers of granting leases for twenty-one years, conferred upon tenants in tail by the Fines and Recoveries Act (3 & 4 Will. 4, c. 74), ss. 15, 41, and upon tenants for life and other limited owners by the Settled Estates Act, 1877 (40 & 41 Vict. c. 18), s. 46, are practically superseded by the wider provisions of the present Act, except that as a tenant in dower is not included among the "limited owners" entitled to exercise the powers of a tenant for life (s. 58), it may still be necessary for her to avail herself of the 46th section of the Settled Estates Act.

Trustees'
powers.

It is to be observed that any leasing powers which may be vested in trustees are not taken away by this Act, but they cannot now be exercised without the consent of the tenant for life (s. 56).

The tenant for life cannot by assignment, release or contract deprive himself of the powers here conferred upon him; and although he is precluded from exercising them to the prejudice of his assignee, he may, unless the assignee is in possession, grant leases (without fine) as if no assignment had taken place: s. 50, *post*.

On comparing the provisions of this and the next section, with s. 18 of the Conveyancing Act, 1881, it will be noticed that a tenant for life has as against the mortgagee of his life interest actually larger powers of granting leases than if he were a person absolutely entitled to the equity of redemption.

If a tenant for life purports to grant a lease for a longer term than is here authorized, the lease will be good *pro tanto: Campbell* v. *Leach*, Amb. 740; Sugden on Powers, 519, 567, 8th ed.

"Whether
involving
waste or
not."

The words "whether involving waste or not" do not, it is submitted, authorize the tenant for life to grant a lease expressed to be "without impeachment of waste," for the insertion of these words would enable the lessee to cut timber, plough up ancient meadow or pasture and open mines which would be opposed to the general scheme of the Act. See, however, s. 7 of the Act of 1890, which implies that in some leases for twenty-one years the lessee may be "exempted from punishment for waste." The meaning to be attached to these words probably is that the lease is to be valid notwithstanding that the commission of waste is necessarily involved in the *purpose* for which it is granted, as, for example, the opening of mines, or the destruction of old houses with a view to building on their site. The position of the lessee as regards waste is independent of whether the tenant for life is himself impeachable or unimpeachable; but depends entirely on what is reasonably necessary to carry out the purpose for which the lease is granted. He is liable for acts of waste, except so far as they are expressly or impliedly sanctioned by the lease, but not, it seems, for permissive waste. *Re Cartwright*, 41 Ch. D. 532. See, however, *Davies* v. *Davies*, 38 Ch. D. 499.

§ 6.

7.—(1.) Every lease shall be by deed, and be made to take effect in possession not later than twelve months after its date.

(2.) Every lease shall reserve the best rent that can reasonably be obtained, regard being had to any fine taken, and to any money laid out or to be laid out for the benefit of the settled land, and generally to the circumstances of the case.

(3.) Every lease shall contain a covenant by the lessee for payment of the rent, and a condition of re-entry on the rent not being paid within a time therein specified not exceeding thirty days.

(4.) A counterpart of every lease shall be executed by the lessee and delivered to the tenant for life; of which execution and delivery the execution of the lease by the tenant for life shall be sufficient evidence.

(5.) A statement, contained in a lease or in an indorsement thereon, signed by the tenant for life, respecting any matter of fact or of calculation under this Act in relation to the lease, shall, in favour of the lessee and of those claiming under him, be sufficient evidence of the matter stated.

§ 7. Regulations respecting leases generally.

The regulations here laid down differ from the conditions annexed to the ordinary power, by permitting a fine to be taken, and by enabling the tenant for life to sign a conclusive statement respecting any matter of fact or of calculation, under the 5th sub section.

Sect. 7. Regulations respecting leases.

E 2

§ 7.

It would seem that whether the conditions of this section are complied with, or not, the power will be well exercised; and the lease valid, if the lessee is a person dealing in good faith within the meaning of s. 54; the remedy of the remainderman being confined to an action against the tenant for life in respect of a breach of trust. See s. 53. But if the lessee knows of the irregularity the lease may be set aside. See *Selwyn* v. *Garfit*, 38 Ch. D. 273.

Relief against defective execution.

If a tenant for life acting *bonâ fide* purports to grant a lease in excess of his powers, it may in some cases be upheld with such variations as may be necessary to bring it into conformity with the statutory power, for by 12 & 13 Vict. c. 26, every lease under a power, which is invalid by reason of the non-observance or omission of some condition or restriction, or by reason of any other deviation from the terms of such power, will, if made *bonâ fide*, and the lessee has entered under it, operate as a contract for a lease, subject to any variation which may be necessary to bring it into conformity with the power. See also as to the confirmation of invalid leases by the remainderman, 13 & 14 Vict. c. 17.

If a building lease is invalid as a building lease on account of the omission of a covenant to build, the defect is not one which can be regarded as falling within the terms of the statute, and cannot be cured by treating the lease as an ordinary one for twenty-one years. *Hallett* to *Martin*, 24 Ch. D. 624. See also *Gas Light and Coke Company* v. *Towse*, 35 Ch. D. 519.

Sub-s. 1. "By deed."

Section 7 of the Act of 1890 modifies this sub-section by enacting that a tenant for life may grant a lease by writing under hand only, "when the term does not extend beyond three years from the date of the writing." The tenant for life has, however, under s. 31, *post*, power to contract to grant a lease, and such a contract, when capable of being specifically enforced, places the parties in the same position as if a lease had been made under seal. *Walsh* v. *Lonsdale*, 21 Ch. D. 9; *Swain* v. *Ayres*, 21 Q. B. D. 289.

Sub-s. 2. Best rent.

Whether the "best rent" is reserved or not, is a question for the jury: *Wright* v. *Smith*, 5 Esp. 203. See also *Roe* v. *Archbishop of York*, 6 East, 86, where it was held that improvements made by the tenant would not justify a lease at an undervalue. This doctrine is abolished by the present enactment, since it expressly provides that money laid out for the benefit of the settled land may be taken into account in determining the rent: but it is of course to be understood that the improvements must be permanent in their nature, and not such as would be exhausted during the term of the lease. See Sugden on Powers, 779, 8th ed. The tenant for life is not bound to accept the highest offer made to him, "for in the choice of a tenant there are many things to be regarded besides the mere amount of the rent offered:" *Doe* v. *Radcliffe*, 10 East, 278; *Dyas* v. *Cruise*, 2 Jo. & Lat. 460.

According to Lord Eldon, the "leading criterion" in these cases is, "whether the man who makes the lease has got as much for others as he has got for himself;" Sugden on Powers, 785, 8th ed. See also *Doe* v. *Bettison*, 12 East, 305.

The value of a lease surrendered under s. 13, *post*, may, it seems, be taken into account in estimating the rent to be reserved: see *Re Rawlins' Estate*, L. R. 1 Eq. 286.

Except in building and mining leases (see ss. 8, 9), the rent should be uniform throughout the term. The reservation of a progressively increasing rent is not authorized by the power. See *Hallett* to *Martin*, 24 Ch. D. 624 at p. 632; and a progressively diminishing rent would be open to still graver objections.

A covenant of renewal at a specified rent is not void, but it cannot be enforced unless when the time comes for renewal the rent is the best that could then be reasonably obtained. See *Gas Light and Coke Company* v. *Towse*, 35 Ch. D. 519.

Where a lease of a holding to which the Agricultural Holdings Act, 1883, applies, is made to the tenant of the same, it is by that Act provided that it shall not be necessary in estimating the rent to be reserved to take into account against the tenant the increase (if any) in the value of such holding arising from any improvements made or paid for by him on such holding. 46 & 47 Vict. c. 61, s. 43.

The Housing of the Working Classes Act, 1890, enacts that any lease of land in pursuance of the Settled Land Act, when made for the purpose of the erection on such land of dwellings for the working classes, may be made at such rent as having regard to the said purpose, and to all the circumstances of the case, is the best that can be reasonably obtained, notwithstanding that a higher rent might have been obtained if the land were leased for another purpose. 53 & 54 Vict. c. 70, s. 74. And see s. 18 of the Act of 1890, which extends the meaning of the expression "working classes."

§ 7.

A fine received on the grant of a lease is to be deemed capital money arising under the act: Act of 1884, s. 4. It should accordingly be paid either to the trustees of the settlement or into Court, as provided by s. 22, *post*.

Fine.

The covenant for payment of rent will, as a general rule, be entered into with the tenant for life; and, whether he has a legal estate or not, the benefit of the covenant will, under s. 10 of the Conv. Act, 1881, be annexed and incident to and go with the reversionary estate in the land.

Sub-s. 3. Covenant by lessee.

The counterpart is, for many purposes, evidence against the lessee: *Roe* v. *Davis*, 7 East, 363; *Houghton* v. *Kœnig*, 18 C. B. 235; Taylor on Evidence, 393, 8th ed.; and where there is a manifest

Sub-s. 4. Counterpart.

§ 7.

Sub-s. 5.
Statement signed by tenant for life.

error in the lease, the counterpart may be looked at to correct the mistake: *Burchell* v. *Clark*, 2 C. P. D. 88.

The object of sub-s. 5 seems to be to enable the lessee to sell his interest without being subject to inquiry as to compliance with the statutory regulations. Section 54 protects him "as against all parties entitled under the settlement," a "conclusive statement" under this sub-section furnishes him with evidence against all the world. The onus lies on the purchaser of a lease of showing that the lease was not duly granted, Conv. Act, 1881, s. 3 (4); and the "statement" which, it is to be observed, must be either contained in, or indorsed upon the lease, thus answers possible requisitions by way of anticipation. The "matter of calculation" here referred to appears to be the determination of the minimum rent, under a building agreement in the manner provided by s. 8 (3); and, of course, cannot refer to "matter of calculation" properly so called, viz., purely arithmetical processes. The conclusive statements signed by the tenant for life may also be advantageously employed, when the lessee wishes to preserve evidence of the fact that he has erected buildings, or expended a certain amount in repairs, or improvements, in accordance with a previous agreement. See s. 8.

Building and Mining Leases.

§ 8.

Regulations respecting building leases.

8.—(1.) Every building lease shall be made partly in consideration of the lessee, or some person by whose direction the lease is granted, or some other person, having erected, or agreeing to erect, buildings, new or additional, or having improved or repaired, or agreeing to improve or repair, buildings, or having executed, or agreeing to execute, on the land leased, an improvement authorized by this Act, for or in connection with building purposes.

(2.) A peppercorn rent or a nominal or other rent less than the rent ultimately payable, may be made payable for the first five years or any less part of the term.

(3.) Where the land is contracted to be leased in lots, the entire amount of rent to be ultimately payable may be apportioned among the lots in any manner; save that—

(i.) The annual rent reserved by any lease shall not be less than ten shillings; and

(ii.) The total amount of the rents reserved on all leases for the time being granted shall not be less than the total amount of the rents which, in order that the leases may be in conformity with this Act, ought to be reserved in respect of the whole land for the time being leased; and

(iii.) The rent reserved by any lease shall not exceed one fifth part of the full annual value of the land comprised in that lease with the buildings thereon when completed.

§ 8.

Compare the definitions of "Building purposes" and "Building lease" in s. 2 (10) iii., *ante*, p. 26, with the more elaborate description of a building lease contained in this section. It is important to observe that no distinction is drawn between a building lease and a repairing lease. The erection of new, and the improvement or repair of existing buildings are both "building purposes," and equally authorize the grant of a lease for 99 years. In *Truscott* v. *Diamond Rock Boring Co.*, 20 Ch. D. 251, there was power to lease the premises " to any person or persons who shall improve or repair the same, or covenant or agree to improve or repair the same," and it was held that an agreement that the lessee should " do necessary repairs " sufficiently complied with the terms of the power. See also *Easton* v. *Pratt*, 2 H. & C. 676; Sugden on Powers, 829, 8th ed. It would seem, having regard to the foregoing decisions, that if the lease contains the common covenant to repair it is a building lease within the meaning of this section, although there may be no expenditure of capital by the lessee on the demised premises.

Sect. 8. Regulations as to building leases.

It is enacted by the Act of 1889 that any building lease and any agreement for granting building leases under this Act may contain an option, to be exercised at any time within an agreed number of years not exceeding ten, for the lessee to purchase the land leased at a price fixed at the time of the making of the lease or agreement for the lease, such price to be the best which, having regard to the rent reserved, can reasonably be obtained, and to be either a fixed sum of money or such a sum of money as shall be equal to a stated number of years purchase of the highest rent reserved by the lease or agreement : 52 & 53 Vict. c. 36, s. 2.

Option of purchase.

As to the extent of ground which may be included in a building lease, see *Cooper* v. *Denne*, 4 Bro. C. C. 80; *Higgins* v. *Rosse*, 3 Bli. 112; and Chance on Powers (2399). It seems that if an ordinary building agreement provides that one plot is to be left vacant of buildings, the agreement will not be valid within the meaning of this section : *Re Sabin's Settled Estates*, 30 S. J. 62.

Extent of ground.

No additional duty is payable in respect of improvements on, or additions to the demised property : The Stamp Act, 1870 (33 & 34

Vict. c. 97), s. 98 ; and see 33 & 34 Vict. c. 44, overruling the decision in *Re Bolton's Lease*, L. R. 5 Ex. 82.

Sub-s. 3. Leases in pursuance of building contract.

It is not uncommon in building contracts to provide that the builder, instead of taking a lease of the premises in his own name, may require leases of the separate houses to be granted direct to his nominees, the rent being apportioned by the architect of the lessor; and this sub-section is probably intended to provide for such a case. See *Cust* v. *Middleton*, 3 D. F. & J. 33. The object seems to be, to prevent an unequal apportionment of the rent, and to secure a certain outlay upon each plot of ground comprised in a separate lease. If all the land were comprised in a single lease, the lessor, on non-payment of any part of the rent, might re-enter upon any part of the premises. The effect of sub-division is to diminish this security, and to make each plot liable only for its apportioned rent; but, so long as the apportionment is made with a due regard to the relative values of the several parts of the property, the arrangement is advantageous to the occupier, without materially affecting the interests of the lessor.

Provisions to secure a fair apportionment.

The provisions of this sub-section are somewhat crabbed, but appear to be effective. The first is, of course, intended to prevent excessive subdivision of the rent, whereby the cost of collection would be considerably increased. The second fixes a minimum rent, not for each individual lease, but for the group of leases granted up to any particular date; so that if more than the "best rent," within the meaning of s. 7 (2), is reserved by the first lease, an equivalent reduction may be made in that reserved by the second; and similarly as to the third and subsequent leases. The builder is precluded by this clause from disposing of the houses first completed, except upon the terms of a fair ground-rent being reserved to the lessors.

The third clause of this sub-section in effect requires that the letting value of the house, when built, shall be at least five times the amount of the ground rent.

This section does not provide for the apportionment of rent upon the assignment of part of the premises, where the builder, instead of entering into a contract for a lease, takes a lease in his own name in the first instance.

§ 9. Regulations respecting mining leases.

9.—(1.) In a mining lease—

(i.) The rent may be made to be ascertainable by or to vary according to the acreage worked, or by or according to the quantities of any mineral or substance gotten, made merchantable, converted, carried away, or disposed of, in or from the settled land, or any other land, or by or according to any facilities given in that behalf; and

(ii.) A fixed or minimum rent may be made payable, with or without power for the lessee, in case the rent, according to acreage or quantity, in any specified period does not produce an amount equal to the fixed or minimum rent, to make up the deficiency in any subsequent specified period, free of rent other than the fixed or minimum rent.

(2.) A lease may be made partly in consideration of the lessee having executed, or his agreeing to execute, on the land leased, an improvement authorized by this Act, for or in connexion with mining purposes.

§ 9.

Sect. 9. Regulations as to mining leases.

The manner of ascertaining the rent in a mining lease varies with the nature of the mineral, and the district in which the mine is situated.

"Rents are generally payable in money in demises of quarries or open workings, and are often so payable for mines. In mines of coal the render is also usually in money, and, in many instances, made to vary with the market price of the article. The rents made payable in respect of metalliferous mines are almost invariably proportioned to the quantity of ore actually raised, and without any stipulated certain rent in money. It is a common practice to stipulate that the rent shall be paid in money, according to the market price of the day, or by delivery of the metals in a manufactured state:" Bainbridge on Mines, 471—2, 4th ed.

In order to enable leases to be made under the Act in conformity with the practice as stated above, this section has been amended by the Act of 1890 in the following manner :—

"8. In a mining lease—

(i.) The rent may be made to vary according to the price of the minerals or substances gotten, or any of them :

(ii.) Such price may be the saleable value, or the price or value appearing in any trade or market or other price list or return from time to time, or may be the marketable value as ascertained in any manner prescribed by the lease (including a reference to arbitration), or may be an average of any such prices or values taken during a specified period."

Provision as to mining leases.

Although "rent" is by s. 2 (10) defined so as to include "duty," or a render of rent in kind, it seems doubtful from the language of this section whether a proportion of the mineral, either in its natural

Render in kind.

§ 9.

or in its manufactured condition, may be reserved under this Act. See *Campbell* v. *Leach*, Amb. 743, where ore was said to be "analogous to money;" and *Basset* v. *Basset*, ibid. 843. A render of mineral in its natural state is an exception and not a reservation, and consequently no distress can be levied for such a rent: Bainbridge, 471, 4th ed. See also s. 11, *post*, which provides that part of the mining rent is to be set aside as "capital money," a provision inapplicable to a payment in kind.

On the other hand it is stated by Lord St. Leonards that "the word *rent*, in powers of leasing, is with great propriety construed to mean not money merely, but any return or equivalent adapted to the nature of the subject demised; therefore, upon a lease of mines, a due proportion of the produce may be reserved as a render in lieu of money, although the power requires a 'rent' generally to be reserved": Sugden on Powers, 791, 8th ed. See also Dav. Conv. iii. 489, 3rd ed.

Minimum rent.

The payment of the fixed rent is, in some districts, made to depend upon the capabilities of the mine, so that if it is worked out, or its productiveness diminished, or accidents occur, the fixed or minimum rent can no longer be exacted. Here, if a fixed or minimum rent is reserved, it must continue to be paid throughout the term whether the mine can be worked or not: *Marquis of Bute* v. *Thompson*, 13 M. & W. 487; *Clifford* v. *Watts*, L. R. 5 C. P. 577; *Mellers* v. *Duke of Devonshire*, 16 Beav. 252; *Jefferys* v. *Fairs*, 4 Ch. D. 448.

It is also important to observe that there is no power to remit the "dead rent" during the first years of the term while the minerals are being "won" (see *Lewis* v. *Fothergill*, L. R. 5 Ch. 103), or to insert a provision that the lessee shall be entitled to determine the lease when the mine is incapable of being worked at a profit. It has, indeed, been recently decided that the latter provision, in the absence of a special custom, is not a usual clause in the lease of a colliery: *Strelley* v. *Pearson*, 15 Ch. D. 113; and see *Gowan* v. *Christie*, L. R. 2 H. L. Sc. 273.

Acreage rent.

The "acreage" rent referred to in this section is not, it may be remarked, that payable in respect of the surface; but is what is commonly called a "footage rent," which is merely a mode of determining the quantity of mineral extracted by a combination of the acreage with the thickness of the seam.

Outstroke royalty.

When a mine, instead of having a separate communication with the surface, is worked through another, an "outstroke royalty" is generally reserved in respect of the minerals brought to bank through the demised mine. This is the meaning of the words "or any other land" in the first sub-section. See *G. W. Ry. Co.* v. *Rous*, L. R. 4 H. L. 650.

Facilities given.

The rent may also vary with the "facilities given" for the working,

&c., of the mines. A surface rent (*Re Reveley*, 11 W. R. 744), and the royalties usually payable in respect of wayleaves are included in this provision. As to facilities given in respect of "any other land," see *G. W. Ry. Co.* v. *Rous, ubi supra*; *Bidder* v. *North Staffordshire Ry. Co.*, 4 Q. B. D. 413.

§ 9.

The improvements authorized by the Act are specified in s. 25, *post*; and those which are connected with mining purposes appear to be (xiv.) tramways, railways, canals, and docks; (xv.) jetties, piers, and landing-places for facilitating transport of things required for mining purposes; and (xix.) trial pits for mines and other preliminary works necessary or proper in connection with development of mines.

Sub-s. 2. Improvement in connexion with mining purposes.

10.—(1.) Where it is shown to the Court with respect to the district in which any settled land is situate, either—

(i.) That it is the custom for land therein to be leased or granted for building or mining purposes for a longer term or on other conditions than the term or conditions specified in that behalf in this Act, or in perpetuity; or

(ii.) That it is difficult to make leases or grants for building or mining purposes of land therein, except for a longer term or on other conditions than the term and conditions specified in that behalf in this Act, or except in perpetuity;

the Court may, if it thinks fit, authorize generally the tenant for life to make from time to time leases or grants of or affecting the settled land in that district, or parts thereof, for any term or in perpetuity, at fee-farm or other rents, secured by condition of re-entry, or otherwise, as in the order of the Court expressed, or may, if it thinks fit, authorize the tenant for life to make any such lease or grant in any particular case.

§ 10. Variation of building or mining lease according to circumstances of district.

(2.) Thereupon the tenant for life, and, subject to any direction in the order of the Court to the contrary, each of his successors in title being a tenant for life, or having the powers of a tenant for life under this Act, may make in any case, or in the particular case, a lease or grant of or affecting the settled land, or part thereof, in conformity with the order.

THE SETTLED LAND ACT, 1882.

§ 10.
Sect. 10.
Circumstances of the district.

The discretionary power conferred upon the Court by this section is somewhat larger than that contained in the 4th section of the Settled Estates Act, which provides that a lease may be for such term of years as the Court shall direct, when the Court shall be satisfied that it is the usual custom of the district and beneficial to the inheritance to grant such a lease for a longer term than the term thereinbefore specified in that behalf. Under this Act the variation may be authorized either in accordance with local custom, or on account of any particular difficulty affecting the grant of leases in the ordinary form.

Under the Settled Estates Act, the Court, upon proof of the custom of the district, has sanctioned building leases for 999 years: *Re Carr*, 9 W. R. 776; and 600 years, *Re Cross's Charity*, 27 Beav. 592, in which case the established custom was shown to be to grant leases for 999 years.

Act of 1890.

Where under this section the tenant for life is authorized to make a grant for building purposes in perpetuity at a fee-farm rent, the reservation of the rentcharge operates under s. 9 of the Act of 1890 to create a rentcharge in fee simple with all the powers contained in s. 44 of the Conv. Act, 1881. And the rentcharge is to go and remain to the uses, on the trusts, and subject to the powers and provisions which immediately before the conveyance were subsisting with respect to the land out of which it is reserved.

The application to the Court under this section should be made by Summons in Chambers: S. L. A. Rules, 1882, r. 2, and see Forms III., IV., V. *post;* and should be supported by evidence to establish one or other of the conditions laid down in (i.) and (ii.) *supra* which confer jurisdiction on the Court. Where an infant tenant in tail was eighteen years of age at the date of the application the Court declined to confer a general authority on the Trustees of the Settlement (see s. 60, *post*) to grant leases for 200 years under this section, but required them to make a special application in respect of each lease. The ground of this decision was that as the minor would so soon be of age it was inexpedient to deprive him further than was necessary of the full dominion over his property: *Cecil* v. *Langdon*, 54 L. T. 418.

§ 11.
Part of mining rent to be set aside.

11. Under a mining lease, whether the mines or minerals leased are already opened or in work or not, unless a contrary intention is expressed in the settlement, there shall be from time to time set aside, as capital money arising under this act, part of the rent as follows, namely,—where the tenant for life is impeachable for waste in respect of minerals, three fourth parts of the rent, and otherwise one

fourth part thereof, and in every such case the residue of the rent shall go as rents and profits.

§ 11.

If the tenant for life makes use of the powers of the Act to grant mining leases, he is by this section put upon terms to capitalize a portion of the annual profits; and the principle upon which the enactment is founded is, that working mines is not merely reaping the fruit of the land, but is a consumption of the inheritance.

Sect. 11. Mining rent.

In the case of a settlement by way of trust for sale within s. 63, *post*, the tenant for life takes only an equitable interest in the proceeds of sale; and not being in a position to commit waste the expression "impeachable for waste" becomes meaningless as to him. What then is the proportion of the mining rent which must be set aside under those circumstances? The Court of Appeal has decided that the tenant for life must be treated as if he were impeachable for waste and accordingly that three-fourths of the rent must be set aside: *Re Ridge*, 31 Ch. D. 504. Lindley, L. J., who delivered the judgment of the Court, said, "If s. 11 is taken literally and by itself then as Mrs. Moody is not a tenant for life impeachable for waste (such expression not being properly applicable to her) one fourth only of the rents ought in this case to be capitalized. But so to construe the section, is in our opinion to sacrifice its true meaning, and under cover of adhering to the words, to miss the object sought to be attained by them."

Settlements by way of trust for sale.

A direction to the trustees to receive the rents and apply them for certain purposes expresses a "contrary intention" within the meaning of this section: *Re Duke of Newcastles' Estates*, 24 Ch. D. 129, 143.

Contrary intention.

The general rules as to the working of mines by a tenant for life may be summarized as follows:—A tenant for life, expressly made unimpeachable for waste, may work for his own profit all the mines and minerals whether they have been already worked or not: but where he is impeachable for waste, he cannot open mines or dig new pits: *Whitfield v. Bewit*, 2 P. Wms. 242. He may, however, continue the working of such as have been opened by the settlor: *Viner v. Vaughan*, 2 Beav. 466; or by a previous tenant in tail: *Clavering v. Clavering*, 2 P. Wms. 388; and he may open new pits or shafts for the purpose of working the old vein (*ibid.*); or a new underlying vein the existence of which was unknown during the testator's lifetime: *Spencer v. Scurr*, 31 Beav. 334; and as to the circumstances under which he may resume the working of a dormant or abandoned mine, see *Bagot v. Bagot*, 32 Beav. 509.

Position of tenant for life.

The Settled Estates Act, 1877 (40 & 41 Vict. c. 18), s. 4, also makes provision for setting aside a certain portion of the rent reserved on a mining lease granted in pursuance of the Act; but the propor-

Mining rent set aside under

§ 11.

the Settled Estates Act.

tion to be set aside is made to depend upon whether the tenant for life is entitled to work the mines and minerals for his own benefit or not. Thus, if a lease of open mines were granted under the Settled Estates Act, the tenant for life, although impeachable for waste, need only relinquish one-fourth of the rent, whereas if he exercises the powers of this Act he must set aside three-fourths thereof; for it does not seem possible to read the words in this section, "impeachable for waste in respect of minerals," as equivalent to "impeachable for waste in respect of *the* minerals," comprised in the lease.

If the settlement is silent on the subject the tenant for life is impeachable for waste (*Re Ridge*, 31 Ch. D. 504), and if the mines are *open* he is allowed to work them, not because he is unimpeachable for waste in respect of these particular minerals, but because such working is not waste. This circumstance renders it probable that applications will continue to be made under the former Act to sanction leases of open mines.

The rents set aside are "land" in the hands of the trustees, and pass by a gift of the surface: see *Re Scarth*, 10 Ch. D. 499. It has been held that a lease of salt-works, where the salt was obtained by the evaporation of brine pumped up from a depth of 150 feet, was not within the above-mentioned provision in the Settled Estates Act, and that no part of the rent need be set aside: *Re Dudley's S. E.*, 26 Sol. J. 359.

To whom rent is payable.

The necessity of setting aside part of the rent as capital money gives rise to questions of some difficulty. Sect. 22 provides that capital money shall be paid either to the trustees, or into court at the option of the tenant for life, which does not seem to contemplate the payment being made by the tenant for life himself: but how can part of the rent be effectually reserved to the trustees who in many cases take no estate in the land ? "No rent (which is properly said a rent) may be reserved upon any lease but only to the lessor, and in no manner it may be reserved to any strange person," Litt. § 346. It is conceived, therefore, that the whole rent must be reserved either generally so as to go with the reversion under s. 10 of the Conveyancing Act, 1881, or else expressly to the lessor. In either case it would in general be recoverable by the tenant for life. In order to carry out the provisions of this section some conveyancers make the trustees parties to the lease, and make the lessee covenant to pay their respective proportions of the rent to the tenant for life and the trustees. But the effect of such a covenant seems very doubtful. Does it deprive the lessor of his right to recover the rent as annexed to the reversion ? If it amounts to an assignment to the trustees of their proportion of the rent, that proportion will become a rent seck in their hands, and will be secured by the sta-

SPECIAL LEASING POWERS.

tutory remedies (Conv. Act, 1881, s. 44) and not by a condition of re-entry in the lease as required by s. 7 (3). If it does not amount to an assignment it would seem only to constitute the trustees the agents of the lessor for the purpose of receiving part of the rent, and such agency might at any time be revoked. A further difficulty arises if a change occurs in the constitution of the trustees of the settlement. The new trustees, not being parties to the deed, will be unable to enforce payment: *Gandy* v. *Gandy*, 30 Ch. D. 57. It may also cause some inconvenience to the lessee on a sale of his interest; for, in order to make the "receipt for the last payment due for rent" effectual under s. 3 (4) of the Conveyancing Act, he will have to shew the title of the trustees of the settlement to give a receipt for part of the rent. The trustees whether they receive their proportion of the rent from the tenant for life or from the lessee have onerous duties to perform if they act under this section, and it would seem to be better in most cases to obtain an order that the lessee should pay the capital portion of the mineral rent into Court. See Form of Summons, Form X., *post*.

§ 11.

Special Powers.

12. The leasing power of a tenant for life extends to the making of—

(i.) A lease for giving effect to a contract entered into by any of his predecessors in title for making a lease, which, if made by the predecessor, would have been binding on the successors in title; and

(ii.) A lease for giving effect to a covenant of renewal, performance whereof could be enforced against the owner for the time being of the settled land; and

(iii.) A lease for confirming, as far as may be, a previous lease, being void or voidable; but so that every lease, as and when confirmed, shall be such a lease as might at the date of the original lease have been lawfully granted, under this Act, or otherwise, as the case may require.

§ 12.
Leasing powers for special objects.

This section does not confer upon *lessees* any rights which they did not previously possess. It merely authorizes the tenant for life in

Sect. 12.
Special objects.

§ 12.

certain cases, by the exercise of his leasing powers, to give legal effect to existing equities; and for that purpose to complete contracts, grant renewals, and cure technical defects in leases which are void or voidable.

It may be observed that this section professes to *extend* the leasing powers of the tenant for life; and it would, therefore, seem that the cases which it contemplates would not, except for its authority, be within the powers of the tenant for life.

i. Contracts.

There are two classes of contracts which a tenant for life or other limited owner may be called upon to complete: viz., (1) those entered into by a previous limited owner under the same settlement; and (2) those entered into by the settlor or testator before the date of the settlement.

As to the former, power is conferred upon the tenant for life by s. 31, *post*, to enter into contracts for leases, which may be enforced against, and carried into effect by any successor in title for the time being of the tenant for life. These leases must be in conformity with the provisions of the Act; and, accordingly, independently of the present section, where one limited owner enters into a valid contract for a lease, any subsequent limited owner may, and indeed must, give effect to that contract by the exercise of his statutory powers. See *Davis* v. *Harford*, 22 Ch. D. 128.

This clause seems to be directed to the second class of cases to which we have referred. If, for example, a testator entered into a contract for a building lease for a term of 999 years, and died before completion, having devised the estate in strict settlement, it is conceived that under this section the tenant for life might grant a lease so as to give effect to such contract. He might in like manner carry out any other contract of the settlor or testator, although not in accordance with the regulations prescribed by this Act. See *Cust* v. *Middleton*, 3 D. F. & J. 33; *Re Kentish Town Estates*, 1 J. & H. 230. The expression "predecessors in title" is ambiguous, and may be confined to persons taking antecedent estates in the chain of limitations under the same settlement. It may, however, include—and this is its proper signification—the testator, settlor, or other person from whom the successor derives title.

Operation of a contract under a power.

Where a contract for valuable consideration has been entered into under a power, it is treated in equity as an execution of the power: *Re Dyke's Estate*, L. R. 7 Eq. 337; *Davis* v. *Harford*, 22 Ch. D. 128. "Contracts are considered as defective executions, and like them require a sufficient consideration to enable the Court to act. The same rules, therefore, apply in each case. As against a remainderman both are equally binding. An instrument in the form of a contract for a lease will be construed as such, and not an actual lease, where the effect of the latter construction would be that upon the face of the instrument it would be a void execution of the power:" Sugden on Powers, 552, 8th ed.

§ 12.

Under the second clause the tenant for life may grant a lease for lives, where, as is generally the case, the covenant for renewal is contained in a lease of that description.

ii. Renewals.

In order to come within this section, the covenant must be capable of being enforced against the owner for the time being of the settled land, and it must therefore have been entered into either by an absolute owner, or a person acting under an exceptional power similar to that set out in *Brigstocke* v. *Brigstocke*, 8 Ch. D. 357.

An ordinary power of leasing does not authorize the insertion of a covenant to renew, but if such a covenant be inserted the validity of the lease will not be affected, for the lessor only, and not those in remainder, will be bound thereby: *Doe* v. *Bettison*, 12 East, 305; and see *Taylor* v. *Stibbert*, 2 Ves. jun. 437; *Gas Light and Coke Company* v. *Towse*, 35 Ch. D. 519.

When the original lease contains a covenant for perpetual renewal, the renewed lease should contain a covenant for renewal in the same words: *Hare* v. *Burges*, 4 K. & J. 45; but when the reversion has become vested in trustees, they cannot be compelled to enter into a covenant to renew, and the proper form in such a case is a demise by the trustees for the new term, reciting the original covenant: *The Copper Mining Co.* v. *Beach*, 13 Beav. 478; *Hodges* v. *Blagrove*, 18 Beav. 404.

The tenant for life under the present section, being a trustee for all parties interested (s. 53), may, it is conceived, insist on adopting the latter form of renewal. As to renewal by guardians of infants, see 11 Geo. 4 and 1 Will. 4, c. 65; and by the committees of lunatics, 53 Vict. c. 5, s. 120; and generally as to the renewal of leases, Woodfall, pp. 337–345, 12th ed.

Clause iii. seems to meet the two cases of (1) a demise by the settlor, which is void in consequence of not being under seal; and (2) a lease under a power which is defective "by reason of the non-observance or omission of some condition or restriction, or by reason of some other deviation from the terms of such power:" 12 & 13 Vict. c. 26.

iii. Confirmation of void or voidable leases.

"It seems to be now settled that all instruments void at law as leases, but so expressed as to be capable of being construed as agreements for leases, are good as such agreements both at law and in equity:" Dav. Conv. v., pt. i., 17, 3rd ed.; *Parker* v. *Taswell*, 2 De G. & J. 559; *Stranks* v. *St. John*, L. R. 2 C. P. 376.

Void demise.

If the settlor was absolutely entitled, *any* void lease, which is capable of being construed as an agreement, may be confirmed under this section by the tenant for life.

Where a lease was granted under a power, and all the terms of the

Lease under a power.

§ 12.

power were not strictly observed, the Courts of Equity were accustomed to aid the lessee if the defect was one of form and not of substance. See Sugden on Powers, 714, 8th ed.

Now under "the Act for granting relief against defects in leases, made under powers of leasing, in certain cases" (12 & 13 Vict. c. 26), leases which are invalid, by reason of the non-observance or omission of some condition or restriction, or by reason of any other deviation from the terms of the power, are, if the lease has been made *bonâ fide* and the lessee has entered, to be deemed valid contracts for leases, "save so far as any variation may be necessary in order to comply with the terms of such power."

By the Act to amend the last-mentioned Act (13 & 14 Vict. c. 17), the acceptance of rent amounts to confirmation of an invalid lease, if the person receiving the same by a note in writing shows an intention to confirm the lease (s. 2); and where the reversioner is able and willing to confirm the invalid lease, the lessee is bound to accept a confirmation accordingly (s. 3).

Surrenders.

§ 13.
Surrender and new grant of leases.

13.—(1.) A tenant for life may accept, with or without consideration, a surrender of any lease of settled land, whether made under this Act or not, in respect of the whole land leased, or any part thereof, with or without an exception of all or any of the mines and minerals therein, or in respect of mines and minerals, or any of them.

(2.) On a surrender of a lease in respect of part only of the land or mines and minerals leased, the rent may be apportioned.

(3.) On a surrender, the tenant for life may make of the land or mines and minerals surrendered, or of any part thereof, a new or other lease, or new or other leases in lots.

(4.) A new or other lease may comprise additional land or mines and minerals, and may reserve any apportioned or other rent.

(5.) On a surrender, and the making of a new or other lease, whether for the same or for any extended or other term, and whether or not subject to the same or to any other covenants, provisions, or conditions, the value of the lessee's interest in the lease surrendered may be taken into account in the determination of the amount of the rent to be reserved, and of any fine to be taken, and of the nature of the covenants, provisions, and conditions to be inserted in the new or other lease.

§ 13.

(6.) Every new or other lease shall be in conformity with this Act.

"Surrender, properly, is a yielding up of an estate for life or years to him that hath an immediate estate in reversion or remainder, wherein the estate for life or years may drown by mutual agreement:" Co. Litt. 337 b.

Sect. 13. Surrender.

Where the tenant for life has only an equitable interest (s. 2 (5)), or the land is settled by way of trust for sale (s. 63), a transaction carried out under this section is not a "surrender" within the meaning of the foregoing definition, unless the trustees in whom the legal estate is vested are made parties to the deed. This, however, is probably not necessary; as, although the term may not "drown by mutual agreement," it will be annihilated by force of the statute.

Leases may be surrendered under the Settled Estates Act (40 & 41 Vict. c. 18), s. 7, and it has been held that a lease granted upon a surrender takes effect "in possession," so as to satisfy the requirements of the Act in that behalf, although an underlease granted by the surrendering lessee is unexpired: *Re Ford's S. E.*, L. R. 8 Eq. 309.

Settled Estates Act.

As to the surrender of contracts for leases, see s. 31, *post*, p. 114.

The consideration referred to in the first sub-section seems to be payable by the lessee, implying that he pays to get rid of the lease. If, on the other hand, the lease is a beneficial one, there is no power to give consideration for the surrender, except under sub-s. 5, by taking it into account in the grant of a new lease. It may be mentioned that under the Stamp Act, 1870 (33 & 34 Vict. c. 99), s. 98, a lease is not to be charged with any duty by reason of being made in consideration of the surrender of any existing lease.

Sub-s. 1. Consideration.

Stamp Duty.

The remedies against sub-lessees are now unaffected by the surrender of the lessee's interest: 8 & 9 Vict. c. 106, s. 9; and, on the other hand, their rights will not be prejudiced thereby: *Mellor* v. *Watkins*, L. R. 9 Q. B. 400.

Sub-lessees.

By the Conveyancing Act, 1881, s. 12, every condition or right of re-entry will, in case of a partial surrender, be apportioned and remain annexed to the reversionary estate in the land which has not been surrendered.

Apportionment of conditions.

Sub-s. 5 overthrows the doctrine stated by Lord St. Leonards in these terms:—" But the existence of a lease, beneficial to the lessee, will not justify the grant of a new one at a less rent than the pro-

Sub-s. 5. Conditions of new lease.

F 2

§ 13.

perty is worth at the time :" Sugden on Powers, 787, 8th ed., citing *Wright* v. *Smith*, 5 Esp. Ca. 203; *Lefroy* v. *Walsh*, 1 Ir. C. L. Rep. N. S. 313.

The surrender of a beneficial lease is equivalent to the payment of a fine, and may be taken into account in the reduction of the rent under the new lease. See *Re Rawlins' Estate*, L. R. 1 Eq. 286.

Copyholds.

§ 14.

Power to grant to copyholders licences for leasing.

14.—(1.) A tenant for life may grant to a tenant of copyhold or customary land, parcel of a manor comprised in the settlement, a licence to make any such lease of that land, or of a specified part thereof, as the tenant for life is by this Act empowered to make of freehold land.

(2.) The licence may fix the annual value whereon fines, fees, or other customary payments are to be assessed, or the amount of those fines, fees, or payments.

(3.) The licence shall be entered on the court rolls of the manor, of which entry a certificate in writing of the steward shall be sufficient evidence.

Sect. 14. Licences to copyholders.

The provisions of this section are analogous to those of the 9th section of the Settled Estates Act; and it is to be observed, that the copyhold tenant may himself be a tenant for life, in which case the powers of this Act would be called into requisition, as well for the lease as for the licence in pursuance of which it was granted. There is, however, no power given to the tenant for life of the copyhold to concur in fixing the amount of the fines.

According to the custom of the manor of Ealing, the lord cannot license a lease for a longer term than twenty-one years: *Hanbury* v. *Litchfield*, 2 My. & K. 629. Where such a custom prevails it will not, it is conceived, be overridden by the present section.

Operation of licences.

Except by licence or special custom, a lease by a copyholder for more than a year is a cause of forfeiture, and the licence operates as a dispensation. "The terms of obtaining the lord's licence depend upon the custom of each particular manor, just as the fine on admittance; but the licence is usually given as a matter of course, on payment of a certain fixed sum for each house or acre of land for each year of the term of the proposed lease:" Scriven, 193, 6th ed.

Semble, any payment made for the grant of a licence would be "capital money arising under the Act."

The power here conferred does not extend, like the ordinary form, to a licence to build or pull down houses, or to improve the premises. But this omission does not seem important, as the tenant generally enfranchises previously to incurring any serious outlay, and "meliorating waste," as it is called, does not seem to be a ground of forfeiture: *Hardy* v. *Reeves*, 4 Ves. 466, 480; *Doe* v. *The Earl of Burlington*, 5 B. & Ad. 507.

§ 14.

Referring to the power of fixing the annual value for the purpose of assessing fines, Mr. Davidson remarks that "this may be the most important part of the power, especially as it would often be impracticable to make improvements, if the lord could not effectually remit the customary right to have the fines assessed on the improved value during a certain term:" Dav. Conv. iii. 542, 3rd ed. As to the power of the lord of a manor, being a limited owner, to grant licences otherwise than in pursuance of a power authorizing him in that behalf, see Watkins on Copyholds, ii. 111.

Sub-s. 2. Fixing the annual value.

V.—Sales, Leases, and other Dispositions.

Mansion and Park.

15. *Notwithstanding anything in this Act, the principal mansion-house on any settled land, and the demesnes thereof, and other lands usually occupied therewith, shall not be sold or leased by the tenant for life, without the consent of the trustees of the settlement, or an order of the Court.*

§ 15. Restriction as to mansion-house, park, &c.

The section has been repealed and re-enacted with amendments by s. 10 of the Act of 1890 which is in the following terms:—

Sect. 15.

Mansion and Park.

"10.—(1.) From and after the passing of this Act s. 15 of the Act of 1882, relating to the sale or leasing of the principal mansion-house, shall be and the same is hereby repealed.

Restriction on sale of mansion.

"(2.) Notwithstanding anything contained in the Act of 1882, the principal mansion-house (if any) on any settled land, and the pleasure grounds and park and lands (if any) usually occupied therewith, shall not be sold, exchanged, or leased by the tenant for life without the consent of the trustees of the settlement or an order of the Court.

"(3.) Where a house is usually occupied as a farmhouse, or where the site of any house and the pleasure grounds and park and lands (if any) usually occupied therewith do not together exceed twenty-

§ 15.

Sub-s. 1. Repeal.

five acres in extent, the house is not to be deemed a principal mansion-house within the meaning of this section."

The words in sub-s. 1 " relating to the sale or leasing of the principal mansion-house" seem to be surplusage, and do not limit the generality of the repeal. S. 15 relates not only to the "principal mansion-house" but also to "the demesnes thereof, and other lands usually occupied therewith," but the substituted provisions in sub-s. 2 of the Act of 1890 are clearly intended to supersede the whole of the earlier enactment.

Sub-s. 2. Discretion.

Notwithstanding an express direction by the settlor that the mansion-house shall not be sold, the trustees of the settlement or the Court may sanction a sale under this section: *Re Brown's Will*, 27 Ch. D. 179; see also *Re Thompson's Will*, 21 L. R., Ir. 109. In the former case it was also decided that if chattels are annexed to the mansion-house as heirlooms, they must either be included in the application for a sale (see s. 37), or proper provision must be made for their custody.

The discretion vested in the trustees of the settlement and the Court by this section should be guided by the consideration whether the rest of the estate will sell to greater advantage with the mansion-house than without it : *Re Brown's Will*, 27 Ch. D. 179. But this is not the only circumstance to be taken into account; and where the tenant for life has mortgaged his life estate to its full value the Court will not make an order authorizing a sale without the consent of the mortgagees: *Re Sebright's Settled Estates*, 33 Ch. D. 429.

The changes introduced by this sub-section are (1) The words "pleasure grounds and park" replace "demesnes," and (2) The restriction imposed by the section is extended to the power of exchange. "Park" seems to be used in its popular not in its legal signification.

Specific performance with compensation.

If the tenant for life enters into a contract for the sale of the settled land, including the mansion-house, and fails to obtain the consent of the trustees, or an order of the Court as required by this section, specific performance as to the rest of the land, with compensation in respect of the mansion-house, cannot be enforced either by vendor or purchaser.

"If a purchase was made of a mansion-house in one lot, and farms, &c, in others, and no title could be made to the lot containing the mansion-house, it would be a ground to rescind the whole contract:" *Poole* v. *Shergold*, 1 Bro. C. C. 118.

The converse case is put by Lord St. Leonards, who states that "a seller could not at the election of the purchaser be deprived of his mansion-house and park, to which he could make a good title, whilst a large adjoining estate held and sold with it would be left on his hands with a proclaimed bad title :" Sug. V. & P. 316, 14th ed.

Sub-s. 3.

The third sub-section is intended to remove the doubt felt under the repealed enactment, whether any dwelling house on any plot of ground might not be a principal mansion-house within the meaning of the Act; but it seems that the question of fact whether "a house is usually occupied as a farmhouse" may in particular cases be difficult to determine. It was decided in an Irish case under the repealed section that a house and grounds in one county, settled upon the same trusts as lands in another, was the principal mansion-house on the settled land : *Re Thompson's Will*, 21 L. R., Ir. 109.

§ 15.
Principal mansion-house.

The principles involved in this decision are important, and may be thus stated : (1) There can be only one principal mansion-house included in a settlement; (2) The limitations of the instrument and not geographical position determine the extent of the settled land. It is thus quite possible that the principal mansion-house with reference to Irish land might be situate in England or *vice versâ*. Questions may arise when several residences are included in the same settlement as to which is entitled to the honour of being within this section. It is conceived that it is not competent to the settlor to declare by the settlement which of several houses is to be regarded as "the principal mansion-house;" for if the one selected did not in fact satisfy this description the declaration would as to this particular house amount to an attempted restriction on the exercise of the powers of the Act by the tenant for life and would be void under s. 51, *post*.

For Forms of Summons, see Forms under S. L. Act, 1882, Nos. IV., V., VI., VIII.

Forms.

Streets and Open Spaces.

16. On or in connection with a sale or grant for building purposes, or a building lease, the tenant for life, for the general benefit of the residents on the settled land, or on any part thereof,—

§ 16.
Dedication for streets, open spaces, &c.

(i.) May cause or require any parts of the settled land to be appropriated and laid out for streets, roads, paths, squares, gardens, or other open spaces, for the use, gratuitously or on payment, of the public or of individuals, with sewers, drains, watercourses, fencing, paving, or other works necessary or proper in connexion therewith ; and

(ii.) May provide that the parts so appropriated shall be conveyed to or vested in the trustees of the

§ 16.

settlement, or other trustees, or any company or public body, on trusts or subject to provisions for securing the continued appropriation thereof to the purposes aforesaid, and the continued repair or maintenance of streets and other places and works aforesaid, with or without provision for appointment of new trustees when required; and

(iii.) May execute any general or other deed necessary or proper for giving effect to the provisions of this section (which deed may be inrolled in the Central Office of the Supreme Court of Judicature), and thereby declare the mode, terms, and conditions of the appropriation, and the manner in which and the persons by whom the benefit thereof is to be enjoyed, and the nature and extent of the privileges and conveniences granted.

Sect. 16. Streets and open spaces.

The powers here conferred upon the tenant for life are similar to those which the Court was authorized to exercise by the Settled Estates Act, s. 20.

It is important to observe, that the tenant for life cannot, out of generosity or public spirit, dedicate gratuitously a portion of the estate to the purposes of this section. The dedication must be made "on or in connexion" with a building scheme, the rents to be obtained being naturally increased by the advantages offered to the residents. The power is presumably conferred for the purpose of disposing of the settled land on more advantageous terms than could otherwise have been obtained. It seems that if roads are dedicated to the public it must be gratuitously, there being no power to charge tolls for the user of the road : *Austerberry* v. *Corporation of Oldham*, 29 Ch. D. 750.

Raising expenses.

The execution of the works authorized by this section may be paid for out of capital moneys arising under the Act (s. 25, xvii.) ; and, accordingly, the tenant for life may sell part of the settled land to pay for making roads on another part; but he has no power to raise capital money by mortgage except for the special purposes enumerated in s. 18 of this Act and s. 11 of the Act of 1890. If, therefore, there are no funds available, and if a sale is inexpedient, application must still be made to the Court, under the Settled Estates Act, to sanction the execution of the works, and the raising of the money by charge or mortgage. 40 & 41 Vict. c. 18, ss. 20, 21.

§ 16.

By s. 28, *post*, the tenant for life is bound, if the Board of Agriculture (which has taken the place of the Land Commissioners) order him to do so, "to maintain and repair at his own expense" every improvement executed under the Act. The special provision made for repairs by this section, seems only to apply where the improvement is self-supporting, as in the case of a square for which the residents subscribe. As to what will amount to a dedication of a highway to the public, and the liability for repairs in such a case, see *Healey v. Corporation of Batley*, L. R. 19 Eq. 375; *Austerberry v. Corporation of Oldham*, 29 Ch. D. 750.

Repairs.

The dedication of an open space for the gratuitous use of the public would seem to be a "charity" (see *Townley v. Bedwell*, 6 Ves. 194); but by the Mortmain and Charitable Uses Act, 1888 (51 & 52 Vict. c. 42), s. 6, assurances by deed of land for the purposes only of a public park (defined as including any park, garden, or other land dedicated or to be dedicated to the recreation of the public) are excepted from the operation of Parts I. and II. of the Act. If, however, the deed is "made otherwise than in good faith for full and valuable consideration, it must be executed not less than twelve months before the death of the assuror . . . and must be enrolled in the books of the Charity Commissioners within six months after the execution of the deed." It is conceived that a conveyance of a park or square by the tenant for life to trustees for the benefit of the public under this section as part of a general building scheme constitutes an assurance for "full and valuable consideration" within the meaning of the Mortmain and Charitable Uses Act, 1888; and accordingly that none of the restrictions of that Act have any application.

Inrolment of deed.

Surface and Minerals apart.

17.—(1.) A sale, exchange, partition, or mining lease, may be made either of land, with or without an exception or reservation of all or any of the mines and minerals therein, or of any mines and minerals, and in any such case with or without a grant or reservation of powers of working, wayleaves or rights of way, rights of water and drainage, and other powers, easements, rights, and privileges for or incident to or connected with mining purposes, in relation to the settled land, or any part thereof, or any other land.

§ 17.

Separate dealing with surface and minerals, with or without wayleaves, &c.

§ 17.

(2.) An exchange or partition may be made subject to and in consideration of the reservation of an undivided share in mines or minerals.

Sect. 17. Surface and minerals apart.

This section is framed in the most general and comprehensive terms so as to authorize dealings with the surface and the minerals as if they formed separate inheritances, with the same powers of granting or reserving easements rights and privileges for the benefit of one over the other, as if the several strata had been contiguous farms instead of lying one above the other.

The express mention of "mining lease" in this section was unnecessary (see s. 2 (10) iv.), and mystifies the reader who finds that "a mining lease may be made of land with an exception or reservation of all or any of the mines and minerals therein."

Confirmation of Sales Act.

Under a power to make sale of all or any part of the settled estate it was held by Lord Romilly that the trustees could not sell the lands with a reservation of the minerals: *Buckley* v. *Howell*, 29 Beav. 546. In consequence of this decision the law was altered by the Confirmation of Sales Act (25 & 26 Vict. c. 108), which enacted in effect that every trustee and other person having a power of sale over land might, with the sanction of the Court of Chancery, dispose of the land or minerals separately, unless forbidden to do so by the instrument creating the trust or power.

It is important to observe that, by virtue of s. 51, *post*, the tenant for life cannot be deprived by the settlement of the power of separate disposition herein conferred; and that, where he is unimpeachable for waste, he may (as pointed out by the late Master of the Rolls in *Buckley* v. *Howell*, *ubi supra*), work the reserved minerals for his own benefit, and invest the proceeds of sale of the surface in another estate with valuable minerals under it. He would thus get the minerals from under the two estates. There is, indeed, no reason why the process should stop there. He might in like manner sell the surface of the second estate reserving the minerals, and re-invest in a third mineral property; a course of dealing which would, of course, prejudice the interests of the remainderman.

Perhaps the answer to this difficulty is to be found in s. 53, which places the tenant for life in exercising any power under the Act in the position of a trustee. If he should endeavour to reap an undue advantage for himself the Court would probably at the instance of the remainderman or of the trustees of the settlement interfere to prevent such an abuse of his powers.

By s. 3, *ante*, p. 38, the mines or minerals may be reserved on enfranchisement.

Restrictions imposed by the settlement on the exercise of the powers thereby conferred upon the trustees do not affect the statutory powers, even when these are to be exercised by the trustees on behalf of an infant. Thus, where there was power conferred by the settlement upon the trustees to sell or exchange with the consent of the tenant for life if of age, and if not of his guardians, it was held that the trustees (the tenant in tail in possession being an infant), could, under this section and s. 60, sell the surface apart from the minerals without the consent of the infant's testamentary guardians: *Re Duke of Newcastle's Estates*, 24 Ch. D. 129, 142.

§ 17.

It is difficult to say whether under this section the tenant for life can give the purchaser or lessee of the minerals the right to "let down" the surface, or whether he can on a sale of the surface reserve to himself and his successors in title a similar right. The general law is that the owner of the upper stratum is entitled as of common right to support from the subjacent strata, but the mineral owner may shew that on the construction of his grant or reservation he has acquired the right to let down the surface either with or without compensation to the owner: *Rowbotham* v. *Wilson*, 8 H. L. Cas. 348; *Aspden* v. *Seddon*, L. R. 10 Ch. 394; 1 Ex. D. 496; *Dixon* v. *White*, 8 App. Cas. 833; *Love* v. *Bell*, 9 App. Cas. 286. The words of this section—"a grant or reservation of powers of working and other powers, &c., incident to mining purposes" certainly seem wide enough to authorize such a contract on the part of the tenant for life; but there is no provision as to compensation for such injuries either when the surface is sold, or when it is retained.

Letting down the surface.

Mortgage.

18. Where money is required for enfranchisement, or for equality of exchange or partition, the tenant for life may raise the same on mortgage of the settled land, or of any part thereof, by conveyance of the fee simple, or other estate or interest the subject of the settlement, or by creation of a term of years in the settled land, or otherwise, and the money raised shall be capital money arising under this Act.

§ 18. Mortgage for equality money, &c.

The tenant for life is empowered by s. 11 of the Act of 1890, to raise money by mortgage of the settled land for the purpose of paying off incumbrances, but with this exception it is only for the special object mentioned in this section, namely, enfranchisement and equality of exchange or partition, that the tenant for life is expressly authorized to raise money by mortgage. The mortgagee, however, under s. 40, is not bound "to see that any money is wanted for any purpose of this Act, or that no more than is wanted is raised," and

Sect. 18. Raising money by mortgage.

§ 18.

the Act itself seems to contemplate more money being raised than is actually wanted; for s. 21, referring no doubt to the provisions of the present section, provides for the investment of capital money, subject to "application for any special authorized object for which the same was raised."

Cross references.

Notice should be given by the tenant for life to the trustees of the settlement of his intention to raise money under this section in accordance with s. 45, *post*, p. 137, and the trustees should in general be parties to the mortgage deed to give a receipt for the money (s. 40); which must either be paid to them or into Court (s .22). In the absence of special provision in the settlement authorizing one trustee to receive capital money there must be at least two trustees, s. 39. The power to complete the transaction by the execution of the mortgage deed is conferred by s. 20, and it may be observed that the tenant for life acting under the statutory power can vest the legal estate in the mortgagee, although he himself is only equitably entitled.

Enfranchisement money.

The "money required for enfranchisement" mentioned in this section is that payable by the copyholder, and does not include the expenses of the lord under s. 3 (ii.) in effecting an enfranchisement. See the Copyhold Act, 1852 (15 & 16 Vict. c. 51), s. 31, which provides that these expenses, where the lord has but a limited interest, may be charged on the manor, or other lands settled or held therewith. No provision is in this Act made for their payment, but it is presumed that they may be deducted out of the enfranchisement consideration.

Capital money arising under the Act from whatever source it springs may be applied to the purposes here specially provided for (see s. 21 (iv.) and (v.)), and when such money is available it will of course be unnecessary to make use of this power.

Undivided Share.

§ 19.

Concurrence in exercise of powers as to undivided share.

19. Where the settled land comprises an undivided share in land, or, under the settlement, the settled land has come to be held in undivided shares, the tenant for life of an undivided share may join or concur, in any manner and to any extent necessary or proper for any purpose of this Act, with any person entitled to or having power of right of disposition of or over another undivided share.

Sect. 19. Undivided share.

"Land" by the definition in s. 2 (10) includes an "undivided share in land:" and, accordingly, where an undivided share is settled, it constitutes the "settled land," within the meaning of the powers conferred by this Act. Without the assistance of this section the tenant for life could thus have exercised such of the powers conferred by the Act as are applicable to an undivided share. He could have sold his share, or made partition (s. 3), or he could have concurred with the owners of the other shares in selling the entirety: *Re Cooper & Allen's Contract*, 4 Ch. D. 802; but he would have been unable to grant or to concur in granting a lease: *Tolson* v. *Sheard*, 5 Ch. D. 19.

§ 19.

It is important to observe the distinction between the two cases of an undivided share being comprised in the original settlement, and of the settled land coming to be held in undivided shares. In the latter case the tenant for life of one of such shares has none of the statutory powers in respect of his undivided share; for the determination of the question whether land is "settled land" is governed by the state of facts and the limitations of the settlement at the time of the settlement taking effect s. 2 (4); and in the case under consideration the entirety and not an undivided share constituted the "settled land" when the settlement took effect. See *Re Collinge's Settled Estates*, 36 Ch. D. 516. An exchange or partition may be made subject to and in consideration of the reservation of an undivided share in mines or minerals (s. 17) and the powers of this section will then be available in respect of such undivided share.

The Court will permit (see s. 62, *post*) the committee of a lunatic tenant in tail under this section to sell his share to his co-owners: *Re Gaitskell*, 40 Ch. D. 416: although there was no jurisdiction to sanction such an arrangement when the lunatic was absolutely entitled: *Re Weld*, 28 Ch. D. 514. See now, however, the Lunacy Act, 1890 (53 Vict. c. 5), ss. 120, 341.

Lunatic's share.

Conveyance.

20.—(1.) On a sale, exchange, partition, lease, mortgage, or charge, the tenant for life may, as regards land sold, given in exchange or on partition, leased, mortgaged, or charged, or intended so to be, including copyhold or customary or leasehold land vested in trustees, or as regards easements or other rights or privileges sold or leased, or intended so to be, convey or create the same by deed, for the estate or interest the subject of the settlement, or for any less estate or interest, to the uses and in the manner requisite for giving effect to the sale, exchange, partition, lease, mortgage, or charge.

§ 20.

Completion of sale, lease, &c., by conveyance.

(2.) Such a deed, to the extent and in the manner to and in which it is expressed or intended to operate and can

§ 20. operate under this Act, is effectual to pass the land conveyed, or the easements, rights, or privileges created, discharged from all the limitations, powers, and provisions of the settlement, and from all estates, interests, and charges, subsisting or to arise thereunder, but subject to and with the exception of—

    (i.) All estates, interests, and charges having priority to the settlement; and

    (ii.) All such other, if any, estates, interests, and charges as have been conveyed or created for securing money actually raised at the date of the deed; and

    (iii.) All leases and grants at fee-farm rent or otherwise, and all grants and easements, rights of common, or other rights or privileges granted or made for value in money or money's worth, or agreed so to be, before the date of the deed, by the tenant for life, or by any of his predecessors in title, or by any trustees for him or them, under the settlement, or under any statutory power, or being otherwise binding on the successors in title of the tenant for life.

(3.) In case of a deed relating to copyhold or customary land, it is sufficient that the deed be entered on the court rolls of the manor, and the steward is hereby required on production to him of the deed to make the proper entry; and on that production, and on payment of customary fines, fees, and other dues or payments, any person whose title under the deed requires to be perfected by admittance shall be admitted accordingly; but if the steward so requires, there shall also be produced to him so much of the settlement as may be necessary to show the title of the person executing the deed; and the same may, if the steward thinks fit, be also entered on the court rolls.

Sect. 20. Conveyance in exercise of powers.

This section furnishes the machinery whereby the powers, previously conferred upon the tenant for life, are to be carried into effect by conveyance. In strict settlements, *i.e.* where the limitations are legal, the conveyance under an express power operates by revocation of the uses of the settlement, and an appointment by the trustees to the new uses. This power of revocation and new appointment, which is always annexed to such a power, enables the trustees by virtue of the Statute of Uses to vest the legal estate in the purchaser, the declaration of the use being fed by the original seisin of the grantees to uses in the settlement.

Under this Act the operation of the statutory conveyance is entirely different. The estate is transferred by virtue of this statute alone; and, upon the execution of the conveyance, it goes over from the person in whom it was previously vested to the person named in such conveyance, so as to give effect to the sale, exchange, partition, lease, or mortgage.

The first sub-section, indeed, speaks of a conveyance to uses as if there were an implied power of revocation and new appointment, but the second sub-section makes it clear that the conveyance is to operate as a statutory power quite irrespectively of the Statute of Uses.

"A power given by a will or by an Act of Parliament to sell an estate is a common law authority. The estate passes by force of the will, or Act of Parliament, and the person who executes the power merely nominates the party to take the estate." Sugden on Powers, 45, 8th ed. The distinction is of importance with reference to the form of the conveyance. Where the appointment operates under the Statute of Uses, the legal estate vests by a rule of law and without reference to the intention of the parties in the first person named as an appointee. In the case of a common law authority the appointment of the estate to A. and his heirs to the use of other persons, "would not of itself vest the legal estate in A., but would give the legal estate to the real objects of the appointment." Sug. on Powers, 196, 8th ed.

§ 20.

In order to provide expressly for the completion of contracts entered into by a deceased tenant for life (s. 31 (2)) it has been enacted that a tenant for life may make any conveyance which is necessary or proper for giving effect to a contract entered into by a predecessor in title which if made by such predecessor would have been valid as against his successors in title. Act of 1890, s. 6.

Amendment Act of 1890, s. 6.

The words "including copyhold or customary or leasehold land *vested in trustees*" are presumably inserted here with special reference to the case of a strict settlement in which copyholds and leaseholds are vested in trustees upon trusts corresponding with the uses of the freeholds. They do not limit the generality of the section, and accordingly freeholds vested in trustees, and copyholds and leaseholds not so vested may be conveyed by the tenant for life for all the estate and interest the subject of the settlement.

Sub-s. 1. Copyholds and leaseholds.

The tenant for life has power to sell (s. 3) or to lease (s. 6) any easement, right, or privilege over or in relation to the settled land;

Easements, rights, or privileges.

§ 20.   and this section enables him to give effect to such sale or lease by conveyance. In the Act of 1882 there was no provision for the grant or reservation of easements on exchange or partition, except in the special case of the surface and the minerals being separately disposed of under s. 17, and it will be observed that the conveyance or creation of easements on exchange or partition is ignored by this section.

The Act of 1890 provides (s. 5) that on an exchange or partition any easement, right, or privilege of any kind may be reserved or may be granted over or in relation to the settled land or any part thereof, or other land; or an easement, right, or privilege of any kind may be given or taken in exchange or on partition for land or for any other easement, right, or privilege of any kind. The first part of the foregoing section seems to deal with the creation of easements, rights, or privileges, *de novo*, and as they only come into existence by the conveyance no further power is necessary. The second part of the section refers to existing easements, rights or privileges, and the tenant for life will probably be held to take an implied power of conveying in such a manner as to give effect to the intention of the parties.

As to the creation of easements, rights, or privileges, by way of use, see the Conveyancing Act, 1881, s. 62.

Sub-s. 2. Incumbrances.   One of the chief difficulties in the practical working of this Act "for facilitating sales, leases, and other dispositions of settled land" is that many settled estates are subject to incumbrances which fetter the power of alienation. With the consent of the incumbrancer the tenant for life may under s. 5 charge an incumbrance upon any other part of the settled land in exoneration of the part sold; but if this cannot be done the conveyance can only be made subject to the estates, interests, charges, and incumbrances specified in sub-s. (2). It was pointed out by Mr. Justice Stirling in *Re Lord Stamford's Settled Estates* (43 Ch. D. 84, 93), that the word "charges" in this sub-section is used with reference as well to those which take priority over the settlement as to those which are created by the settlement itself; and this wide meaning should be borne in mind when the same word has to be construed in other parts of the Act. The statutory powers operate only on the "settled land," and accordingly the conveyance is by clause i. made subject to "all estates, interests, and charges having priority to the settlement." Thus if a reversion, or an equity of redemption is the subject of a settlement the rights of the prior owner, or of the mortgagee, are not affected by a conveyance under the Act.

The second clause of the sub-section excepts from the conveyance "all such other, if any, estates, interests and charges as have been conveyed or created for securing money actually raised at the date of the deed." It would seem not unnatural to limit this clause to estates, interests, and charges subsisting or to arise under the settlement, such as mortgages or charges which have been made for raising portions; but Mr. Justice North in *Re Sebright's Settled Estates* (33 Ch. D. 429, 438) has laid it down that "these words" (*i.e.*, the words of this clause) "include all estates and interests created subsequently to the settlement for the purpose of securing money, and that they therefore include a mortgage of his life interest made by the tenant for life for the purpose of raising money. Therefore, the conveyance by the tenant for life under the 20th section can only pass the estates subject to any charge by mortgage or otherwise of his life estate which has been made by the tenant for life for the purpose of raising money." This *dictum* does not seem easily reconcileable with the provisions of s. 50, *post*, which in substance enacts that a tenant for life who has assigned or incumbered his life estate may exercise the powers of this Act as if he had not done so, provided he obtains the consent of his assignee or incumbrancer. Again, if the clause applies to mortgages of the life interest it must equally apply to mortgages of the reversion; and it would be contrary to the whole scope of the Act to hold that a reversioner by raising money on his reversion could in any way hamper the tenant for life in the exercise of his statutory powers.

§ 20.

Life estate charges.

With respect to copyholds the statutory conveyance resembles a bargain and sale in pursuance of a power given by will, which is sufficient *without any surrender* to vest the right to admittance in the purchaser.

Sub-s. 3. Copyholds.

The admittance, it will be observed, is to be made on payment of "customary fines, fees, and other dues or payments," and Cotton, L.J., has said that in his opinion "the Act was not intended to take away any of the rights of the lord, but was not intended to give him any." *Re Naylor and Spendla's Contract*, 34 Ch. D. 217 at p. 221. In this case a testator, who was tenant on the court rolls of a manor, devised all his real estate to trustees upon trust to occupy or let it at their discretion, and to pay the net profits or rents to his wife for life. Shortly after the death of the testator the widow contracted to sell the copyhold under the powers of the Settled Land Act. The trustees had not been admitted, but the lord was not yet entitled to seize for want of a tenant. The question was raised on a summons under the Vendor and Purchaser Act, on which the lord and steward appeared and agreed to be bound by the decision, whether the lord was bound to admit the purchaser on payment of a single fine and set of fees, or whether another fine and set of fees were payable as if the trustees or the customary heir had been admitted. The Court (Cotton and Bowen, L.JJ., Fry, L.J., dissenting) held that the lord could claim only one fine on the ground that "the lord would have no right to a fine for the admittance of trustees who never were

Fines and fees.

C.S.L.A. G

§ 20.

admitted, and from whom the purchaser's right to be admitted is not derived."

The principle of this decision would seem to apply equally to a devise to the tenant for life without the intervention of trustees, and also to a settlement of copyholds by deed.

Production of the settlement.

Difficulties may occasionally arise in practice as to the production of the settlement to the steward of the manor. The legal tenant for life of freeholds is entitled as a matter of right to the possession of the title-deeds: *Garner* v. *Hannyngton,* 22 Beav. 627; *Allwood* v. *Heywood,* 1 H. & C. 745; *Leathes* v. *Leathes,* 5 Ch. D. 221; except when he has been guilty of misconduct with respect to the deeds: *Jenner* v. *Morris,* L. R. 1 Ch. 603; or there is a pending suit, *Stanford* v. *Roberts,* L. R. 6 Ch. 307; or they have been impounded by the Court for safe custody: *Ford* v. *Peering,* 1 Ves. jun. 72. And see *Wright* v. *Robotham,* 33 Ch. D. 106.

If the tenant for life is only equitably entitled, the *right* seems greatly to depend upon the *fact* of possession. In other words, in the absence of special circumstances, the person who has got the deeds may keep them: *Taylor* v. *Sparrow,* 4 Giff. 703; and see *Lady Langdale* v. *Briggs,* 8 D. M. & G. 391, 416. There may be cases, therefore, in which the tenant for life neither has the deeds nor has a right to call for them, though he may be entitled to inspect them; and if they are, for example, in the custody of the remainder-men, of the Court, or of mortgagees, he may not be able to comply with the steward's requisition.

This Act, however, has so materially altered the position of an equitable tenant for life that under ordinary circumstances the Court will commit the custody of the deeds to him. *Re Burnaby's Settled Estates,* 42 Ch. D. 621.

Covenant for production.

It may also be observed that where the tenant for life has not the possession of the deeds, he cannot, since he does not " retain possession," give an acknowledgment and undertaking under s. 9 of the Conv. Act, 1881.

Succession duty.

Where a tenant for life and remainderman join in the sale of an estate, it remains liable in the hands of the purchaser to succession duty on the death of the tenant for life; *secus* where the sale takes place under a power, or by virtue of the Settled Estates Act: *Re Warner's S. E.,* 17 Ch. D. 711, the duty being in those cases shifted from the land to the purchase-money or its investments. The same principles seem to apply here and to free the land from the succession duty payable on the death of the tenant for life, but not from that payable in respect of terminable charges anterior to the settlement. See, however, *Dugdale* v. *Meadows,* L. R. 6 Ch. 501, and the remarks thereon in Dav. Conv. ii., pt. i., 313, 4th ed., where it is stated that "the decision is not recognised as valid by the Crown, and is manifestly wrong." See also *Re Cooper & Allen's Contract*, 4 Ch. D. 802.

§ 20.

A tenant in tail (s. 58) exercising the powers of this Act can do so without an enrolled deed; and in like manner a married woman (s. 61) whenever married, and whether she is entitled for her separate use or not, can convey by virtue of her statutory power without a deed acknowledged.

Tenant in tail. Married woman.

The tenant for life is, of course, bound to enter into express or implied covenants for title and further assurance. See *Re The London Bridge Acts*, 13 Sim. 176; *Earl Poulett v. Hood*, L. R. 5 Eq. 115, where it seems to have been held that the tenant for life, whose consent is required to the exercise of a power of sale by trustees, must give the ordinary covenants. It is, however, the practice under this Act to qualify the statutory covenants of the tenant for life, implied by his conveying as "*beneficial owner*," by a proviso that, as regards the remainder or reversion expectant on his life estate, the covenants of the tenant for life shall extend only to his own acts and defaults and those of his heirs, and of persons claiming under or in trust for him or them. See Dart. V. & P. 620, 6th ed.; Prideaux, Conv. i., 301, 14th ed.; Key & Elphinstone i., 440, 3rd ed.; Davidson, Concise Prec. 121, 15th ed.

Covenants for title.

The following references as to matters incidental to the conveyance may be found useful:—As to payment of the purchase-money, s. 22 (1); as to trustees' power to give receipts, s. 40; as to the discharge of the purchaser paying his purchase-money to the trustees, s. 40; or into Court, s. 46 (2); as to the general protection of *bonâ fide* purchasers, s. 54; as to the power to execute the deed, s. 55 (2); and as to the investment of the purchase-money, s. 21.

References to incidental matters.

VI.—INVESTMENT OR OTHER APPLICATION OF CAPITAL TRUST MONEY.

21. Capital money arising under this Act, subject to payment of claims properly payable thereout, and to application thereof for any special authorized object for which the same was raised, shall, when received, be invested or otherwise applied wholly in one, or partly in one and partly in another or others, of the following modes (namely):

§ 21. Capital money under Act; investment, &c., by trustees or Court.

(i.) In investment on Government securities, or on other securities on which the trustees of the settlement are by the settlement or by law authorized to invest trust money of the settle-

§ 21.

ment, or on the security of the bonds, mortgages, or debentures, or in the purchase of the debenture stock, of any railway company in Great Britain or Ireland incorporated by special Act of Parliament, and having for ten years next before the date of investment paid a dividend on its ordinary stock or shares, with power to vary the investment into or for any other such securities :

(ii.) In discharge, purchase, or redemption of incumbrances affecting the inheritance of the settled land, or other the whole estate the subject of the settlement, or of land-tax, rentcharge in lieu of tithe, Crown rent, chief rent, or quit rent, charged on or payable out of the settled land :

p. 98. (iii.) In payment for any improvement authorized by this Act :

(iv.) In payment for equality of exchange or partition of settled land :

(v.) In purchase of the seignory of any part of the settled land, being freehold land, or in purchase of the fee simple of any part of the settled land, being copyhold or customary land :

(vi.) In purchase of the reversion or freehold in fee of any part of the settled land, being leasehold land held for years, or life, or years determinable on life :

(vii.) In purchase of land in fee simple, or of copyhold or customary land, or of leasehold land held for sixty years or more unexpired at the time of purchase, subject or not to any exception or reservation of or in respect of mines or minerals therein, or of or in respect of rights or powers relative to the working of mines or minerals therein, or in other land :

(viii.) In purchase, either in fee simple, or for a term of sixty years or more, of mines and minerals convenient to be held or worked with the settled land, or of any easement, right or privilege convenient to be held with the settled land for mining or other purposes :

(ix.) In payment to any person becoming absolutely entitled or empowered to give an absolute discharge :

(x.) In payment of costs, charges, and expenses of or incidental to the exercise of any of the powers, or the execution of any of the provisions, of this Act :

(xi.) In any other mode in which money produced by the exercise of a power of sale in the settlement is applicable thereunder.

As to the various sources whence "capital money" may arise under the Act, see *ante* p. 14. It should be observed that a distinction is drawn between "investment" and "application" of the capital money, the former expression being confined to the securities specified in clause i., the latter embracing the other modes in which the money may be applied.

The words "subject to payment of claims properly payable thereout" must be meant to apply to the discharge of incumbrances, and the payment of costs, charges, and expenses incidental to the exercise of the powers of the Act, although they seem to be surplusage, since those objects are specially provided for under clauses ii. and x. of this section.

The cases provided for in s. 18 seem to be referred to by the words "for any special authorized object for which the same was raised."

Trustees are "by law authorized" to invest trust monies, unless expressly forbidden by the instrument creating the trust, in any of the numerous investments specified in "The Trust Investment Act, 1889" (52 & 53 Vict. c. 32), s. 3, including "the Debenture or Rentcharge or Guaranteed or Preference Stock of any railway company in Great Britain or Ireland incorporated by special Act of Parliament, and having during each of the ten years last past before the date of investment paid a dividend at the rate of not less than three per centum per annum on its ordinary stock."

As, however, the same section includes "any of the stocks, funds, or securities for the time being authorized for the investment of cash under the control of the Court," and as the Rules of the Supreme Court, Ord. xxii. r. 17, authorize an investment of such funds in Guaranteed or Preference Stock of railway companies which have

§ 21.

Sect. 21. Investment of capital money.

"Payment of claims properly payable thereout."

"Special authorized object."

i. Investment.

§ 21. paid any dividend on the ordinary stock for the ten previous years, the restriction as to a three per cent. dividend is practically abolished.

The Court will not take judicial cognizance of the fact, however notorious, that any railway company has for the required period paid dividends on its ordinary stock; and an affidavit verifying that fact must in all cases be produced: *Re Byron's Charity*, 31 W. R. 517.

Trustees have the same power under the Local Loans Act, 1875 (38 & 39 Vict. c. 83), s. 27, of investing in debentures or debenture stock issued under the Act, as they have of investing in debentures or debenture stock of any railway company; and it was held that Liverpool Corporation Stock was not, in the absence of evidence that a dividend had been paid on it for ten years, an authorized security for capital moneys arising under the Settled Land Act: *Re Maberly*, 33 Ch. D. 455. So far, however, as municipal corporations and county councils are concerned, this decision has been superseded by s. 3 (m) of the Trust Investment Act, 1889. The Court in one case allowed capital moneys to be applied in recouping the four trustees of a will (three of whom were appointed trustees of the settlement created thereby) the amount by which they had overdrawn their trust account for the purpose of investing a large sum on mortgage of freeholds, upon the terms that the trustees of the will should execute in favour of the trustees of the settlement a declaration of trust of so much of the mortgage money as represented the capital money advanced to them: *Re Harrop's Trusts*, 24 Ch. D. 717.

The Court will not, without the consent of all parties interested, allow capital money to be sent to a foreign country where the beneficiaries reside, for the purpose of investment there: *Re Lloyd*, 54 L. T. 643.

ii. Incumbrances. The power conferred by this section of applying capital money in the discharge, purchase, or redemption of incumbrances may be exercised notwithstanding that the incumbrance affects only a part of the settled land: *Re Chaytor's Settled Estate Act*, 25 Ch. D. 651; *Re Navan and Kingscourt Railway Co.*, 21 L. R. Ir. 369.

The proceeds of sale of heirlooms may be applied in discharging incumbrances without keeping them on foot for the benefit of the infant remainderman who would have been absolutely entitled to the heirlooms on attaining twenty-one years of age: *Re Duke of Marlborough's Settlement*, 32 Ch. D. 1.

When a loan is contracted under the Public Money Drainage Act (9 & 10 Vict. c. 101), or the Improvement of Land Act, 1864 (27 & 28 Vict. c. 114), it is charged on the inheritance of the land; but is repayable, both principal and interest, by a limited number of periodical instalments. Both Acts expressly throw upon the tenant

APPLICATION OF CAPITAL MONEY. 87

§ 21.

for life or other limited owner the duty of paying these instalments as they accrue due, upon the ground that drainage, and many of the other improvements sanctioned by the later Act, are not permanent but after a certain number of years require to be renewed. In *Re Knatchbull's Settled Estate*, 29 Ch. D. 588, the Court of Appeal, while recognizing that there was a charge on the inheritance for the sum expended under the Improvement of Land Act, yet held that the charge was not an incumbrance which in its nature was capable of being discharged or redeemed, and refused to sanction the application of capital moneys for that purpose. This decision has been overruled by the Act of 1887, the 1st section of which is in the following terms:—

"1. Where any improvement of a kind authorized by the Act of 1882 has been or may be made either before or after the passing of this Act, and a rentcharge, whether temporary or perpetual has been or may be created in pursuance of any Act of Parliament, with the object of paying off any moneys advanced for the purpose of defraying the expenses of such improvement, any capital money expended in redeeming such rentcharge, or otherwise providing for the payment thereof, shall be deemed to be applied in payment for an improvement authorized by the Act of 1882."

Amendment of sect. 21 of the Settled Land Act, 1882.

In a case where the order, whereby the settled lands were charged with a drainage rentcharge, distinguished the amount of capital and interest in each instalment, it was held by Mr. Justice Kay that capital moneys arising under the Settled Land Act could be applied in paying such portions of the instalments then remaining to be paid as from time to time represented capital, but not such portions as represented interest: *Re Lord Sudeley's Settled Estates*, 37 Ch. D. 123; *Re Newton's Settled Estate*, 61 L. T. 787; on appeal W. N. 1890, 24. But in *Re Lord Egmont's Settled Estates*, 45 Ch. D. 395, the Court of Appeal expressed an opinion that Mr. Justice Kay took too limited a view of the Act in Lord Sudeley's case, and failed to give effect to the words "or otherwise providing for the payment thereof," and in accordance with the more liberal interpretation of the Act, the court sanctioned the application of capital money in paying all the expenses of redeeming a terminable rentcharge, including a bonus to the lender in order to purchase his consent to the redemption. See also *Re Duke of Leinster's Settled Estates*, 23 L. R. Ir. 152.

It might seem at first sight that if money has been raised by the mortgage of a long term of years, or by "creation of a term of years in the settled land," under the provisions of ss. 5, 18, or 47 of this Act, or of s. 11 of the Act of 1890, or if leaseholds have been mortgaged by sub-demise, the powers hereby conferred would not be available; as such incumbrances, although they practically fall upon

§ 21.

the successive owners of the estate, yet do not "affect the inheritance or *other* the whole estate the subject of the settlement."

It has, however, been decided in several cases that a strict interpretation need not be put on these words. Thus where an annuity was by a marriage settlement directed to be paid out of certain tithes for a term of 1000 years, it was held that the tithes in question being an incorporeal hereditament, were "land" within the meaning of this Act, and that the annuity was an incumbrance affecting the inheritance within the meaning of this clause. The trustees were accordingly authorized to apply capital moneys in their hands in purchasing the annuity with a view to its discharge: *Re Esdaile*, 54 L. T. 637. Some difficulty was created in this case by the fact that the annuity was personal estate, and when purchased by the trustees might be held to vest absolutely in the first tenant in tail. The order seems to have been made only on the condition that the tenant in tail should be bound to admit the extinguishment of the annuity.

In another case Mr. Justice North sanctioned the application of capital moneys in the discharge of a mortgage by the trustees of a term of 2000 years created by the will to secure portions: *Re Frewen*, 38 Ch. D. 383.

The grounds of the decision in this case were : (1) that the mortgagee might foreclose, and if he did he might acquire the fee under s. 65 of the Conveyancing Act, 1881 ; and (2) that the tenant for life had power to sell the entire fee free from incumbrances, and unless the incumbrance in question was one which could be paid off this could not be done. But this latter reason does not appear to be satisfactory, as the tenant for life can only sell subject to such charges as have been created for securing money actually raised at the date of the deed. See s. 20 (2), ii., *ante*, p. 78.

Land tax, tithe rent-charge, &c.

As to the redemption of land tax, see 42 Geo. 3, c. 116, s. 22 ; 16 & 17 Vict. c. 117, s. 1 ; as to the proof of redemption, Dart, V. & P. 398, 6th ed. ; as to tithe rentcharge, see 6 & 7 Will. 4, c. 71 ; and as to redemption thereof, 9 & 10 Vict. c. 73 ; 23 & 24 Vict. c. 93 ; 41 & 42 Vict. c. 42 ; as to the redemption of chief-rent, quit-rent, or other perpetual charges, the Conveyancing Act, 1881, s. 45, under which these small payments may sometimes be redeemed through the agency of the Board of Agriculture, to whom the powers of the Copyhold Commissioners were transferred by 52 & 53 Vict. c. 30.

Raising money on mortgage.

There is now power to raise money on mortgage for the purpose of discharging incumbrances on the Settled Land (Act of 1890, s. 11), but for the purposes of the section "incumbrance" does not include an annual sum payable only during a life or lives, or during a term of years absolute or determinable.

Agricultural

Capital money may by virtue of the Agricultural Holdings Act,

1883 (46 & 47 Vict. c. 61, s. 29), be applied in payment of any moneys expended and costs incurred by a landlord under or in pursuance of the Act in or about the execution of any improvement mentioned in the first or second Schedule thereto, and also in discharge of any charge created on a holding under or in pursuance of the Act in respect of any such improvement.

§ 21.

Holdings Act, 1883.

For an enumeration of the improvements authorized by this Act, see s. 25, to which an addition has been made by s. 13 of the Act of 1890.

iii. Improvements.

The tenant for life may require capital moneys to be expended in authorized improvements even when the trustees are in possession of the property in pursuance of a trust for management as if they were absolute owners, and are empowered or directed to pay for such improvements out of income: *Clarke v. Thornton*, 35 Ch. D. 307. And the position of the tenant for life as a trustee under s. 53 does not prevent him from securing this advantage for himself: *Re Lord Stamford's Estate*, 56 L. T. 484.

Capital money arising from one estate may be applied towards payment for improvements on another, if the two estates are settled by the same instrument to uses which only differ by the limitation as to one estate of a term of years to trustees upon trust to raise money by the accumulation of the rents: *Re Lord Stamford's Settled Estates*, 43 Ch. D. 84.

Special power is conferred by s. 18 to raise by mortgage any money wanted for the purpose of enfranchisement, or equality of exchange or partition.

iv. Equality money.

The words "or freehold" did not occur in clause vi. as originally introduced, but the Parliamentary history of a clause cannot be properly referred to as a guide to its interpretation. The language as it now stands is obscure and seems to authorize, by implication, the purchase of a leasehold reversion, where a sub-term is comprised in the settlement.

vi. Reversion of leaseholds.

It must also be observed that the words "so as to merge the leasehold interest in the reversion," which originally qualified the clause in the Bill, have been omitted in the Act. The directions contained in s. 24, as to the settlement of purchased land, make it clear that no merger can take place. The freehold is to be conveyed to the uses of the settlement, the leasehold interest will continue to be vested in the trustees upon trusts corresponding as nearly as may be with the limitations of the freeholds; the result of which would seem to be that, notwithstanding the purchase of the reversion under this clause, the leasehold interest may vest absolutely in a tenant in tail, while the reversion goes over to the next taker under the limitations of the settlement.

The principle of treating the mines and minerals as a distinct

vii. viii. Mines and minerals.

§ 21.

inheritance from the surface, which is recognised in s. 17, is still further exemplified by the power of investment in clauses vii. and viii.

ix. Person absolutely entitled.

The Court will not pay out capital money representing settled land to a tenant in tail as a person "absolutely entitled," unless he executes a disentailing assurance : *Re Reynolds*, 3 Ch. D. 61 (following *Re Butler's Will*, L. R. 16 Eq. 479, and *Re Broadwood's S. E.*, 1 Ch. D. 438 ; and overruling *Re Row*, L. R. 17 Eq. 30), and the authorities there cited.

If the fund is in the hands of the trustees of the settlement they cannot, it is conceived, safely pay it over to the tenant in tail.

The Court is now empowered to order that capital money in Court may be paid out to the trustees of the Settlement (Act of 1890, s. 14). Before that Act it had no power to do so : *Cookes* v. *Cookes*, 34 Ch. D. 498, except where it had been paid in under the Lands Clauses Consolidation Act, 1845, or some similar Act of Parliament, and came within the provisions of s. 32, *post*: *Re Wright's Trusts*, 24 Ch. D. 662 ; *Re Smith*, 40 Ch. D. 386.

x. Costs, charges, and expenses.

This clause provides that capital money may be applied " in payment of costs charges and expenses of or incidental to the exercise of any of the powers, or the execution of any of the provisions of this Act." Where the money is in the hands of the trustees of the settlement they are bound to obey any direction of the tenant for life as to the payment of costs, s. 22 (2) ; or else bring the matter before the Court under s. 44. When the money is in Court the order directing its application generally follows the terms of this clause, leaving for the determination of the taxing master the question whether any particular items are "incidental" or not: *Re Rudd*, W.N. 1887, 251.

The "costs charges and expenses" here referred to should be carefully distinguished from the costs charges and expenses incurred on an application to the Court over which it has an absolute discretion, s. 46 (6). The payment of the former "costs charges and expenses " is on the contrary one of the many ways in which capital money may be applied. The Court of Appeal has decided that the tenant for life cannot insist, as of right, on capital money being so applied ; but that the Court has a discretion in the matter. The question arose in the case of *Cardigan* v. *Curzon-Howe* (41 Ch. D. 375), with reference to the costs of obtaining the concurrence in a sale of the mortgagees of the life estate. Mr. Justice Chitty held (40 Ch. D. 338), that such costs were not incidental to the exercise of the powers of the Act ; but the Court of Appeal took a different view, and Lord Halsbury, L. C., said : "What I think the learned judge has not sufficiently observed is that the thing done under the

APPLICATION OF CAPITAL MONEY.

§ 21.

powers of the Act is the sale; and if for the purposes of the sale, and the most beneficial exercise of the power of sale, it is necessary to get the consent of the mortgagees, it seems to me a straining of language to say that the costs of obtaining such consent are not costs incidental to the exercise of the power of sale, which is a power given only by the Act." The manner in which the Court arrived at the conclusion that the payment of these costs, although an authorized application of capital money, lay in the discretion of the Court, does not appear satisfactory.

No reference was made to s. 22, which seems to give the tenant for life almost absolute authority, for he can in all cases require capital money to be paid to the trustees, and can "direct" them as to the manner in which it is to be invested or applied. However, Lord Justice Cotton has laid it down as a general rule that "the costs of obtaining, on a sale under the Act, the concurrence of mortgagees of the life estate, ought not to be allowed out of capital, and that will be a rule for trustees to act upon when the capital money is not in Court, and they have to deal with it," 41 Ch. D. at p. 380. See also *Re Beck*, 24 Ch. D. 608, where the costs of such mortgagees were allowed.

In *Re Beck, supra*, the property offered for sale was not sold at the auction, but was on the same day, through the instrumentality of the auctioneer, sold by private contract. The transactions were in these circumstances treated as substantially one, and scale charges were allowed to the solicitors of the tenant for life for conducting the sale and deducing title to the property as if the amount of the purchase money had been bid at the auction.

The costs of the tenant for life and his solicitor and surveyor in the preparation and carrying out of schemes for improvements under s. 26, may be paid out of capital money : *Re Lord Stamford's Settled Estates*, 43 Ch. D. 84. But if the survey is more elaborate or extensive than is necessary for the purpose, the costs may be disallowed : *Re Eyton's Settled Estate*, W. N. 1888, 254. Where an action by the remaindermen against the tenant for life, seeking to restrain a sale by him under the Act, was dismissed with costs, it was held on a subsequent application by the tenant for life that he was entitled to be paid the difference between solicitor and client, and party and party costs, as costs incidental to the exercise of his powers : *Re Llewellin*, 37 Ch. D. 317.

Schemes.

Survey.

Defending action.

The Court has no jurisdiction to sanction a mortgage of the proceeds of sale of a farm in order to provide funds for its cultivation, until the completion of the purchase. The present section states what is to be done with capital money "when received," but there is no power to create a charge on capital money which has not been received : *Round v. Turner*, 60 L. T. 379.

Mortgage.

It seems that the settlor cannot "by a declaration of a contrary

xi. In any other

§ 21.
authorized mode.

intention," *exclude* any of the foregoing modes of investment. See s. 51, *post*, p. 149.

Where the settlement is by way of trust for sale, capital money cannot be applied in the purchase of land unless such application is authorized by the settlement. See s. 63 (2), ii., *post*, p. 174.

§ 22.
Regulations respecting investment, devolution, and income of securities, &c.

22.—(1.) Capital money arising under this Act shall, in order to its being invested or applied as aforesaid, be paid either to the trustees of the settlement or into Court, at the option of the tenant for life, and shall be invested or applied by the trustees, or under the direction of the Court, as the case may be, accordingly.

(2.) The investment or other application by the trustees shall be made according to the direction of the tenant for life, and in default thereof, according to the discretion of the trustees, but in the last-mentioned case subject to any consent required or direction given by the settlement with respect to the investment or other application by the trustees of trust money of the settlement; and any investment shall be in the names or under the control of the trustees.

(3.) The investment or other application under the direction of the Court shall be made on the application of the tenant for life, or of the trustees.

(4.) Any investment or other application shall not during the life of the tenant for life be altered without his consent.

(5.) Capital money arising under this Act while remaining uninvested or unapplied, and securities on which an investment of any such capital money is made, shall, for all purposes of disposition, transmission and devolution, be considered as land, and the same shall be held for and go to the same persons successively, in the same manner and for and on the same estates, interests, and trusts, as the land wherefrom the money arises would, if not disposed of, have been held and have gone under the settlement.

(6.) The income of those securities shall be paid or applied as the income of that land, if not disposed of, would have been payable or applicable under the settlement.

§ 22.

(7.) Those securities may be converted into money, which shall be capital money arising under this Act.

Sect. 22. Regulations respecting investment, &c.

The policy of the Act, which seems to be to entrust the tenant for life with all the administrative powers of an absolute owner, is strikingly exemplified in this section. At *his* option the capital money is to be paid to the trustees or into Court; according to *his* direction the trustees are bound to apply any money in their hands in any of the authorized modes; and no change can be made in the investments without *his* consent.

Sub-s. 1. Option of tenant for life.

The option conferred upon the tenant for life of directing capital money to be paid to the trustees of the settlement or into Court, is one which may in the case of an infant tenant for life be exercised on his behalf by the trustees themselves. See *Re Duke of Newcastle's Estate*, 24 Ch. D. 129, 140. As to the procedure on payment of the money into Court, see Rules 10 to 14, inclusive, and Forms IX., X., and XI.

Where the tenant for life exercised his option by directing capital money to be paid into Court, it could not formerly be paid out to the trustees of the settlement to be applied by them: *Cookes* v. *Cookes*, 34 Ch. D. 498; but now this may be done "if the Court thinks fit." Act of 1890, s. 14.

Sub-s. 2. Investment or application.

The distinction between "investment" and "application" should be carefully noticed with reference to the concluding words of this sub-section. The former is the particular mode of application authorized by s. 21, clause i., whereas the latter includes all the various ways in which capital money may be applied. It should be observed that the trustees under this sub-section must obey the direction of the tenant for life, and that their discretion arises only in default of such direction; and it seems that the tenant for life cannot be fettered by the settlement in directing the mode of investment, or other application of the capital money; for it is only where the trustees are exercising their discretion that regard is to be had to "any consent required on direction given by the settlement."

The power of the tenant for life to direct in what manner the trustees of the settlement shall apply capital money in their hands has been fully recognised in *Re Duke of Marlborough's Settlement*, 30 Ch. D. 127; 32 Ch. D. 1; *Clarke* v. *Thornton*, 35 Ch. D. 307; and *Re Lord Stamford's Estate*, 56 L. T. 484; but seems to have been restricted or ignored in *Cardigan* v. *Curzon-Howe*, 41 Ch. D. 375.

Deposit.

When the tenant for life has entered into a contract for the purchase of land as an investment of capital money, the trustees of

§ 22.

the settlement cannot, it is conceived, be called upon by the tenant for life to pay the deposit out of the capital money, as the deposit is not a part payment of the purchase-money until the contract is completed. *Howe* v. *Smith*, 27 Ch. D. 89.

Sub-s. 3. Application to the Court.

The Court will, it is presumed, in applications under this sub-section, give effect to the reasonable wishes of the tenant for life, for "it would be a strange thing that the legislature should be held, upon the construction of this Act of Parliament, to have meant that the rights of the tenant for life should depend upon the accident whether the money is or is not in Court: per Chitty, J., *Clarke* v. *Thornton*, 35 Ch. D. 307, 314.

The application, which should be by summons (s. 46 (3) and rule 2, *post*), may be made either by the tenant for life, or by the trustees. If the former is the applicant the trustees need not be served in the first instance (Rules 4 and 5, *post*); but the tenant for life must always be brought before the Court.

It is to be observed that the remainderman has no *locus standi* with respect to investment, or other application of the capital money, and should not be served unless the Court under s. 46 (5) and rule 6, should so direct.

Sub-s. 5. Constructive reconversion.

Even where capital money has been invested on the securities referred to in s. 21 (i), it is to be regarded as constructively reconverted into land; but this sub-section does not apply to any "application" as distinguished from "investment" of the money; and thus if the purchase-money of freeholds is applied in the purchase of leaseholds (s. 21, vii), or *vice versâ*, the quality of the settled land is permanently changed. And it would also seem that where the purchase-money arising from the sale of leaseholds has been applied in the improvement of freeholds, a tenant in tail, who would have been absolutely entitled to the leaseholds, is not entitled to a charge upon the freeholds for the amount expended.

The latter words of this sub-section are inappropriate to money arising from the sale of heir-looms under s. 37; and while such money is "invested," as distinguished from "applied," the investment remains as it was before personal estate: *Re Duke of Marlborough's Settlement*, 32 Ch. D. 1.

§ 23. Investment in land in England.

23. Capital money arising under this Act from settled land in England shall not be applied in the purchase of land out of England, unless the settlement expressly authorizes the same.

"England" in an Act of Parliament includes Wales, and Berwick-upon-Tweed: 20 Geo. II., c. 42, s. 3.

24.—(1.) Land acquired by purchase or in exchange, or on partition, shall be made subject to the settlement in manner directed in this section.

(2.) Freehold land shall be conveyed to the uses, on the trusts, and subject to the powers and provisions which, under the settlement, or by reason of the exercise of any power of charging therein contained, are subsisting with respect to the settled land, or as near thereto as circumstances permit, but not so as to increase or multiply charges or powers of charging.

(3.) Copyhold, customary, or leasehold land shall be conveyed to and vested in the trustees of the settlement on trusts and subject to powers and provisions corresponding, as nearly as the law and circumstances permit, with the uses, trusts, powers, and provisions to, on, and subject to which freehold land is to be conveyed as aforesaid; so nevertheless that the beneficial interest in land held by lease for years shall not vest absolutely in the person who is by the settlement made by purchase tenant in tail, or in tail male, or in tail female, and who dies under the age of twenty-one years, but shall, on the death of that person under that age, go as freehold land conveyed as aforesaid would go.

(4.) Land acquired as aforesaid may be made a substituted security for any charge in respect of money actually raised, and remaining unpaid, from which the settled land, or any part thereof, or any undivided share therein, has theretofore been released on the occasion and in order to the completion of a sale, exchange or partition.

(5.) Where a charge does not affect the whole of the settled land, then the land acquired shall not be subjected thereto, unless the land is acquired either by purchase with money arising from sale of land which was before the sale subject to the charge, or by an exchange or partition of land which, or an undivided share wherein, was before the exchange or partition subject to the charge.

(6.) On land being so acquired, any person who, by the direction of the tenant for life, so conveys the land as to

§ 24. subject it to any charge, is not concerned to inquire whether or not it is proper that the land should be subjected to the charge.

(7.) The provisions of this section referring to land extend and apply, as far as may be, to mines and minerals, and to easements, rights, and privileges over and in relation to land.

Sect. 24. Settlement of purchased lands.

This section follows very closely the provisions usually inserted in "real" settlements for the purpose of making the purchased lands subject to the trusts of the settlement: see Dav. Conv. iii., 1020, 3rd ed. It should be read with s. 20, *ante*, the object of the present section being to impose upon the purchased land "the limitations, powers, and provisions of the settlement, and the estates, interests, and charges subsisting or to arise thereunder," but none of the "estates, interests, and charges," subject to which the land (assuming that the capital money has arisen from the sale of land) was previously sold.

Sub-s. 2. Freeholds.

There are some dangers incurred by a referential settlement which cannot well be avoided. For example, if the trustees of the portions term be dead, no new term will be created by a conveyance to the uses of the settlement; and in like manner, if the tenant for life or reversioner has sold or mortgaged his interest, the legal estate in the purchased land will pass to the tenant for life or the reversioner, as the case may be, and not to the assignee or mortgagee. Lewin on Trusts, 507, 8th ed.

The assignee of the tenant for life is protected by s. 50, *post*, but the assignee of the reversioner cannot by any precaution prevent the legal estate vested in him from being divested by an exercise of the statutory powers.

As to the effect of a conveyance to the uses of a will, where a recovery had been suffered by a tenant in tail, see *Wortham* v. *Mackinnon*, 4 Sim. 485; 8 Bing. 564; and it seems that if a tenant in tail converts his estate into a base fee, or an estate in fee simple, a subsequent conveyance to the uses of the settlement would vest in him a like estate in the purchased lands.

The words, "but not so as to increase or multiply charges or powers of charging," are still retained, *ex abundanti cautelâ*, to prevent a conveyance to uses giving, for example, to the widow a second jointure rent-charge, or to the portionists a second set of portions out of the newly acquired lands: see Williams on Settlement, p. 222. It has been laid down that "it is not a reasonable way of reading a trust, created by reference to other trusts, to consider everything as there repeated, and so to make it a duplication, as it were, of trusts in the nature of charges." *Per* Lord Cranworth, L. C., in *Hindle* v. *Taylor*, 5 D. M. & G. 577, at p. 594.

§ 24.

The proviso in this sub-section, that leaseholds shall not vest absolutely in a tenant in tail by purchase who dies under twenty-one, corresponds closely with the common form : Dav. Conv. iii., 1131, 3rd ed. See also the Conv. Act, 1881, s. 42. An omission in the corresponding clause in Lord Cranworth's Act (23 & 24 Vict. c. 145, s. 4, repealed by s. 64, *post*) is here supplied by a gift over of the leaseholds on the death of the infant tenant in tail.

Sub-s. 3. Leaseholds.

Chattels cannot be entailed ; and, if they were subjected to the same limitations as freeholds, they would vest absolutely in the first tenant in tail. The object of the present clause is to keep the freehold and leasehold estates together as long as possible. See Jarman on Wills, ii., 577, 4th ed. The words *by purchase* are rendered necessary by the rule against perpetuities ; for it is conceivable that there should be an indefinite series of tenants in tail all dying under twenty-one, in which case the vesting of the chattels would be clearly postponed beyond the legal limit. Jarman on Wills, i., 274, 4th ed. ; *Christie* v. *Gosling*, L. R. 1 H. L. 279 ; *Harrington* v. *Harrington*, L. R. 5 H. L. 87 ; *Martelli* v. *Holloway*, *Ibid.*, 532.

The object of these three sub-sections, which must be read together, seems to be to facilitate the sale of settled land free from incumbrances, by enabling the land acquired in its place to be substituted as a security for certain charges. Section 5, *ante*, empowers the tenant for life, with the consent of an incumbrancer, to transfer the incumbrance from the land sold or given in exchange or on partition to any other part of the settled land, whether already charged therewith or not, and in some cases the consent of the incumbrancer would be more readily given if the acquired land, as well as that retained (if any), were charged in his favour. By virtue of subsection 4 this can be done, and it will be remembered that, in the absence of agreement with the incumbrancer, settled land can only be conveyed subject to "any charge in respect of money actually raised and remaining unpaid." See s. 20 (2), ii.

Sub-ss. 4, 5 and 6. Substituted securities.

Although the words "actually raised" point to charges (such as portions) arising under the settlement itself, yet there seems no reason to exclude from the operation of this section charges having priority to the settlement.

The fifth sub-section seems to be needlessly scrupulous as to the incidence of the charge, inasmuch as the whole of the settled land must be subject to identical limitations. See *Lord Stamford's Settled Estates*, 43 Ch. D. 84. Moreover, s. 5, *ante*, authorizes the transfer of incumbrances from one part of the settled land to another, whether the latter was already charged or not. If, for example, two farms, A. and B., are settled, A. being subject to a charge from which B. is

C.S.L.A.   H

§ 24. free, and the charge on A. is with a view to a sale transferred to B., can the land subsequently acquired with the purchase-money of A. be made subject to the charge? It is conceived that it can, inasmuch as A. was, before the sale, subject to the charge.

It must be observed that in many cases "capital money arising under the Act" will be a mixed fund, coming from several sources, and that, if it is desired to charge the purchased land under this section, evidence should be preserved that the purchase-money was *wholly* provided by the land formerly subject to the charge.

It is also important to observe that when capital money, which has not arisen from the sale of land (*e.g.*, fines on leases, Act of 1884, s. 4, or money produced by sale of securities, s. 22 (7), *ante*), is invested in the purchase of land, there is no power to subject the last-mentioned land to any charge or incumbrance.

Sub-s. 6.
Conveyance to mortgagees.

Sub-s. 6 seems to indicate that the conveyance may be taken direct to the mortgagee or other incumbrancer, and subject thereto to the uses of the settlement.

VII.—IMPROVEMENTS.

Improvements with Capital Trust Money.

§ 25.
Description of improvements authorized by Act.

25. Improvements authorized by this Act are the making or execution on, or in connection with, and for the benefit of settled land, of any of the following works, or of any works for any of the following purposes, and any operation incident to or necessary or proper in the execution of any of those works, or necessary or proper for carrying into effect any of those purposes, or for securing the full benefit of any of those works or purposes (namely):

(i.) Drainage, including the straightening, widening, or deepening of drains, streams, and watercourses:

(ii.) Irrigation; warping:

(iii.) Drains, pipes, and machinery for supply and distribution of sewage as manure:

(iv.) Embanking or weiring from a river or lake, or from the sea, or a tidal water:

(v.) Groynes; sea walls; defences against water:

(vi.) Inclosing; straightening of fences; re-division of fields:

(vii.) Reclamation; dry warping:

(viii.) Farm roads; private roads; roads or streets in villages or towns:

(ix.) Clearing; trenching; planting:

(x.) Cottages for labourers, farm-servants, and artisans, employed on the settled land or not:

(xi.) Farmhouses, offices, and out-buildings, and other buildings for farm purposes:

(xii.) Saw-mills, scutch-mills, and other mills, water-wheels, engine-houses, and kilns, which will increase the value of the settled land for agricultural purposes or as woodland or otherwise:

(xiii.) Reservoirs, tanks, conduits, watercourses, pipes, wells, ponds, shafts, dams, weirs, sluices, and other works and machinery for supply and distribution of water for agricultural, manufacturing, or other purposes, or for domestic or other consumption:

(xiv.) Tramways; railways; canals; docks:

(xv.) Jetties, piers, and landing places on rivers, lakes, the sea, or tidal waters, for facilitating transport of persons and of agricultural stock and produce, and of manure and other things required for agricultural purposes, and of minerals, and of things required for mining purposes:

(xvi.) Markets and market-places:

(xvii.) Streets, roads, paths, squares, gardens, or other open spaces for the use, gratuitously or on payment, of the public or of individuals, or for dedication to the public, the same being necessary or proper in connexion with the conversion of land into building land:

(xviii.) Sewers, drains, watercourses, pipe-making, fencing, paving, brick-making, tile-making,

§ 25.

and other works necessary or proper in connexion with any of the objects aforesaid:

(xix.) Trial pits for mines, and other preliminary works necessary or proper in connexion with development of mines:

(xx.) Reconstruction, enlargement, or improvement, of any of those works.

Sect. 25.
Improvements.

This section extends in several important particulars the list of "improvements" in "The Improvement of Land Act, 1864" (27 & 28 Vict. c. 114), s. 9 : *Re Newton's Settled Estate,* 61 L. T. 787.

All the works there enumerated are comprised in this section, and, in addition, we find that provision is made for the distribution of sewage manure, for groynes and sea-walls, artisans' cottages, docks, markets, and market-places, streets and open spaces in connexion with a building scheme, and trial pits for mines. Further, the former Act was wholly confined to agricultural purposes, whereas the works mentioned in clause xiii. may be undertaken for manufacturing or other purposes; and those in xv. for facilitating the transport of minerals as well as of agricultural stock.

" Planting," in clause ix., is not confined as in the former Act to "planting for shelter." Several of these improvements are such as might best be undertaken in conjunction with other landowners; and accordingly by s. 27, *post,* power is conferred on the tenant for life, as by the Land Improvement Act, s. 12, to join or concur with other persons in the execution of the improvements.

Repairs.

The provisions of the section have been still further extended by the several enactments presently referred to; but in none of them will be found any authority for the expenditure of capital money in repairs. Independently of statute, money which is subject to a trust for investment in the purchase of land, may with the sanction of the Court be employed in erecting new buildings on the settled land, but not in repairs or in permanent improvements which do not put new buildings on the ground : *Drake* v. *Trefusis,* L. R. 10 Ch. 364 ; but the Court may direct money to be raised on mortgage of an infant's estate for the purpose of paying for such repairs as are certified to be absolutely necessary : *Re Jackson,* 21 Ch. D. 786 ; and see *Conway* v. *Fenton,* 40 Ch. D. 512. Sale monies of one estate have been applied in paying for improvements on another, although the two estates were settled by different instruments : *Re Houghton Estate,* 30 Ch. D. 102. In this case Bacon, V.-C., sanctioned the expenditure of capital money (1) in providing a water supply for the principal mansion-house (xiii) ; (2) in renewing the drainage of the same house (i) ;

(3) in repairing the stables (xi) ? ; and (4) in enlarging and improving the agent's house (xi)? It would not, however, be safe to rely implicitly on the soundness of this decision.

§ 25.

Silos were considered by the Court of Appeal, in *Re Broadwater Estate*, 33 W. R. 738, not to be improvements within the meaning of this section. The formation of silos is however included in the schedule to the Agricultural Holdings Act, *post*, as an improvement in which capital money may be expended.

Silos.

Clause (xx) read with clause (xix) has the effect, it seems, of striking out of the latter the word "preliminary," so that all works necessary or proper for the development of mines may be paid for out of capital money : *Re Mundy's Settled Estates*, 63 L. T. 311.

Mines.

It will be remembered that, under the Public Money Drainage Acts, limited owners may obtain Government loans for drainage works, but as such loans are repayable by a rent-charge of £6½ per cent. in twenty-two years, the machinery of the present Act is clearly more advantageous to the tenant for life ; and for the same reason the Improvement of Land Act (extended by s. 30, *post*) will be only adopted when capital money is not available for the purposes of this section.

Drainage Acts.

Capital money may also be applied in payment of any moneys expended and costs incurred by a landlord in or about the execution of any improvement mentioned in the first or second parts of the schedule to the Agricultural Holdings Act, 1883, as for an improvement authorized by this Act. 46 & 47 Vict. c. 61, s. 29.

Agricultural Holdings Act, 1883.

The schedule here referred to is in the following terms :—

Part I.

"Improvements to which consent of landlord is required :

(1.) Erection or enlargement of buildings.
(2.) Formation of silos.
(3.) Laying down of permanent pasture.
(4.) Making and planting of osier beds.
(5.) Making of water meadows or works of irrigation.
(6.) Making of gardens.
(7.) Making or improving of roads or bridges.
(8.) Making or improving of watercourses, ponds, wells, or reservoirs, or of works for the application of water-power or for supply of water for agricultural or domestic purposes.
(9.) Making of fences.
(10.) Planting of hops.
(11.) Planting of orchards or fruit bushes.

§ 25.
(12.) Reclaiming of waste land.
(13.) Warping of land.
(14.) Embankment and sluices against floods.

Part II.

Improvement in respect of which notice to landlord is required:

(15.) Drainage."

Housing of the Working Classes.
This section has also been extended by the Housing of the Working Classes Act, 1890 (53 & 54 Vict. c. 70), s. 74, which (in substitution for s. 11 of the repealed Act of 1885, 48 & 49 Vict. c. 72) enacts that the improvements on which capital money may be expended enumerated in this section shall include any dwellings available for the working classes, the building of which in the opinion of the Court is not injurious to the estate.

Act of 1890, s. 13.
The Act of 1890, s. 13, adds to the improvements authorized by the Act of 1882 the following; namely,

" (i.) Bridges;
" (ii.) Making any additions to or alterations in buildings reasonably necessary or proper to enable the same to be let;
" (iii.) Erection of buildings in substitution for buildings within an urban sanitary district taken by a local or other public authority, or for buildings taken under compulsory powers, but so that no more money be expended than the amount received for the buildings taken and the site thereof;
" (iv.) The rebuilding of the principal mansion-house on the settled land: Provided that the sum to be applied under this sub-section shall not exceed one-half of the annual rental of the settled land."

Bridges.
The making or improving of bridges is an improvement included in the schedule to the Agricultural Holdings Act which of course only applies when the land is in the occupation of tenants.

Buildings.
The buildings mentioned in s. 25 are all connected with farming purposes, but the later Act is more general and extends to any addition to or alteration in a single house in a town necessary or proper to enable it to be let.

The latter portion of clause iii., *supra*, appears to apply to buildings wherever situate, and not to be confined to such as are within an urban sanitary district. If any land is taken over and above the actual site of the buildings there must be an apportionment of the purchase money for the purposes of this clause.

Mansion-house.
The Improvement of Land Act was extended by the Limited Owners' Residences Acts (33 & 34 Vict. c. 56, and 34 & 35 Vict. c. 84), so as to include in the list of "improvements" the erection, completion,

or improvement of a suitable mansion-house, but the amount which might be raised for this purpose was limited to two years' rental of the estate.

§ 25.

The above enactment is still more strictly limited as regards the amount which may be expended; and whether the estate is large or small, one-half the annual rental would seem to be insufficient to rebuild the mansion-house in suitable style.

Independently of statutory authority the Courts have not been accustomed to sanction an expenditure of this kind unless clearly for the benefit of all parties concerned: *Hibbert* v. *Cooke*, 1 S. & S. 552; *Dent* v. *Dent*, 30 Beav. 363; but where the sole trustee had expended a considerable sum in restoring a mansion-house which had been burnt down, and it appearing that the estate had been benefited by the outlay to the full amount of certain funds in Court subject to reinvestment in land, those funds were ordered to be paid out to the trustee so that he might be recouped to that extent the moneys that he had spent: *Jesse* v. *Lloyd*, 48 L. T. 656; but as a rule personal estate settled on the same trusts as the real estate will not be applied in rebuilding a mansion-house: *Dunne* v. *Dunne*, 7 D. M. & G. 207; nor will the tenant for life be declared entitled to a charge for moneys expended by him in that manner; *Horlock* v. *Smith*, 17 Beav. 572; *Caldecott* v. *Brown*, 2 Hare 144; see also *Dixon* v. *Peacock*, 3 Drew. 288.

26.—(1.) Where the tenant for life is desirous that capital money arising under this Act shall be applied in or towards payment for an improvement authorized by this Act, he may submit for approval to the trustees of the settlement, or to the Court, as the case may require, a scheme for the execution of the improvement, showing the proposed expenditure thereon.

§ 26.
Approval by Land Commissioners of scheme for improvement and payment thereon.

(2.) Where the capital money to be expended is in the hands of trustees, then, after a scheme is approved by them, the trustees may apply that money in or towards payment of the whole or part of any work or operation comprised in the improvement, on—

> (i.) A certificate of the Land Commissioners certifying that the work or operation, or some specified part thereof, has been properly executed, and what amount is properly payable by the trustees in respect thereof, which certificate shall be conclusive in favour of the

§ 26.

trustees as an authority and discharge for any payment made by them in pursuance thereof; or on

(ii.) A like certificate of a competent engineer or able practical surveyor nominated by the trustees and approved by the Commissioners, or by the Court, which certificate shall be conclusive as aforesaid; or on

(iii.) An order of the Court directing or authorizing the trustees to so apply a specified portion of the capital money.

(3.) Where the capital money to be expended is in Court, then, after a scheme is approved by the Court, the Court may, if it thinks fit, on a report or certificate of the Commissioners, or of a competent engineer or able practical surveyor, approved by the Court, or on such other evidence as the Court thinks sufficient, make such order and give such directions as it thinks fit for the application of that money, or any part thereof, in or towards payment for the whole or part of any work or operation comprised in the improvement.

Sect. 26. Approval of scheme.

The scheme for improvement is to be approved by the trustees or by the Court, not by the Land Commissioners, as stated in the marginal note. The duties of the Commissioners, now replaced by the Board of Agriculture, 52 & 53 Vict. c. 30, are not discretionary but ministerial, and are confined to seeing that the work has been properly executed and certifying what sum is to be paid in respect thereof.

Preliminary scheme.

This section is not retrospective, and it was held that capital money could not be applied in paying off charges for improvements executed before the Act came into operation: *Re Knatchbull's Settled Estate*, 27 Ch. D. 349 (affirmed C. A. 29 Ch. D. 588). It was also held in a later case that if the tenant for life executed the improvements without submitting a scheme for the approval of the trustees or of the Court there was no power to recoup to him the amount of his expenditure: *Re Hotchkin's Settled Estates*, 35 Ch. D. 41, and see *Re Broadwater Estate*, 33 W. R. 738. In the former case the land on which the improvements had been executed had been sold; and Cotton, L. J., expressed a doubt whether there was power to authorize the trustees to pay out of capital money the expense of improvements on land no longer in settlement. By the 15th section of the Act of 1890 it is, however, enacted as follows:—

§ 26.

"15. The Court may, in any case where it appears proper, make an order directing or authorizing capital money to be applied in or towards payment for any improvement authorized by the Settled Land Acts, 1882 to 1890, notwithstanding that a scheme was not, before the execution of the improvement, submitted for approval, as required by the Act of 1882, to the trustees of the settlement or to the Court."

Court may order payment for improvements executed.

This section it will be observed reverses the decision in *Re Hotchkin's Settled Estates* only so far as the Court is concerned. The trustees have still no power to pay moneys in their hands for work which has been done without the submission of a scheme, although the Court has a discretionary power of "directing" capital money in Court, or of "authorizing" capital money in the hands of the trustees to be so applied. Where, however, extra work has to be done in carrying out a scheme the trustees may apply capital moneys in their hands in payment for such extra work if it was incidental to the original scheme and has been properly executed, and they are not limited to the particular amount of the estimated expenditure: *Re Bulwer Lytton's Will*, 38 Ch. D. 20.

Extra work.

It is important to observe that the work, or at least so much as is to be paid for, must be executed before the money is paid; and that there is no power to advance money to the tenant for life to be expended by him in improvements. But the preliminary costs of preparing the scheme, including surveyor's charges, seem to be payable under s. 21 (x.), as "incidental to the execution of the provisions of the Act;" and may accordingly be defrayed by the trustees out of any capital moneys in their hands.

Where the money to be expended is in the hands of trustees, it is highly important that they should accurately follow the course of procedure here prescribed, which consists of the following steps :—

(1.) The scheme must be submitted to the trustees and approved by them.

(2.) The works must be executed.

(3.) A certificate of the Board of Agriculture or of an engineer or surveyor, nominated by the trustees, and approved by the Board or by the Court, or an order of the Court must be obtained, as an authority for the trustees to pay over the money to the tenant for life.

The procedure, where the money is in Court, follows the same lines; the Court, however, taking an unfettered discretion as to the evidence which it will accept in proof of the execution of the works.

It is to be observed that the scheme must be approved by the "trustees of the settlement," and therefore where money is in the

§ 26.

hands of trustees (*e.g.* under s. 33) who do not come within the definition of "trustees of the settlement" in s. 2, *ante*, they should be appointed to that office before undertaking the duties imposed by this section. See as to the appointment of "trustees of the settlement," s. 38, *post*, and s. 17 of the Act of 1890.

Improvement of Land Act.

In proceedings under the Improvement of Land Act, 1864, the Board of Agriculture, before giving their sanction, must be satisfied that a permanent increase of the yearly value of the lands exceeding the yearly amount proposed to be charged thereon, will be effected by the proposed works (27 & 28 Vict. c. 114, s. 25). The discretion of the trustees and the Court is not similarly fettered under this Act.

§ 27.

Concurrence in improvements.

27. The tenant for life may join or concur with any other person interested in executing any improvement authorized by this Act, or in contributing to the cost thereof.

Sect. 27. Concurrence in improvements.

Compare with this section the similar provisions in the Improvement of Land Act, 1864 (27 & 28 Vict. c. 114), s. 12. This section does not expressly authorize the trustees of the settlement to apply capital money in payment for the joint improvement; or to provide for the apportionment of the cost between the several estates, but these powers are probably conferred by implication.

The scheme for the whole work, whether it is an artificial harbour, a railway, or a system of "arterial drainage," must, it is conceived, be submitted to the trustees or the Court, and approved in the manner pointed out in the last section.

It is clear that the tenant for life may join or concur with the limited owners of other settled estates, or with persons absolutely entitled in the execution of joint improvements under this Act; but there is no power to proceed partly under this Act, and partly under the Improvement of Land Act. The former requires the expenses to be defrayed out of capital money in Court or in the hands of trustees, while the latter contemplates the money being raised by way of loan to be secured as a terminable charge; and in the case of a joint application requires "the sum to be charged in pursuance of any joint application, so that a separate and distinct sum may become charged on the land of each landowner:" s. 12.

§ 28.

Obligation on tenant for life and

28.—(1.) The tenant for life, and each of his successors in title having, under the settlement, a limited estate or interest only in the settled land, shall, during such period, if any, as the Land Commissioners by certificate in any case prescribe, maintain and repair, at his own expense, every improvement executed under the foregoing provisions of this Act; and where a building or work in its nature insurable against damage by fire is comprised in the improvement, shall insure and keep insured the same, at his own expense, in such amount, if any, as the Commissioners by certificate in any case prescribe.

§ 28. successors to maintain, insure, &c.

(2.) The tenant for life, or any of his successors as aforesaid, shall not cut down or knowingly permit to be cut down, except in proper thinning, any trees planted as an improvement under the foregoing provisions of this Act.

(3.) The tenant for life, and each of his successors as aforesaid, shall from time to time, if required by the Commissioners, on or without the suggestion of any person having, under the settlement, any estate or interest in the settled land in possession, remainder, or otherwise, report to the Commissioners the state of every improvement executed under this Act, and the fact and particulars of fire insurance, if any.

(4.) The Commissioners may vary any certificate made by them under this section, in such manner or to such extent as circumstances appear to them to require, but not so as to increase the liabilities of the tenant for life, or any of his successors as aforesaid.

(5.) If the tenant for life, or any of his successors as aforesaid, fails in any respect to comply with the requisitions of this section, or does any act in contravention thereof, any person having, under the settlement, any estate or interest in the settled land in possession, remainder, or reversion, shall have a right of action, in respect of that default or act, against the tenant for life; and the estate of the tenant for life, after his death, shall be liable to make good to the persons entitled under the settlement any damages occasioned by that default or act.

The powers and duties of the Land Commissioners have been transferred to the Board of Agriculture, 52 & 53 Vict. c. 30.

Unless the Board issue a certificate prescribing the period during

Board of Agriculture. Sub-s. 1.

§ 28.

Repairs and Insurance.

which the improvements are to be maintained and repaired, or the amount for which the buildings are to be insured, the first sub-section seems to have no operation; in fact the obligation to maintain, repair, and insure is imposed upon the limited owners of settled land partly by the act and partly by the certificate of the Board. Where the improvements are effected without the intervention of the Board, as for example when the money is in Court and the order for payment is made on the report of a surveyor, a special application will have to be made for a certificate under this section, if it is desired to impose the obligation upon the tenant for life.

General rule as to repairs.

In the absence of any such certificate, the relative rights and liabilities of the tenant for life, remaindermen, and trustees seem to stand on the same footing as if the improvements had been effected before the settlement. Thus, if the legal estate be in the trustees, the Court will not, unless there is an express trust to repair, interfere at the instance of a remainderman, in cases of permissive waste, against an equitable tenant for life in possession: *Powys* v. *Blagrave*, 4 D. M. & G. 448.

In the case of legal limitations the tenant for life is not liable to the remainderman for permissive waste: *Barnes* v. *Dowling*, 44 L. T. 809; *Re Cartwright*, 41 Ch. D. 532.

Where an obligation to repair is imposed by the settlement (*Re Skingley*, 3 M. & G. 221; *Woodhouse* v. *Walker*, 5 Q. B. D. 404; *Andrew* v. *Williams*, 52 L. T. 41), or a contract or covenant to that effect is entered into by the tenant for life (*Marsh* v. *Wells*, 2 S. & S. 87), the tenant for life or his personal representatives will be liable for dilapidations.

Leaseholds.

Leaseholds in general stand in a different position from freeholds on account of the liability to the lessor in respect of repairs; and where they are vested in trustees upon trust for persons in succession it is the duty of the trustees to preserve the property for the remainderman, and to apply the rents and profits in executing such repairs as may be necessary to save a forfeiture of the lease: *Re Fowler*, 16 Ch. D. 723. But as between tenant for life and remainderman the former is not bound at his own expense to put the premises in repair so as to comply with the terms of the lease: *Re Courtier*, 34 Ch. D. 136.

Insurance.

The position of the tenant for life as regards insurance has been thus stated. "Though, in the absence of special contract or obligation, the tenant for life is not bound to rebuild in case of fire, and by parity of reasoning is not bound to insure, yet it seems that if he insured he would be bound to lay out the insurance money in rebuilding:" Dav. Conv. iii. 290 (e), 3rd ed. But the remainderman has in such a case no lien on the insurance monies: Bunyon on

Fire Insurance, 196, 2nd. ed. ; and see *Warwicker* v. *Bretnall*, 23 Ch. D. 188.

§ 28.

If the tenant for life, however, is bound to insure by an order of the Board of Agriculture made under this section, his position would appear to be different from that of a tenant for life who voluntarily effects an insurance ; and the insurance must be taken to have been made for the benefit of all parties as if the obligation to insure had been imposed by the settlement : *Seymour* v. *Vernon*, 16 Jur. 189 ; and see *Norris* v. *Harrison*, 2 Mad. 268.

Where improvements have been effected under the Improvement of Land Act, 1864, the person for the time being bound to make the periodical payments in respect of the charge is bound to uphold the improvements and works, and insure buildings "susceptible of damage by fire" in an amount equal to the principal sum originally charged. He is further made liable to an action for any damage occasioned by his default ; and machinery is provided whereby the maintenance of the improvements may be enforced : 27 & 28 Vict. c. 114, ss. 72-76.

Improvement of Land Act.

This section is by the Act of 1887 applied to improvements effected under the Improvement of Land Act, or any similar Act, when the rent-charge created in pursuance of such Act has been redeemed by the expenditure of capital money ; but drainage, which is the improvement most commonly effected in this manner, is in its nature incapable of being kept in repair : *Re Lord Sudeley's Settled Estates*, 37 Ch. D. 123.

A tenant in tail may commit with impunity every species of waste (Co. Litt. 224, a.), and may, it is conceived, cut down any trees even if planted as an improvement, although he comes within the literal meaning of the prohibition in sub-s. 2. As to the disposition of the proceeds of sale of timber wrongfully cut, see *Seagram* v. *Knight*, L. R. 2 Ch. 628 ; *Higginbotham* v. *Hawkins*, L. R. 7 Ch. 676 ; *Honywood* v. *Honywood*, L. R. 18 Eq. 306 ; *Baker* v. *Sebright*, 13 Ch. D. 179.

Sub-s. 2. Cutting down trees.

The duties of the Commissioners (now replaced by the Board of Agriculture) prescribed by s. 26 end with their report on the works ; by this sub-section they are constituted overseers of the improvements during the continuance of the settlement. It is not stated what steps are to be taken by them for the protection of the estate in the event of the works being dilapidated, or the buildings uninsured ; and it would seem that the object of sub-s. 3 is merely to obtain information, the right of action being conferred, if at all, by sub-ss. (1) and (5).

Sub-s. 3. Land Commissioners.

The Board of Agriculture have no power to make a mandatory order for the repair of the works, or even to direct a surveyor to inspect and report thereon.

§ 28.

The provisions of the Improvement of Land Act, 1864, s. 75, whereby the Commissioners are empowered after default to execute repairs, are not applicable to the present case, even if incorporated by s. 48 (6), *post*.

Sub-s. 4. Varying the certificate.

The contents of the certificate under this section are not expressed to extend beyond a specification of the *period* during which the tenant for life is to maintain the works, and the *amount* in which he is to insure; and by this sub-section the term may be shortened, or the amount diminished: but the language seems to imply that the certificate is intended to contain more elaborate provisions than are above referred to with reference to the maintenance of the works.

Sub-s. 5. Right of action.

It is to be observed that under this sub-section a right of action is conferred upon everybody, "having, under the settlement, any estate or interest in the settled land in possession, remainder, or reversion;" and it may be a question what damages are recoverable in such an action—are they the total injury to the inheritance? and if so, how are they to be impounded for the benefit of "the persons entitled under the settlement?" or, must each successive remainderman bring an action for his own apportioned damage? A palpable absurdity (produced by an "amendment" of the bill in its passage through the House of Commons) is apparent on the face of this sub-section, for the tenant for life is made answerable in damages for the acts and defaults of his successors in title. Thus if an estate were limited to A. for life, remainder to B. in tail, remainder to C. in fee. If B. after the death of A. committed default and died without barring his estate tail, the remedy of C. would, on the words of the statute, be against the estate of A. and not against that of B. It is not likely that the Courts would give effect to such a claim, but it is difficult to see how any "successor in title" or his estate can be made answerable under this sub-section.

Tort or contract.

The right of action hereby conferred seems to be founded partly on tort partly on the statutory obligation, inasmuch as the damages are recoverable in respect of the wrongful act or omission of the tenant for life in disobeying or not complying with the requisitions of the section. See *Batthyany* v. *Walford*, 36 Ch. D. 269, 279. As demands in the nature of unliquidated damages arising otherwise than by reason of a contract, promise, or breach of trust, are not provable in bankruptcy (Bankruptcy Act, 1883, 46 & 47 Vict. c. 52, s. 37), no claim can be made under this section in the bankruptcy of the tenant for life (*Re Newman*, 3 Ch. D. 494), or against his estate if it is insolvent and is being administered by the Court. Jud. Act, 1875, s. 10.

County Court.

Where the damage claimed is not more than £50 the action may, it seems, be brought against the tenant for life in the County Court under s. 56 of the County Courts Act, 1888 (51 & 52 Vict. c. 43);

and the rules laid down by s. 116 of the same Act as to the costs of actions unnecessarily brought in the High Court apply to actions under this section.

§ 28.

"All actions for penalties, damages or sums of money given to the party grieved by any statute now or hereafter to be in force, ... shall be commenced . . . . within two years after the cause of such actions, but not after." 3 & 4 Will. 4, c. 42, s. 3. If the tenant for life, therefore, persistently neglects to perform his duty as to repairs under this section, the reversioner, in order to obtain complete compensation, would have to bring actions every two years, unless it should be held that in such a case the cause of action is one and indivisible although increasing *de die in diem*. Where the wrongful act consists of the cutting down trees (sub-s. 2), the action should be brought within two years from the time at which they were cut.

Statute of Limitations.

The measure of damages is, it would seem, the diminution in the value of the reversion, or the plaintiff's interest in the reversion, due to the wrongful act or default of the tenant for life, less a discount for immediate payment (see *Whitham* v. *Kershaw*, 16 Q. B. D. 613), and not the sum necessary to put the property in repair, and it is clear that the amount recovered is not to be expended on the property, for that would be to give the tenant for life for a time the enjoyment of the damages which he had been compelled to pay.

Measure of damages.

If the tenant for life is an infant, there seems to be no remedy under this section in case of default.

Infant.

The second part of the clause is obscure, since it does not appear whether there is a right of action against the executors or administrators of the tenant for life, or whether there is conferred merely a right to prove for the "damages." By 3 & 4 Will. 4, c. 42, s. 2, actions may be brought against the executors of the wrongdoer for an injury to property real or personal, but the injury must have been committed within six months of the person's death, and within six months after administration has been taken out. See *Woodhouse* v. *Walker*, 5 Q. B. D. 404.

Execution and Repair of Improvements.

29. The tenant for life, and each of his successors in title having, under the settlement, a limited estate or interest only in the settled land, and all persons employed by or under contract with the tenant for life, or any such successor, may from time to time enter on the settled land, and, without impeachment of waste by any remainderman or reversioner, thereon execute any improvement authorized

§ 29.

Protection as regards waste in execution and repair of improvements.

§ 29. by this Act, or inspect, maintain, and repair the same, and, for the purposes thereof, on the settled land, do, make, and use all acts, works, and conveniences proper for the execution, maintenance, repair, and use thereof, and get and work freestone, limestone, clay, sand, and other substances, and make tramways and other ways, and burn and make bricks, tiles, and other things, and cut down and use timber and other trees not planted or left standing for shelter or ornament.

Sect. 29. Waste in execution and repair of improvements.

This section applies, it is conceived, only as between the persons successively entitled under the settlement. If the land is in the occupation of tenants, the improvements must be executed with their consent. The execution of the improvements is to be "without impeachment of waste by any remainderman or reversioner," and it can scarcely be intended by the statute that the tenant for life is to be at liberty to take the "freestone, limestone, clay, &c.," of a lessee, and cut down and use the timber and other trees on his farm without giving him any compensation; but the power conferred on the tenant for life "to enter on the Settled Land" is unnecessary, unless it refers to land in the occupation of tenants.

The power here conferred upon each of the "successors in title" of the tenant for life must, it is presumed, be qualified by adding the words "when his estate or interest is in possession" (see s. 58). If he could enter and inspect, maintain and repair the works while he was a remainderman or reversioner, the section would have made him unimpeachable for waste by the tenant for life. Compare this section with the analogous provisions of s. 34 of "The Improvement of Land Act."

Improvement of Land Act, 1864.

§ 30. *Extension of 27 & 28 Vict. c. 114, s. 9.*

30. The enumeration of improvements contained in section nine of the Improvement of Land Act, 1864, is hereby extended so as to comprise, subject and according to the provisions of that Act, but only as regards applications made to the Land Commissioners after the commencement of this Act, all improvements authorized by this Act.

Sect. 30. Improvement of Land Act, 1864.

The Improvement of Land Act, 1864, the scope of which is here extended, enables limited owners to effect loans for the improvement of settled estates. But as these loans are repayable, by instalments of mixed principal and interest, in, at most, 25 years, the terms are not as advantageous as those provided by the present Act. Still, there may be cases in which it is not possible or convenient to raise, by a sale of part of the property, capital money for improvements under this Act; and it therefore seems expedient to indicate briefly the manner in which that object may be effected by a loan under the Improvement of Land Act. The procedure is as follows:—If a "landowner" (s. 8) desires to borrow money for an "improvement" (s. 9), he applies to the Inclosure Commissioners (now the Board of Agriculture) for their sanction (s. 11); who after investigation (s. 15), may, if satisfied that the proposed improvement will effect a permanent increase of the yearly value of the land, exceeding the yearly amount of the charge, make an order sanctioning the improvement, and specifying the number of years, not exceeding 25, in which the loan is to be repaid by half-yearly instalments. The order sanctioning an improvement is called a "Provisional Order," and confers a right on the completion of the works to an "absolute order," which the Commissioners are empowered (s. 49) to execute, charging the inheritance with the repayment of the loan by a rent-charge for the term of years mentioned in the provisional order, so as to repay principal and interest by half-yearly instalments (s. 51). The money is generally provided by a Land Improvement Company, to whom the benefit of the charge is assigned (s. 53).

§ 30.

Where two Land Improvement Companies had advanced money on the same estate, and each was by its incorporating statute declared to be entitled to a first charge upon the inheritance of the improved land in priority over every other then existing or future charge, it was held that the charge which was first in order of time was entitled to priority. *Pollock* v. *Lands Improvement Company*, 37 Ch. D. 661. The Act contains elaborate provisions as to security for expenses, maintenance of improvements, saving clauses and other matters to which it is unnecessary further to refer, as its importance is greatly diminished by the facilities conferred upon limited owners by the present Act.

Priority.

The Improvement of Land Act has been also extended by former statutes, so as to include as "improvements" the following works:—

Previous extensions of the Improvement of Land Act.

(1.) A suitable mansion-house and offices; but only two years' rental of the settled land can be expended. This, however, means the rental of the whole of the settled land, and not merely that part on which the house is to be built: *Re Dunn's S. E.*, W. N. 1877, 39. See the Limited Owners, Residences Acts, 1870 & 1871, 33 & 34 Vict. c. 56; 34 & 35 Vict. c. 84.

§ 30.

(2.) Sewage works under "The Public Health Act" (38 & 39 Vict. c. 55), s. 31.

(3.) Reservoirs and other works for the supply of water under 40 & 41 Vict. c. 31.

VIII.—Contracts.

§ 31.

Power for tenant for life to enter into contracts.

31.—(1.) A tenant for life—

(i.) May contract to make any sale, exchange, partition, mortgage, or charge; and

(ii.) May vary or rescind, with or without consideration, the contract, in the like cases and manner in which, if he were absolute owner of the settled land, he might lawfully vary or rescind the same, but so that the contract as varied be in conformity with this Act; and any such consideration, if paid in money, shall be capital money arising under this Act; and

(iii.) May contract to make any lease; and in making the lease may vary the terms, with or without consideration, but so that the lease be in conformity with this Act; and

(iv.) May accept a surrender of a contract for a lease, in like manner and on the like terms in and on which he might accept a surrender of a lease; and thereupon may make a new or other contract, or new or other contracts, for or relative to a lease or leases, in like manner and on the like terms in and on which he might make a new or other lease, or new or other leases, where a lease had been granted; and

(v.) May enter into a contract for or relating to the execution of any improvement authorized by this Act, and may vary or rescind the same; and

(vi.) May, in any other case, enter into a contract to do any act for carrying into effect any of the purposes of this Act, and may vary or rescind the same. § 31.

(2.) Every contract shall be binding on and shall enure for the benefit of the settled land, and shall be enforceable against and by every successor in title for the time being of the tenant for life, and may be carried into effect by any such successor; but so that it may be varied or rescinded by any such successor, in the like case and manner, if any, as if it had been made by himself.

(3.) The Court may, on the application of the tenant for life, or of any such successor, or of any person interested in any contract, give directions respecting the enforcing, carrying into effect, varying, or rescinding thereof.

(4.) Any preliminary contract under this Act for or relating to a lease shall not form part of the title or evidence of the title of any person to the lease, or to the benefit thereof.

"Contracts are considered as defective executions, and like them require a sufficient consideration to enable the Court to act. The same rules, therefore, apply to each case. As against a remainderman both are equally binding. The principal distinctions between them are, that a contract to execute a power might be enforced against the donee of the power himself, where a defective execution without any contract, although capable of being enforced against a remainderman, could not be aided against the party who made it:" Sugden on Powers, 552, 8th ed.; *Re Dyke's Estate*, L. R. 7 Eq. 337. *Contracts.*

Although under the general law, the tenant for life might have entered into binding contracts to exercise the powers of the Act, yet the safer course has been here followed of expressly authorizing him to do so; and it may be observed that, by virtue of s. 19, *ante*, the tenant for life of an undivided share may concur with the owners of the other shares in a joint contract for the sale of the property as a whole.

It will be noticed that "enfranchisement" is not expressly mentioned in this clause; but it seems to be virtually included in " Sale." See s. 3, *ante*, p. 38. *Sub-s. 1. Enfranchisement.*

If a purchase goes off through default of the purchaser, the vendor, in the absence of stipulation to the contrary, may retain the deposit: *Depree* v. *Bedborough*, 4 Giff. 479; *Ex parte, Barrell*, L. R. 10 Ch. 512; *Howe* v. *Smith*, 27 Ch. D. 89, and a forfeited deposit would seem to be within the spirit of this clause, and to be "capital money *Deposit.*

§ 31.

Leases.

arising under the Act." See *Shrewsbury* v. *Shrewsbury*, 18 Jur. 397, where it was held that a tenant for life was not entitled to retain a deposit, but that it belonged to the settled estates.

A contract to grant a lease, if it is capable of being specifically enforced by a Court of equity, places both parties in the same position as if a lease had been actually granted. *Walsh* v. *Lonsdale*, 21 Ch. D. 9 ; *Swain* v. *Ayres*, 21 Q. B. D. 289 ; *Lowther* v. *Heaver*, 41 Ch. D. 248. The power here conferred therefore seems to render practically inoperative the condition in s. 7, *ante*, that every lease shall be by deed.

The tenant for life may also enter into a valid contract to grant a lease at a future day, or to renew a lease on its expiration : *Gas Light and Coke Company* v. *Towse*, 35 Ch. D. 519. Lord Justice, (then Mr. Justice) Kay in that case said :—" Such a contract is not a reversionary lease in any sense : it is a contract at a future time to grant a lease ; and provided that, when that future time comes, the lease is in all respects in conformity with the power—that is that it reserves the best rent, and contains proper covenants, and so on— there is no harm in the contract ; it is a perfectly good contract. So, when a lease is granted, if in the lease there is a covenant that when that lease expires the lessor will renew the lease, be it for one year, ten years, or any number of years within the power, *primâ facie* there is nothing bad in that covenant."

It does not, however, seem clear that if the tenant for life dies before the term fixed for granting or renewing the lease, the contract is within sub.-s. 2 of this section, so as to be enforceable against the successor in title of the tenant for life. The remedy of the lessee might reasonably be held to be an action for damages for breach of contract against the personal representatives of the tenant for life.

iv. Surrenders.

As to the terms on which the tenant for life may accept surrenders of leases, see s. 13, *ante*, p. 66.

v. Improvements.

The list of " improvements " will be found in s. 25, and the manner in which they are to be executed is described in s. 29.

Sub-s. 2. Specific performance.

" The general rule with regard to suits to enforce contracts is, that the parties to the contract or their representatives are the necessary and sufficient parties to the suit :" Fry, Sp. Perf. 62.

Under this section the right of action, so to speak, runs with the estate ; and neither the executors of the tenant for life, nor the trustees of the settlement, need be made parties. Although this sub-section provides that the contract of a tenant for life may be " carried into effect " by the successors in title, express power to complete such a contract is conferred by s. 6 of the Act of 1890, which is as follows :—

Completion of Contracts.

"6. A tenant for life may make any conveyance which is necessary or proper for giving effect to a contract entered into by a predecessor in title, and which, if made by such predecessor, would have been valid as against his successors in title." *Power to complete predecessor's contract.*

Independently of the special provisions of this Act, it seems to be settled that the remainderman is bound by the contract of a tenant for life made *pursuant to his power: Shannon* v. *Bradstreet,* 1 Sch. & Lef. 52. *Secus,* if the terms of the contract are not authorized by the power : *Ricketts* v. *Bell,* 1 De G. & S. 335.

"Where the contract to execute the power is merely by parol, or the written agreement is not effectual under the Statute of Frauds, it seems that it will not bind the remainderman, *although it is in part performed* by the intended appointee": Sugden on Powers, 554, 8th ed. See *Blore* v. *Sutton,* 3 Mer. 237 ; but acquiescence will prevent the remainderman from repudiating the contract : *Stiles* v. *Cowper,* 3 Atk. 692. *Parol contracts.*

It seems doubtful, when the contract is not in conformity with the Act, whether the purchaser or lessee can compel specific performance, with compensation for what he loses by the contract being reduced to conformity.

The powers conferred by the Act on a tenant for life may by virtue of s. 58, *post,* be exercised by a tenant in tail in possession ; and notwithstanding ss. 40, 47 of the Fines and Recoveries Act, a contract by a tenant in tail under this section may be enforced after his death against the next tenant in tail. *Contracts by tenants in tail.*

Although "any person interested in any contract" may apply to the court for "directions respecting the enforcing, carrying into effect, varying, or rescinding thereof, "yet hostile actions for specific performance or rescission of the contract do not seem to be contemplated by this sub-section. See Rule 4 and Form XVII. *post.* *Sub-s. 3. Directions by the Court.*

A provision similar to sub-s. (4) is contained in s. 4 of the Conveyancing Act, 1882 (45 & 46 Vict. c. 39), which enacts that "where a lease is made under a power contained in a settlement, will, Act of Parliament, or other instrument, any preliminary contract for or relating to the lease shall not for the purpose of the deduction of title to an intended assign form part of the title, or evidence of title, to the lease." See *Salaman* v. *Glover,* L. R. 20 Eq. 444 ; where the grant of light and easements in a lease was controlled by the words of the antecedent agreement. *Sub-s. 4. Preliminary contract.*

IX.—MISCELLANEOUS PROVISIONS.

§ 32.

Application of money in Court under Lands Clauses and other Acts.
8 & 9 Vict. c. 18.
23 & 24 Vict. c. 106.
32 & 33 Vict. c. 18.
40 & 41 Vict. c. 18.

32. Where, under an Act incorporating or applying, wholly or in part, the Lands Clauses Consolidation Acts, 1845, 1860, and 1869, or under the Settled Estates Act, 1877, or under any other Act, public, local, personal, or private, money is at the commencement of this Act in Court, or is afterwards paid into Court, and is liable to be laid out in the purchase of land to be made subject to a settlement, then, in addition to any mode of dealing therewith authorized by the Act under which the money is in Court, that money may be invested or applied as capital money arising under this Act, or on the like terms, if any, respecting costs and other things, as nearly as circumstances admit, and (notwithstanding anything in this Act) according to the same procedure, as if the modes of investment or application authorized by this Act were authorized by the Act under which the money is in Court.

Application of money in Court under other Acts.

The object of this section is to enable money in Court, which is liable to be invested in land under the provisions of any Act of Parliament, to be applied as if s. 21 of this Act were incorporated in the investment clause of the Act under which it has been paid in.

Payment out to trustees.

In has been decided in several cases that the Court has power under this section to order the money in Court to be paid out to the trustees of the settlement : *Re Duke of Rutland's Settlement*, 31 W. R. 947 ; *Re Wright's Trusts*, 24 Ch. D. 662 ; *Re The Bolton Estates Act, 1863*, 52 L. T. 728 ; *Ex parte Verschoyle*, 15 L. R. Ir. 576 ; *Re S. Smith*, 40 Ch. D. 386. In the last-mentioned case the Court of Appeal held that the order was in the discretion of the Court, and was justified, not on the ground stated in some of the previous cases, that trustees with a power of sale are persons absolutely entitled, but because the trustees of the settlement are persons " empowered to give an absolute discharge " for capital moneys within the meaning of s. 21 (ix.), *ante*. S. 14 of the Act of 1890, which enables "any capital money paid into Court" to be paid out to the trustees, seems not to apply to this section, but to be confined to capital money arising under the Act which has been paid into Court.

Settlement.

Where the purchase-money of lands belonging absolutely to a charity without power of sale had been paid into Court under the Lands Clauses Consolidation Acts, it was held that the money was "liable to be laid out in the purchase of land to be made subject to a settlement" within the meaning of this section, and might accordingly be invested in debenture stock of a railway company: *Re Byron's Charity*, 23 Ch. D. 171. See also *Re The Chelsea Waterworks Co.*, 56 L. T. 421.

§ 32.

In *Re Arabin's Trusts*, 52 L. T. 728, it was considered doubtful whether the procedure under the Settled Estates Act or under this Act should prevail; and, the tenant for life being a married woman, the Court, to be on the safe side, directed that she should be separately examined under the former Act as to her consent to a re-investment in land by the trustees of the settlement.

Procedure.

It is conceived that, notwithstanding the doubt expressed in *Re Arabin's Trusts, supra*, the procedure to be adopted is that prescribed with reference to the Act of Parliament under which the money has been paid into Court. This seems to have been tacitly assumed in the cases under the Lands Clauses Consolidation Act, where the question whether the costs of a petition should be allowed has always been treated as depending on R. S. C. 1883, Ord. LV. r. 2 (7). By this rule the business to be disposed of in chambers includes:— "Applications for interim and permanent investment, and for payment of dividends under the Lands Clauses Consolidation Act, 1845, and any other Act whereby the purchase-money of any property sold is directed to be paid into Court."

Lands Clauses Consolidation Acts.

It will be observed that this rule does not refer to payment of capital to any person absolutely entitled thereto, nor is any limit fixed as to the amount of the money to be dealt with on summons; but clause (2) of the same rule authorizes payment or transfer on summons to any person of any cash or securities standing to the credit of any cause or matter where the cash does not exceed £1000, or the securities do not exceed £1000 nominal value. This is a general provision and applies to cash or securities in Court under the Lands Clauses Consolidation Act: *Ex parte Maidstone and Ashford Railway Co.*, 25 Ch. D. 168; *Re Calton's Will, ibid.* 240; *Re Madgwick, ibid.* 371. The result is, that as a general rule the application should be by summons except where the fund exceeds £1000, and is not by the order to be applied in interim or permanent investment.

Petition or Summons.

Payment of a sum exceeding £1000 to the applicant on an undertaking to apply it in building, is not within the Rules of Court, and can only be ordered on petition: *Ex parte Jesus College, Cambridge*, 50 L. T. 583; *Re Hargreave's Trust*, 58 L. T. 367.

There are many cases, however, in which both expense and trouble are saved by presenting a petition instead of issuing a summons; and the Court has power to allow the costs of a petition even when there was jurisdiction to make the order on summons: *Re Bethlehem and Bridewell Hospitals*, 30 Ch. D. 541. In cases of complication

§ 32.

Costs.

and difficulty, where a concise statement of facts would be required in chambers, the costs of a petition have been frequently allowed : *Re Arnold*, 31 S. J. 560; *Re Earl de Grey's Entailed Estate*, 32 S. J. 108 ; *Re Stafford's Charity*, 57 L. T. 846 ; *Re Hargreave's Trust*, 58 L. T. 367.

The costs of an interim investment in debenture stock in pursuance of this section must be paid by the public body which has taken the land in the same way as if that form of investment had been authorized by the Private Act : *Re Hanbury*, 52 L. J. Ch. 687. In this case it was held (following *Ex parte Mercer's Co.*, 10 Ch. D. 481) that the Court had an absolute discretion as to costs where the Act was silent on the subject—a doctrine which was overruled by *Re Mill's Estate*, 34 Ch. D. 24 ; and re-established by s. 5 of the Jud. Act, 1890 (53 & 54 Vict. c. 44).

This enactment, which places costs within the discretion of the Court, is made "subject to the express provisions of any statute ; " and s. 80 of the Lands Clauses Act, 1845, throws upon the company the costs of the purchase of the lands, interim investment, re-investment in other land, and of all proceedings relating thereto except such as are occasioned by adverse litigation ; and it has been decided that under this section the costs of paying off incumbrances on other parts of the estate are not payable by the company : *Ex parte Earl of Hardwicke*, '17 L. J. Ch. 422 ; *Re Manchester, &c., Ry. Co.*, 21 Beav. 162 ; but that they are bound to pay those of the redemption of land tax : *Re Bethlem Hospital*, L. R. 19 Eq. 457 ; *Re Hospital of St. Katharine*, 17 Ch. D. 378. The company have also been held liable to pay the costs of applying the fund in the enfranchisement of copyholds : *Re Cheshunt College*, 1 Jur. N. S. 995 ; *Dixon v. Jackson*, 25 L. J. Ch. 588 ; *Re Wilson's Estate*, 11 W. R. 712 ; and in the erection of buildings, or permanent improvements : see *Ex parte Rector of Gamston*, 1 Ch. D. 477 ; *Ex parte Rector of Kirksmeaton*, 20 Ch. D. 203.

It would seem, however, that the company cannot be called upon to pay the costs of schemes and certificates under s. 26 : see *Ex parte Rector of Shipton*, 19 W. R. 549.

Money or securities.

Although the expression in this section is "*Money* in Court," there can be no doubt that it applies where the money has been invested in authorized securities : see *Ex parte Verschoyle*, 15 L. R. Ir. 576 ; *Re Arnold*, 31 S. J. 560 ; *Re Harrop's Trusts*, 24 Ch. D. 717.

§ 33.

Application of money in hands of

33. Where, under a settlement, money is in the hands of trustees, and is liable to be laid out in the purchase of land to be made subject to the settlement, then, in addition to such powers of dealing therewith as the trustees have

independently of this Act, they may, at the option of the tenant for life, invest or apply the same as capital money arising under this Act.

§ 33. trustees under powers of settlement.

It is to be observed that the marginal note introduces the qualifying words "under powers of settlement," which do not occur in the section. The marginal note, however, cannot control the generality of the enactment : *Sutton* v. *Sutton*, 22 Ch. D. 511.

Money in the hands of trustees.

Whatever may be the source whence the money is derived, if it is "liable to be laid out in the purchase of land to be made subject to the settlement," it may be invested or applied as capital money arising under the Act. See *Re Mackenzie's Trusts*, 23 Ch. D. 750; *Re Maberly*, 33 Ch. D. 455.

The trust for investment in land must, however, be imperative. If the trustees have an option of investing in land or on real security (*Atwell* v. *Atwell*, L. R. 13 Eq. 23), or if they have only a power with the consent of the tenant for life, to purchase land (*De Beauvoir* v. *De Beauvoir*, 3 H. L. Cas. 524), or if they have a discretion as to the time at which they will so invest (*Tempest* v. *Camoys*, 21 Ch. D. 571), it would seem that the section does not apply.

The option here conferred upon the tenant for life is a "power" which may be exercised by tenants in tail and other limited owners under s. 58, *post*; and if the tenant for life is an infant it may be exercised during his minority by the trustees of the settlement : *Re Duke of Newcastle's Estates*, 24 Ch. D. 129, at p. 139.

Option of tenant for life.

Notwithstanding an imperative direction in a will to invest the residue of the testator's personal estate in the purchase of land in Ireland, it was held that under this section the trustees of the will, one of whom was the tenant for life, might invest the money in their hands in any of the securities authorized by s. 21, until they could prudently obey the testator's injunction : *Re Maberly*, 33 Ch. D. 455.

The tenant for life has an option not only to say that money shall be invested or applied as capital money, but to direct *how* it shall be invested or applied : Per Chitty, J., *Clarke* v. *Thornton*, 35 Ch. D. 307, 313. In this case the tenant for life was held entitled to call upon the trustees to apply a fund accumulated by the express direction of the testator in payment for "improvements," although under the will they had full power to pay for them out of rents and profits. See also *Re Earl of Stamford*, 56 L. T. 484.

Under the will of a testator who died in 1880, £200,000 was in the hands of trustees upon trust for investment in the purchase of land to be settled in strict settlement; and it was held, upon the trustees' petition for advice, that they might, at the request of the persons who would be tenants for life of the land when purchased,

§ 33.

invest the money in debenture stock in accordance with s. 21 : *Re Mackenzie's Trusts*, 23 Ch. D. 750.

Here, it will be observed, there was no "settlement" in existence to which the purchased land was to be made subject, but Chitty, J., said : "It is absurd to suppose that that could not now be done which a tenant for life could without question do after an estate had been purchased, by selling the estate and investing the moneys arising from the sale as asked for by this petition."

This case was followed by Mr. Justice North, in *Re Tennant*, 40 Ch. D. 594 ; but the same learned judge in *Re Mundy's Settled Estates*, 63 L. T. 311, doubted the correctness of the former decisions and referred the matter to the Court of Appeal.* If the money is in Court to the credit of an administration action the section does not apply : *Burke v. Gore*, 13 L. R. Ir. 367.

§ 34.
Application of money paid for lease or reversion.

34. Where capital money arising under this Act is purchase money paid in respect of a lease for years, or life, or years determinable on life, or in respect of any other estate or interest in land less than the fee simple, or in respect of a reversion dependent on any such lease, estate, or interest, the trustees of the settlement or the Court, as the case may be, and in the case of the Court on the application of any party interested in that money, may, notwithstanding anything in this Act, require and cause the same to be laid out, invested, accumulated, and paid in such manner as, in the judgment of the trustees or of the Court, as the case may be, will give to the parties interested in that money the like benefit therefrom as they might lawfully have had from the lease, estate, interest, or reversion in respect whereof the money was paid, or as near thereto as may be.

Money paid for lease or reversion.

This section is analogous to s. 74 of the Lands Clauses Consolidation Act (8 & 9 Vict. c. 18), and to s. 37 of the Settled Estates Act, 1877 (40 & 41 Vict. c. 18) ; but differs from both those enactments by authorizing the trustees of the settlement, as well as the Court, to exercise the discretion which under them could be exercised by the Court alone. With this exception the enactments are substantially identical and decisions on the earlier Acts may be regarded as authorities upon the present section : *Cottrell v. Cottrell*, 28 Ch. D. 628.

---

* The Court of Appeal has since approved the earlier decisions, 35 S. J. 191.

Where the purchase-money arises from the sale of a lease for years (and the same observation applies to other limited interests), the whole fund should be exhausted during the period of the lease, so as to give no benefit to the remainderman which he would not have derived from the unconverted leasehold. The object of this section "would clearly be attained by investing the money in the purchase of an annuity having as many years to run as there were years remaining in the term. If an annuity is not actually bought, it must be referred to an actuary to calculate what yearly sum, if raised out of the dividends and corpus of the fund, will exhaust the fund in the number of years which the lease had to run, and the amount so ascertained must be paid to the tenant for life:" Per Jessel, M. R., in *Askew* v. *Woodhead*, 14 Ch. D. 27, 34. This case which follows *Re Phillips' Trusts*, L. R. 6 Eq. 250, and overrules *Re Pfleger*, ibid. 426, may be considered to have settled the principle on which the apportionment between tenant for life and remainderman should take place. See also *Ex parte Wilkinson*, 3 De G. & Sm. 633; *Jeffreys* v. *Conner*, 28 Beav. 328; *Re Money's Trusts*, 2 Dr. & Sm. 94.

§ 34.
Lease.

The principle on which the purchase-money of a reversion is to be laid out is that the income of the tenant for life is not to be increased by the sale. Thus, in *Re Wootton's Estate*, L. R. 1 Eq. 589, land subject to a building lease of which eleven years were unexpired was taken by a railway company, and it was ordered, that only so much of the dividends of the fund in Court should be paid to the tenant for life as would compensate her for the loss of rent, and that the residue should be accumulated till the end of the term. But at the end of the term the tenant for life will be entitled to the income arising from the accumulations as well as from the original purchase-money: *Re Mette's Estate*, L. R. 7 Eq. 72; *Re Wilkes' Estate*, 16 Ch. D. 597. These decisions were approved and followed in *Cottrell* v. *Cottrell*, 28 Ch. D. 628, a case which arose under this section of the Settled Land Act.

Reversion.

Where small parts of an estate subject to leases were taken compulsorily by a railway company, and the tenant for life arranged with the lessees that they should continue to pay the same rents as before, it was held that she should take no benefit from the purchase money until the leases fell in, and that the income should be accumulated in the meantime: *Re Griffiths' Will*, 49 L. T. 161.

Where renewable leaseholds are the subject of a settlement which contains an over-riding trust for renewal, the tenant for life will only be entitled on a sale to the actual income of the purchase-money, whether the leaseholds have ceased to be renewable or not: *Re Wood's Estate*, L. R. 10 Eq. 572; *Hollier* v. *Burne*, L. R. 16 Eq. 163; *Maddy* v. *Hale*, 3 Ch. D. 327; *Re Barber's S. E.*, 18 Ch. D. 624; *Re Lord Ranelagh's Will*, 26 Ch. D. 590.

Renewable leaseholds.

§ 34.

For form of application under this section, see Form XVIII., in the Appendix to the Rules, *post*.

§ 35.

Cutting and sale of timber, and part of proceeds to be set aside.

35.—(1.) Where a tenant for life is impeachable for waste in respect of timber, and there is on the settled land timber ripe and fit for cutting, the tenant for life, on obtaining the consent of the trustees of the settlement or an order of the Court, may cut and sell that timber, or any part thereof.

(2.) Three fourth parts of the net proceeds of the sale shall be set aside as and be capital money arising under this Act, and the other fourth part shall go as rents and profits.

Cutting and sale of timber.

A tenant for life is "impeachable for waste" unless he is expressly made "unimpeachable" by the settlement, in which case he can cut timber as he wishes.

This section confers on a tenant for life, impeachable for waste by analogy to the provision as to mining rent in s. 11, *ante*, p. 60, an interest in the timber which he did not previously possess ; for, when timber was ripe and fit for cutting, and was accordingly cut by the order of the Court, the practice was to invest the whole fund, and allow the tenant for life to receive only the dividends and no part of the capital : *Tooker* v. *Annesley*, 5 Sim. 235 ; Seton, 1259, *et seq*. It may also be observed that the Court would not, on the application of a tenant for life, order timber to be cut merely because it was *ripe*, unless it was decaying or injuring the growth of other timber : *Seagram* v. *Knight*, L. R. 2 Ch. 628.

"Timber" properly signifies oak, ash, and elm, twenty years old and upwards, and in particular districts other trees are "timber" by local custom : *Honywood* v. *Honywood*, L. R. 18 Eq. 306 ; a case which may be also usefully consulted as to the rights of the tenant for life in respect of trees which are not timber. There seems no reason why the word "timber" in this section should receive any but its proper and technical meaning, and if so there is no power to cut and sell timber—like trees.

The proportion of the proceeds of sale which is set aside, being "capital money," must follow the trusts of the settlement, and does not belong absolutely to the first person who comes into possession of the estates as tenant in tail or tenant for life unimpeachable for waste. It is different where timber is wrongfully cut by a tenant for life impeachable for waste, or under an order of the Court. In those cases the person who first takes an estate unimpeachable for waste is entitled to receive the capital : *Waldo* v. *Waldo*, 12 Sim. 107 ; *Lowndes* v. *Norton*, 6 Ch. D. 139.

PROTECTION OR RECOVERY OF SETTLED LAND.

§ 35. In a recent case a tenant for life of an estate in strict settlement, who had express power to cut and sell timber or other trees which were beginning to decay, and to apply the produce to his own use, sold the estate under the Settled Land Act, subject to conditions of sale which provided that the purchaser should, "in addition to his purchase-money," pay for all timber and timberlike trees at a valuation. The tenant for life claimed payment, (1) of so much of the amount of the valuation as represented timber beginning to decay which he might have sold under his power, and (2) one-fourth of the balance by virtue of this section. It was, however, held that he was not entitled to either; for there was but one sale, the amount of the valuation being merely an addition to the purchase-money of the estate, and the timber until severance being part of the inheritance: *Re Llewellin*, 37 Ch. 317. The tenant for life, moreover, in this case had obtained the consent of the trustees only to a sale of the estate with the timber, and was in the same position as a tenant for life under the old law who was impeachable for waste selling by virtue of a power: see *Doran* v. *Wiltshire*, 3 Sw. 699; *Cholmeley* v. *Paxton*, 3 Bing. 207; *Cockerell* v. *Cholmeley*, 6 Bli. N. S. 120. It seems to follow, however, from the judgment in *Re Llewellin*, that the tenant for life, if he obtains the consent of the trustees to a separate sale of the timber, may take the benefit of this section notwithstanding that the estate is sold at the same time.

36. The Court may, if it thinks fit, approve of any action, defence, petition to Parliament, parliamentary opposition, or other proceeding taken or proposed to be taken for protection of settled land, or of any action or proceeding taken or proposed to be taken for recovery of land being or alleged to be subject to a settlement, and may direct that any costs, charges, or expenses incurred or to be incurred in relation thereto, or any part thereof, be paid out of property subject to the settlement.

§ 36. Proceedings for protection or recovery of land settled or claimed as settled.

This section replaces s. 17 of the Settled Estates Act, 1877 (repealed by s. 64, *post*), and extends the provisions of the repealed enactment so as to embrace not only proceedings for *protection*, but also for the *recovery* of settled land.

In *Re Earl of Aylesford's Settled Estates*, 32 Ch. D. 162, Bacon, V.-C., ordered the costs of successful proceedings before the House of Lords Committee for Privileges to establish a peerage claim by the tenant for life to be paid under this section; but it does not seem clear from the report whether the ground of this decision was that the finding of the committee resulted in the inexpensive recovery of the

Proceedings for protection or recovery of land.

§ 36.

Protection from foreclosure.

General jurisdiction.

estates, or (following Mr. Justice Chitty's decision in *Re Sir J. Rivett-Carnac's Will*, 30 Ch. D. 136) that a dignity or title of honour is "land" within the meaning of s. 2, sub-s. 10 (i.).

The costs incurred by a tenant for life in protecting the settled estate from foreclosure, including the costs of obtaining transfers of the mortgages, with interest at 4 per cent. per annum, were charged on the property under this section: *More* v. *More*, 37 W. R. 414. In this case an action was instituted for the purpose by the tenant for life against the infant tenant in tail in remainder, and the order was made on motion for judgment, the action being set down as a short cause, and the allegations in the statement of claim being verified by affidavit. In general, however, the procedure should be by originating summons entitled in the matter of the Act.

Independently of the powers conferred by statute, costs incurred by the tenant for life in defence of the settled estates have been ordered to be defrayed out of capital: *Re Earl De La Warr's Estates*, 16 Ch. D. 587; but the propriety of this order was doubted in *Re Twyford Abbey S. E.*, 30 W. R. 268; where costs incurred by the tenant for life in preventing the construction of a sewage farm, which would have amounted to a nuisance to the tenants of the estate, were, under s. 17 of the Settled Estates Act, ordered to be paid by the trustees, out of capital money in their hands. See also, as to the costs of opposing a Bill in Parliament, *Re Earl of Berkeley's Will*, L. R. 10 Ch. 56; and as to the costs of an application to Parliament before the present Act to enable an infant tenant for life to carry out a sale: *Stanford* v. *Roberts*, 52 L. J. Ch. 50.

§ 37.

Heirlooms.

37.—(1.) Where personal chattels are settled on trust so as to devolve with land until a tenant in tail by purchase is born or attains the age of twenty-one years, or so as otherwise to vest in some person becoming entitled to an estate of freehold of inheritance in the land, a tenant for life of the land may sell the chattels or any of them.

(2.) The money arising by the sale shall be capital money arising under this Act, and shall be paid, invested, or applied and otherwise dealt with in like manner in all respects as by this Act directed with respect to other capital money arising under this Act, or may be invested in the purchase of other chattels, of the same or any other nature, which, when purchased, shall be settled and held on the same trusts, and shall devolve in the same manner as the chattels sold.

(3.) A sale or purchase of chattels under this section shall not be made without an order of the Court.

§ 37.

This is the only section in the Act which relates to personal chattels, and it removes the difficulty experienced in *D'Eyncourt* v. *Gregory*, 3 Ch. D. 635, where it was held that the Court had no jurisdiction to sell chattels settled in strict settlement, even where the sale would be for the benefit of all parties interested.

Heirlooms.

The grammatical construction of the first sub-section is not free from difficulty. If the two alternative modes of settlement are, (1) so as to devolve with land until a tenant in tail by purchase is born or attains the age of twenty-one years; and (2) so as otherwise to vest in some person becoming entitled to an estate of freehold of inheritance in the land, the essential feature of heirlooms, *i.e.*, that they should "devolve with land," is omitted from the second alternative. It seems necessary, therefore, to treat the words "so as to devolve with land" as common to both clauses of the sentence, in which case the second will run thus: "when personal chattels are settled on trust so as to devolve with land so as [otherwise] to vest in some person, &c." This, if inelegant, is intelligible.

Sub-s. 1. Power of sale.

A dignity or title of honour which descends to the heirs general or heirs of the body is an incorporeal hereditament, and is, therefore, "land" within the meaning of this section; and a service of plate bequeathed by will to trustees upon trust to permit the same to be used by the person for the time being entitled to a baronetcy, is an heirloom annexed to the baronetcy, and may be sold with the leave of the Court: *Re Sir J. Rivett-Carnac's Will*, 30 Ch. D. 136. Many difficulties had to be overcome in order to arrive at this conclusion. Thus, in order to create a person entitled to exercise the powers of a tenant for life, the baronet had to be treated as a tenant in tail of the dignity; a conclusion the validity of which depends on such a dignity being a "tenement" within the meaning of the Statute *De Donis*. Mr. Justice Chitty held that it was, on the authority of *Rex* v. *Knollys*, 1 Lord Raym. 10, and *Earl Ferrers' Case*, 2 Eden, 373. It would be out of place to discuss here this interesting question; but reference may be made to the 3rd Report of the Lords Committee on the Dignity of a Peer of the Realm, p. 56, where the cases referred to are stated to be of no authority, and where it is laid down that a dignity or title of honour is not a "tenement" within the meaning of the Statute *De Donis*.

Dignity or title of honour.

It will be observed that in *Sir J. Rivett-Carnac's Case* the "land," *i.e.*, the baronetcy and the "heirlooms," were settled by different instruments. This difficulty, although not referred to, cannot have been overlooked; and it may therefore be assumed that in order to come within this section it is not necessary that the land and the

§ 37.

heirlooms should be comprised in one and the same settlement, but that it is sufficient if the limitations are substantially identical. There were in this case no trustees of the settlement for the purposes of the Act; and a baronetcy being inalienable there could be no such trustees except by the appointment of the Court. It seems to follow that this section is an "isolated enactment," and is not controlled by the provisions of the Act as to such trustees. See also *Constable* v. *Constable*, 32 Ch. D. 233, where it was held that it was not necessary to have trustees of the heirlooms for the purposes of the Act, if there were trustees of the settlement so far as the land was concerned. In that case Mr. Justice Pearson said: "The trustees having power to sell land, are also, *if it is necessary to have such trustees in order to sell the heirlooms under the Act*, trustees for that purpose of the Act."

Where chattels were settled as heirlooms to go with a particular house which had lately become unsuitable to the family, and had been replaced by a larger residence, the Court sanctioned a sale of the old house, together with such of the heirlooms as were unfit for removal, the rest being transferred to the new mansion, and annexed to it as heirlooms: *Browne* v. *Collins*, 62 L. T. 567. As to the question whether a case of election can be raised against the tenant for life by an attempted disposition of heirlooms, see *Re Lord Chesham*, 34 W. R. 321.

Sub-s. 2.
Capital money.

The proceeds of sale of the heir-looms are capital money arising under the Act, and may be applied in discharging incumbrances on the settled land without keeping them on foot for the benefit of the infant remainderman: *Re Duke of Marlborough's Settlement*, 30 Ch. D. 127; affirmed on appeal 32 Ch. D. 1. The result of this section so interpreted was that a remainderman who would on attaining twenty-one years of age have become absolutely entitled to the heirlooms, took only a limited interest in the money produced by their sale, and thus the devolution of the settled property was altered by the operation of the Act. But, as Mr. Justice Chitty pointed out (30 Ch. D. 131), the *Settled Land Act* has made a very great alteration in the law; in fact it has "created a revolution." So long, however, as the proceeds of sale continue invested in personal securities they retain their character of personal estate, and will devolve as such notwithstanding s. 22 (5).

The proceeds of sale may also be applied in payment for improvements on the settled land: *Re Houghton Estate*, 30 Ch. D. 102.

Sub-s. 3.
Discretion of the Court.

The power conferred on the Court of sanctioning a sale of heirlooms under this section is discretionary, and the Act gives no indication of the principles which are to govern the exercise of this discretion. Section 53, which places the tenant for life in the position of a trustee in the exercise of his powers, points to the conclusion that the order should not be made in the interest of the tenant for life alone, but as a general rule the fact that he has incumbered his life estate ought to be excluded from the consideration of the Court: *Re The Earl of Radnor's Will Trusts*, 45 Ch. D. 402; and see *Re Beaumont's Settled Estates*, 58 L. T. 916. In both these cases Mr. Justice Chitty declined to lay down any rules which might fetter the Court in dealing with future cases, and said that the discretion of the Court is one to be fairly exercised according to the exigencies of each particular case.

§ 37.

X.—TRUSTEES.

38.—(1.) If at any time there are no trustees of a settlement within the definition of this Act, or where in any other case it is expedient, for purposes of this Act, that new trustees of a settlement be appointed, the Court may, if it thinks fit, on the application of the tenant for life or of any other person having, under the settlement, an estate or interest in the settled land, in possession, remainder, or otherwise, or, in the case of an infant, of his testamentary or other guardian, or next friend, appoint fit persons to be trustees under the settlement for purposes of this Act.

§ 38. Appointment of trustees by Court.

(2.) The persons so appointed, and the survivors and survivor of them, while continuing to be trustees or trustee, and, until the appointment of new trustees, the personal representatives or representative for the time being of the last surviving or continuing trustee, shall for purposes of this Act become and be the trustees or trustee of the settlement.

The cases in which it will be necessary to apply to the Court under this section for the appointment of trustees of the settlement have been greatly diminished in number by ss. 16 & 17 of the Act of 1890.

Sect. 38. Trustees of the settlement.

"The Trustees of the Settlement," as defined in s. 2 (8), include the following persons:—
 1. Trustees with power of sale of settled land:
 2. Trustees with power of consent to or approval of the exercise of such a power.
 3. The persons who are by the settlement declared to be trustees thereof for purposes of this Act.

To this list must now be added the various persons enumerated in s. 16 of the Act of 1890, which is as follows:—

C.S.L.A.   K

§ 38.

Trustees for the purposes of the Act.

"16. Where there are for the time being no trustees of the settlement within the meaning and for the purposes of the Act of 1882, then the following persons shall, for the purposes of the Settled Land Acts, 1882 to 1890, be trustees of the settlement, namely,

"(i.) The persons (if any) who are for the time being under the settlement trustees, with power of or upon trust for sale of any other land comprised in the settlement and subject to the same limitations as the land to be sold, or with power of consent to or approval of the exercise of such a power of sale, or, if there be no such persons, then

"(ii.) The persons (if any) who are for the time being under the settlement trustees with future power of sale, or under a future trust for sale of the land to be sold, or with power of consent to or approval of the exercise of such a future power of sale, and whether the power or trust takes effect in all events or not."

And s. 17 of the same Act (removing the doubt expressed in *Re Wilcock*, 34 Ch. D. 508 ; *Re Kane*, 21 L. R. Ir. 112) has made the statutory power of appointing new trustees conferred by the Conveyancing Act, applicable to "trustees for the purposes of the Settled Land Acts, 1882 to 1890." The section is in the following terms :—

Application of provisions of 44 & 45 Vict. c. 41, as to appointment of trustees.

"17.—(1.) All the powers and provisions contained in the Conveyancing and Law of Property Act, 1881, with reference to the appointment of new trustees, and the discharge and retirement of trustees, are to apply to and include trustees for the purposes of the Settled Land Acts, 1882 to 1890, whether appointed by the Court or by the settlement, or under provisions contained in the settlement.

"(2.) This section applies and is to have effect with respect to an appointment or a discharge and retirement of trustees taking place before as well as after the passing of this Act.

"(3.) This section is not to render invalid or prejudice any appointment or any discharge and retirement of trustees effected before the passing of this Act otherwise than under the provisions of the Conveyancing and Law of Property Act, 1881."

The expression "trustees for the purposes of the Settled Land Acts, 1882 to 1890" is probably used here instead of "trustees of the settlement," as including only those "trustees of the settlement" who take no estate, and are appointed by the Court, or by or under the settlement. "Trustees of the settlement" in whom property is vested, and who stand in the position of ordinary trustees, were already subject to the provisions of the Conveyancing and Law of Property Act, 1881, and their successors appointed under that Act having the same powers, would be also "trustees of the settlement."

It would, in general, be inexpedient to nominate the tenant for life as the person to exercise the power of appointing new trustees conferred by s. 31 of the Conveyancing Act; for the trustees of the settlement are intended to exercise a general supervision over the acts of the tenant for life, and ought to be persons independent of and unconnected with him. See *Re Kemp's Settled Estates*, 24 Ch. D. 485.

§ 38.

Where there are no "trustees of the settlement," and there is no power in the settlement to appoint them, it will still be necessary to apply to the Court for their appointment before the powers of the Act can be exercised by the tenant for life: *Wheelwright* v. *Walker*, 23 Ch. D. 752, 756; and see *Re Taylor*, 31 W. R. 596. In granting or refusing the application the Court will take into account the object with which it is made: *Burke* v. *Gore*, 13 L. R. Ir. 367.

Appointment by the Court.

Where there are existing trustees in whom the land is vested, but who are not "trustees of the settlement," the Court will, in general, if they are willing to act, appoint them to be trustees for the purposes of the Settled Land Act in preference to strangers: *Re Stoneley's Will*, 27 S. J. 554.

It has been laid down as a rule of practice that in no case can a tenant for life, or a person who might become tenant for life, be appointed a trustee of a settlement for the purposes of the Act: *Re Harrop's Trusts*, 24 Ch. D. 717. Nor will the solicitor of the tenant for life be appointed, though in other respects a fit person, and already a trustee; for "the appointment of trustees is required to impose a check upon the extensive powers conferred by the Act upon the tenant for life." *Per* Cotton, L.J., in *Re Kemp's Settled Estates*, 24 Ch. D. 485, and see *Re John Walker's Trusts*, 31 W. R. 716. As the trustees ought to be independent of each other as well as of the tenant for life, near relatives will not in general be appointed: *Re Knowles' Settled Estates*, 27 Ch. D. 707.

The application to the Court should be made by originating summons (Rule 2, and Form XIX.) entitled in the matter of the estate and in the matter of the Acts, and should be served on the trustees (if any) and on the tenant for life if not the applicant: Rule 4.

Summons.

The authorities at Somerset House having adjudicated that no stamp duty was required on an order appointing trustees of the settlement under this section, the Court directed the order to be passed and entered without a stamp: *Re Potter*, W. N. 1889, 69; see also *Re Kennaway*, W. N. 1889, 70, and the Notice issued by the Board of Inland Revenue, 33 S. J. 366, in which a distinction is drawn as regards stamp duty between appointments of new trustees and original appointments under this section.

Stamp duty.

Although the personal representatives of the last surviving or continuing trustee are constituted "trustees of the settlement;" the section seems to contemplate their immediate removal; but until

Sub-s. 2. Personal representatives.

§ 38.   they exercise the power of appointing new trustees (which they can now in general do under s. 31 of the Conveyancing Act, and s. 17 of the Settled Land Act, 1890), they must be considered as "trustees of the settlement" for all purposes, and, as excluding the persons nominated by s. 16 of the Act of 1890, which only takes effect if "there are no trustees of the settlement within the meaning and for the purposes of the Act of 1882."

A question arises whether in the interval between the death of the last surviving or continuing trustee and the constitution of his personal representative, s. 16 of the Act of 1890 has any operation? Are, for example, persons with a future power of sale trustees of the settlement until such personal representative comes into existence? Or will the grant of probate or letters of administration relate to the death, so as to make the personal representative the trustee of the settlement from the death of the last surviving or continuing trustee? If the latter is the correct view considerable inconvenience may be caused in cases where there is delay in the constitution of a personal representative, and an application will probably have to be made to the Court to exercise the powers of this section.

§ 39.
Number of trustees to act.

39.—(1.) Notwithstanding anything in this Act, capital money arising under this Act shall not be paid to fewer than two persons as trustees of a settlement, unless the settlement authorizes the receipt of capital trust money of the settlement by one trustee.

(2.) Subject thereto, the provisions of this Act referring to the trustees of a settlement apply to the surviving or continuing trustees or trustee of the settlement for the time being.

Sect. 39.
Number of trustees.

As to the various occasions on which capital money may arise under the Act, see *ante*, p. 14.

When a settlement, executed long before the Settled Land Act came into operation, gave powers to the "trustees or trustee" to act, and to receive and give receipts for capital money comprised in the settlement, it was held that "the settlement authorized the receipt of capital trust money of the settlement by one trustee" within the meaning of this section, and that the survivor of the two original trustees came within the exception: *Re Garnett Orme and Hargreaves' Contract*, 25 Ch. D. 595. *A fortiori*, the original appointment of a single trustee would enable him to execute the office of trustee of the settlement.

This enactment is analogous to the provisions in the Conv. Act, 1881, s. 31 (3), and s. 32 (1), their common object being to secure the trust funds from being at the disposal of a single trustee; but although capital money may not be paid to fewer than two persons, there is nothing to prevent the sole survivor of the trustees from dealing with investments under s. 21 (i.).

§ 39.

Compare with this section s. 45 (2), which requires that, when notice is given by the tenant for life under that section, the number of trustees shall not be less than two, "unless a contrary intention is expressed in the settlement." The words of exception adopted here, "unless the settlement authorizes the receipt of capital trust money by one trustee," seem to point to an express rather than an implied authority.

Notice to a sole trustee.

40. The receipt in writing of the trustees of a settlement, or where one trustee is empowered to act, of one trustee, or of the personal representatives or representative of the last surviving or continuing trustee, for any money or securities, paid or transferred to the trustees, trustee, representatives or representative, as the case may be, effectually discharges the payer or transferor therefrom, and from being bound to see to the application or being answerable for any loss or misapplication thereof, and, in case of a mortgagee or other person advancing money, from being concerned to see that any money advanced by him is wanted for any purpose of this Act, or that no more than is wanted is raised.

§ 40.
Trustees' receipts

The personal representatives of a last surviving or continuing trustee appointed by the Court, are by s. 38 (2) declared to be trustees of the settlement, and as such could give receipts under this section without being specially mentioned. When, however, the last surviving or continuing trustee has not been appointed by the Court, his personal representatives may not be trustees of the settlement, and yet are hereby empowered to receive capital money. If, for example, the settlement appointed A. and B., and the survivor of them, trustees or trustee of the settlement for the purposes of the Act; on the death of the survivor his personal representatives would be entitled under this section to receive trust money, and yet would not be trustees of the settlement.

Sect. 40.
Trustees' receipts.

The section is perfectly general in its terms as to the money or securities which may be paid or transferred, and is not even confined to "capital money arising under the Act." It was, indeed, held that this section did not apply when money had been paid into Court so as to enable the Court to pay the money out to the trustees: *Cookes*

§ 40.

Position of mortgagee.

v. *Cookes*, 34 Ch. D. 498. But this can now be done under s. 14 of the Act of 1890.

Persons appointed trustees by the Court under s. 38 are within this section : *Cookes* v. *Cookes*, *supra*.

The only powers to raise money on mortgage for the purposes of the Act are (1) for enfranchisement or equality of exchange or partition, s. 18 ; (2) for payment of costs, charges, and expenses, s. 47 ; and (3) for the discharge of incumbrances, s. 11 of the Act of 1890. Although the section protects the mortgagee only with respect to money advanced by him "for any purpose of *this* Act," *i.e.*, the Act of 1882, yet it seems clear that the protection extends to an advance of money for the purpose of discharging incumbrances under the Act of 1890 ; for by s. 2 of that Act it is provided that the "Settled Land Acts, 1882 to 1889, and this Act, are to be read and construed together as *one Act*." The expression "this Act" seems, therefore, now to include the whole series of Acts.

As to the sources whence capital money may arise, see *ante*, p. 14.

§ 41.

Protection of each trustee individually.

41. Each person who is for the time being trustee of a settlement is answerable for what he actually receives only, notwithstanding his signing any receipt for conformity, and in respect of his own acts, receipts, and defaults only, and is not answerable in respect of those of any other trustee, or of any banker, broker, or other person, or for the insufficiency or deficiency of any securities, or for any loss not happening through his own wilful default.

Sect. 41. Indemnity.

This section is practically identical with the 31st section of Lord St. Leonards' Act (22 & 23 Vict. c. 35).

That enactment incorporates in every deed, will, or other instrument creating a trust the common indemnity clause, which, it may be observed, merely expresses the equitable doctrine of the Courts ; Dav. Conv. iii. 246, 3rd ed. The learned authors of that work remark—and the observation is equally applicable to the present section—that "the protective effect of this rule must not be over-rated, as, though the acknowledgment of the trustee is not conclusive evidence of his having participated in the receipt of the money, it is a breach of trust to permit, without sufficient reason, the co-trustee alone to receive the money : " pp. 246-7.

It may be doubtful whether, having regard to s. 39, *ante*, a trustee of the settlement under this Act will ever be justified in permitting money to be received by a single co-trustee "unless the settlement authorises the receipt of capital trust money by one trustee ; " but in any case he ought not to allow it to *remain* in his hands for a longer period than the circumstances of the case reasonably require.

A trustee who employs a broker to buy authorized securities is justified in paying the purchase-money to the broker if he follows the usual and regular course of business adopted by ordinary prudent men in making such investments : *Speight* v. *Gaunt*, 9 App. Cas. 1. Trustees are never permitted to delegate any part of their trust, but they may always, in cases of necessity, and acting as prudent men of business, employ agents. This rule is, however, subject to the limitation that the agent must not be employed out of the ordinary scope of his business : *Fry* v. *Tapson*, 28 Ch. D. 268.

It is conceived that s. 2 of the Trustee Act, 1888 (51 & 52 Vict. c. 59), does not apply to "trustees of the settlement" under this Act so as to authorize them to delegate to their solicitor the receipt of capital money ; for as a general rule such money would be receivable by the trustees of the settlement under the provisions of the Settled Land Acts, and not "under the trust," within the meaning of s. 2 of the Trustee Act, 1888.

§ 41.

Broker.

Trustee Act, 1888.

42. The trustees of a settlement, or any of them, are not liable for giving any consent, or for not making, bringing, taking, or doing any such application, action, proceeding, or thing, as they might make, bring, take, or do ; and in case of purchase of land with capital money arising under this Act, or of an exchange, partition, or lease, are not liable for adopting any contract made by the tenant for life, or bound to inquire as to the propriety of the purchase, exchange, partition, or lease, or answerable as regards any price, consideration, or fine, and are not liable to see to or answerable for the investigation of the title, or answerable for a conveyance of land, if the conveyance purports to convey the land in the proper mode, or liable in respect of purchase money paid by them by direction of the tenant for life to any person joining in the conveyance as a conveying party, or as giving a receipt for the purchase-money, or in any other character, or in respect of any other money paid by them by direction of the tenant for life on the purchase, exchange, partition or lease.

§ 42.

Protection of trustees generally.

The indemnity here afforded to the trustees embraces three distinct matters :—(1.) Giving consents : (2.) Inaction : (3.) Propriety of dealings.

Sect. 42.

Indemnity.

§ 42.
i. Consents.

As to their powers of consent, see *ante*, p. 69, as to the alienation of the mansion-house and park : and s. 35, relating to the sale of timber by a tenant for life impeachable for waste.

ii. Inaction of trustees.

By s. 45, *post*, notices of the intended exercise of the powers of the Act must be sent to the trustees, and they may by s. 44 apply to the Court if they disapprove of the proposed transaction. But the present section seems to enable them to treat these notices with indifference, and in fact, by exonerating the trustees, sacrifices the interests of the remaindermen.

iii. Propriety of dealings.

In relation to the purchase, exchange, and partition of settled land, and the granting of leases, the trustees are indemnified with respect to matters over which, according to the scheme of the Act, they have no control. The tenant for life is empowered to enter into contracts (s. 31) ; to sell, exchange, make partition, and grant leases (ss. 3, 6), subject to the prescribed regulations (ss. 4, 7) ; to execute conveyances without the concurrence of the trustees (s. 20), and to direct the investment or application of capital money in such manner as he pleases (s. 22). The trustees are, therefore, in the absence of complicity, under no liability for an improper sale by the tenant for life : *Hatten* v. *Russell*, 38 Ch. D. 334, 344.

It should be observed that there are several duties imposed upon the trustees which are not included in this protection clause.

Omissions in section.

They are bound to invest or apply monies in their hands according to the direction of the tenant for life in any of the modes prescribed by s. 21, but this section confers an indemnity only in the case of the purchase of land. Again, the approval of a scheme for improvements (s. 26), the discretionary power of apportioning, between tenant for life and remainderman, the purchase-money of a lease or reversion (s. 34), and the onerous duties to be exercised by them on behalf of infants are not covered by this section. Lastly, it should be noticed that in the case of purchased land they are responsible to a certain extent for the form of the conveyance, which must "purport to convey the land in the proper mode."

§ 43.
Trustees' reimbursement.

43. The trustees of a settlement may reimburse themselves or pay and discharge out of the trust property all expenses properly incurred by them.

Sect. 43. Reimbursement.

A provision similar to this section is contained in the 31st section of Lord St. Leonards' Act (22 & 23 Vict. c. 35), which is merely declaratory of the long-established rule.

The peculiarity of the position of "trustees of the settlement" is, that there may be no property vested in them, but they are not likely to incur any expenses except in connexion with the exercise of the powers of the Act, when, as a general rule, some capital money will be forthcoming from which they may deduct the expenses previously incurred.

§ 43.

44. If at any time a difference arises between a tenant for life and the trustees of the settlement, respecting the exercise of any of the powers of this Act, or respecting any matter relating thereto, the Court may, on the application of either party, give such directions respecting the matter in difference, and respecting the costs of the application, as the Court thinks fit.

§ 44.
Reference of differences to Court.

Although in *Re Mackenzie's Trusts*, 23 Ch. D. 750, a petition was presented, the application under this section should in general be made by originating summons; Rule 2 and Form XX.

The "trustees of the settlement" in this section include trustees for the purposes of the Act, appointed by the Court under s. 38: *Hatten* v. *Russell*, 38 Ch. D. 334, 344. In this case Kay, J., pointed out that although the trustees of the settlement occupied under the Act an irresponsible position, yet that "it would be quite right for them, if a sale were proceeding which they did not approve of, and which they thought was improvident, to submit the matter to the Court under the powers given in s. 44."

A tenant for life will rarely, if ever, have to make an application under this section except for the purpose of obtaining a direction as to the application of capital money in the hands of the trustees as in *Re Knatchbull's S. E.*, 29 Ch. D. 588; *Re Lord Sudeley's S. E.*, 37 Ch. D. 123; *Re Lord Stamford's S. E.*, 43 Ch. D. 84. He can exercise all the powers of the Act independently of the trustees, and if necessary require capital money to be paid into Court instead of to them.

The section is framed in wide terms so as to embrace almost every difference which can arise between the tenant for life and the trustees. Thus if the trustees are in any way dissatisfied with the manner in which the tenant for life is exercising his powers, if they wish to enforce the maintenance, repair or insurance of improvements (s. 28), or to determine the principle on which the costs of a sale are to be allowed, as *In re Beck*, 24 Ch. D. 608, they may avail themselves of this section.

Sect. 44.
Reference of differences to the Court.

The discretion given to the Court as to costs is repeated in s. 46 (6).

Costs.

A somewhat similar reference to the Court is authorized by s. 56 (3), *post*.

45.—(1.) A tenant for life, when intending to make a sale, exchange, partition, lease, mortgage, or charge, shall give notice of his intention in that behalf to each of the

§ 45.
Notice to trustees.

§ 45. trustees of the settlement, by posting registered letters, containing the notice, addressed to the trustees, severally, each at his usual or last known place of abode in the United Kingdom, and shall give like notice to the solicitor for the trustees, if any such solicitor is known to the tenant for life, by posting a registered letter, containing the notice, addressed to the solicitor at his place of business in the United Kingdom, every letter under this section being posted not less that one month before the making by the tenant for life of the sale, exchange, partition, lease, mortgage, or charge, or of a contract for the same.

(2.) Provided that at the date of notice given the number of trustees shall not be less than two, unless a contrary intention is expressed in the settlement.

(3.) A person dealing in good faith with the tenant for life is not concerned to inquire respecting the giving of any such notice as is required by this section.

Sect. 45. Notice to trustees.

Notice under 45 & 46 Vict. c. 38, s. 45, may, as to a sale, exchange, partition, or lease, be general.

The provisions of this section have been to some extent modified by the subsequent Acts. Thus by s. 5 of the Act of 1884 it is enacted that:—

"5. (1.) The notice required by s. 45 of the Act of 1882 of intention to make a sale, exchange, partition, or lease may be notice of a general intention in that behalf.

"(2.) The tenant for life is, upon request by a trustee of the settlement, to furnish to him such particulars and information as may reasonably be required by him from time to time with reference to sales, exchanges, partitions, or leases effected, or in progress, or immediately intended.

"(3.) Any trustee, by writing under his hand, may waive notice either in any particular case, or generally, and may accept less than one month's notice.

"(4.) This section applies to a notice given before, as well as to a notice given after, the passing of this Act.

"(5.) Provided that a notice, to the sufficiency of which objection has been taken before the passing of this Act, is not made sufficient by virtue of this Act."

Moreover in the case of a lease for a term not exceeding twenty-one years at the best rent that can be reasonably obtained without fine, and whereby the lessee is not exempted from punishment for waste, the necessity of notice under this section has been abolished by s. 7 of the Act of 1890; which also provides that such a lease may be granted although there are no trustees of the settlement.

It will be observed that s. 5 of the Act of 1884 does not refer to "mortgage or charge," and therefore the principal section continues to apply in those cases with its original strictness. The first sub-section of s. 5 of the Act of 1884 reversed the rule laid down in *Re Ray's Settled Estates*, 25 Ch. D. 464, where it was also held that the committee of a lunatic tenant for life could not until he had obtained the authority of the judge in lunacy give a valid notice under this section.

§ 45.
Mortgage or charge.

The object, no doubt, of requiring notice to be given to the trustees is to set them upon inquiry as to the propriety of the proposed transaction; but they, not being liable for remaining passive (s. 42), and *bonâ fide* purchasers being expressly protected (sub-s. 3 and s. 54), the notices are probably in most cases an empty formality.

Although the trustees are not bound to take any steps upon receipt of the notice, their clear duty, if they consider the sale, &c., disadvantageous, is to bring the matter before the Court under s. 44.

Notice must be given not only to the trustees but also to their solicitor, and no power is conferred upon him by the Act of 1884 to waive notice, or to accept less than one month's notice. It may be, however, that the notice to the solicitor is only regarded as an indirect notice to the trustees, and that they may waive the indirect as well as the direct notice.

On a sale by the tenant for life the purchaser is not entitled to inquire whether notice has been given or not; the giving of the notice is a matter between the tenant for life and the trustees, and one with which the purchaser is not concerned: per Chitty, J. *Duke of Marlborough* v. *Sartoris*, 32 Ch. D. 616, 623. In this case formal notice was given to the trustees of the settlement and to their solicitor less than one month before the contract for sale, but several months before the time fixed for completion, and specific performance was adjudged at the suit of the tenant for life, the trustees of the settlement being joined as plaintiffs. It appears from this case (1) that the giving of the notices is not a condition precedent to a valid contract; (2) that a distinction is to be drawn between the making of the sale and the making of the contract for sale, and (3) that the notice is good if given one month before either of those two things, the sale or the contract for sale.

Vendor and purchaser.

Where time is not of the essence of the contract as to the date fixed for completion, the fact that there were at the time of the contract no trustees of the settlement, or that no notice had been given to them if there were any, is not a defect of the title of the tenant for life to sell. It is sufficient for the purchaser, if, when he comes to complete his contract, there are trustees to whom he can pay his purchase money if required so to do by the tenant for life; and he is not entitled to rescind the contract on discovering the non-exist-

§ 45. ence of trustees of the settlement. The proper course for the purchaser to pursue in these circumstances is to require the tenant for life to remedy the defect within a specified reasonable time, and to give notice that in case of default he will repudiate the contract: *Hatten* v. *Russell*, 38 Ch. D. 334. Both the cases which have been cited show that the existence of trustees of the settlement is absolutely necessary at the time of completing the contract. See also *Re Taylor*, 31 W. R. 596; *Wade* v. *Wilson*, 33 W. R. 610.

Sub-s. 2.
Number of trustees.

The original appointment of a sole trustee would probably be held to amount to an expression of a contrary intention within the meaning of sub-s. 2. See *Re Garnett Orme and Hargreave's Contract*, 25 Ch. D. 595.

Sub-s. 3.
Protection of purchasers.

As to the general protection of *bonâ fide* purchasers, see s. 54, *post*, p. 154.

XI.—COURT; LAND COMMISSIONERS; PROCEDURE.

§ 46.
Regulations respecting payments into Court, applications, &c.

46.—(1.) All matters within the jurisdiction of the Court under this Act shall, subject to the Acts regulating the Court, be assigned to the Chancery Division of the Court.

(2.) Payment of money into Court effectually exonerates therefrom the person making the payment.

(3.) Every application to the Court shall be by petition, or by summons at Chambers.

(4.) On an application by the trustees of a settlement notice shall be served in the first instance on the tenant for life.

(5.) On any application notice shall be served on such persons, if any, as the Court thinks fit.

(6.) The Court shall have full power and discretion to make such order as it thinks fit respecting the costs, charges, or expenses of all or any of the parties to any application, and may, if it thinks fit, order that all or any of those costs, charges, or expenses be paid out of property subject to the settlement.

39 & 40 Vict. c. 59.
44 & 45 Vict. c. 68.

(7.) General Rules for purposes of this Act shall be deemed Rules of Court within section seventeen of the Appellate Jurisdiction Act, 1876, as altered by section nineteen of the Supreme Court of Judicature Act, 1881, and may be made accordingly.

(8.) The powers of the Court may, as regards land in the County Palatine of Lancaster, be exercised also by the Court of Chancery of the County Palatine; and Rules for regulating proceedings in that Court shall be from time to time made by the Chancellor of the Duchy of Lancaster, with the advice and consent of a Judge of the High Court acting in the Chancery Division, and of the Vice-Chancellor of the County Palatine.

(9.) General Rules, and Rules for the Court of Chancery of the County Palatine, may be made at any time after the passing of this Act, to take effect on or after the commencement of this Act.

(10.) The powers of the Court may, as regards land not exceeding in capital value five hundred pounds, or in annual rateable value thirty pounds, and, as regards capital money arising under this Act, and securities in which the same is invested, not exceeding in amount or value five hundred pounds, and as regards personal chattels settled or to be settled, as in this Act mentioned, not exceeding in value five hundred pounds, be exercised by any County Court within the district whereof is situate any part of the land which is to be dealt with in the Court, or from which the capital money to be dealt with in the Court arises under this Act, or in connexion with which the personal chattels to be dealt with in the Court are settled.

Sect. 46. Practice and procedure.

The regulations contained in this section governing applications to the Court have to some extent been modified by the rules which have been made under sub-s. (7). Thus by the third sub-section an alternative is given of proceeding by petition or by summons, but by Rule 2 the applicant must before he presents a petition obtain the direction of the Judge, or else lose his extra costs. The Court, moreover, seems by the rule to have no discretion as to those costs, which is in direct conflict with sub-s. (6) of this section.

Payment into Court.

Capital money arising under the Act must be paid, at the option of the tenant for life, either to the trustees of the settlement, or into court (s. 22). If it is paid to the trustees, they can, by s. 40 of the Act, give a valid receipt to the person making the payment. Sub-section (2) effects the same purpose when the money is paid into court. As to the practice on payment into court under the Act, see Rules 10 to 14 inclusive, and Forms IX., X., XI.

§ 46.

Service.
Costs.

See Rules, 4, 5, and 6, which repeat and extend the provisions contained in sub.-ss. (4) & (5).

One of the modes in which capital money may be applied is " in payment of costs, charges, and expenses of, or incidental to the exercise of any of the powers or the execution of any of the provisions of this Act"; and it will be remembered that the tenant for life has the right to prescribe the particular mode in which capital money shall be applied. Proper applications to the Court, as for example, a summons for the appointment of trustees of the settlement, are generally incidental to the exercise of the powers of the Act: and accordingly the costs, charges, and expenses of all persons properly before the Court on such applications are a legitimate mode in which to expend capital money. The Court, in the exercise of its discretion under sub s. (6), generally acts on this principle, and orders the costs as between solicitor and client of all proper parties to be paid out of capital, or charged on the corpus of the estate. See Form III. *post*. The Court has jurisdiction under this sub-section to allow the costs of an unsuccessful application: *Re Horne's Settled Estate*, 39 Ch. D. 84, 90; and even the costs of an unsuccessful appeal by a trustee, in a case proper to be settled by the Court of Appeal: *Re Jones*, 26 Ch. D. 736, 744.

The Court may make an order for payment of costs, charges, and expenses, of or incidental to the exercise of any of the powers, or the execution of any of the provisions of the Act, following the words of s. 21 (x.), leaving to the taxing-master to determine what items properly fall within the terms of the order. *Re Rudd*, W. N. 1887, 251, *Re Lord Stamford's Settled Estates*, 43 Ch. D. 84. Costs on the higher scale were allowed in *Re Chaytor's Settled Estates Act*, 25 Ch. D. 651.

Where the applicant sought unsuccessfully to have it declared that he was entitled to exercise the powers of a tenant for life, he was ordered to pay the costs of the trustees and of the remaindermen: *Re Strangways*, 34 Ch. D. 423, 433.

The trustees of the settlement should appear separately from the tenant for life, and in a case where they appeared by the same counsel they were disallowed their costs: *Re Broadwater Estate*, 33 W. R. 738.

See as to the costs of proceedings for protection or recovery of settled land, s. 36; of references to the Court, s. 44; and as to the payment of costs out of the property, s. 47, and the note thereon.

Durham.

The powers of the Court under the Settled Land Acts, 1882 and 1884, may, as regards land and estates in the County Palatine of Durham, be exercised by the Palatine Court of that County; 52 & 53 Vict. c. 47, s. 10.

Sub-s. 10.
County Courts.

As to the equitable jurisdiction of the County Courts, see The County Courts Act, 1888 (51 & 52 Vict. c. 43), s. 67, under which those courts, in administration of estates, execution of trusts, and other matters, have all the powers of the High Court, where the amount or value of the property does not exceed £500.

§ 46.

Under this Act the jurisdiction is conferred by an alternative test of capital or annual value ; and, as property of the annual rateable value of £30 may be worth more than £500, the County Court may have jurisdiction under this Act, although it could not administer the trusts of the settlement. If during the progress of the matter it is made to appear that the subject-matter exceeds the prescribed limit of amount, the validity of any order previously made is not affected, but the matter must be transferred to the High Court, 51 & 52 Vict. c. 43, s. 68.

It seems that the County Court has jurisdiction over capital money if the sum does not exceed £500, whatever may be the value of the unsold realty ; subject to this exception, however, that the County Court cannot in such a case direct the application of the money in "improvements," for that would be dealing with the land, as well as with the capital money. In such a case the jurisdiction would seem to be limited by the aggregate amount of the capital sum and the value of the land.

47. Where the Court directs that any costs, charges, or expenses be paid out of property subject to a settlement, the same shall, subject and according to the directions of the Court, be raised and paid out of capital money arising under this Act, or other money liable to be laid out in the purchase of land to be made subject to the settlement, or out of investments representing such money, or out of income of any such money or investments, or out of any accumulations of income of land, money, or investments, or by means of a sale of part of the settled land in respect whereof the costs, charges, or expenses are incurred, or of other settled land comprised in the same settlement and subject to the same limitations, or by means of a mortgage of the settled land or any part thereof, to be made by such person as the Court directs, and either by conveyance of the fee simple or other estate or interest the subject of the settlement, or by creation of a term, or otherwise, or by means of a charge on the settled land or any part thereof, or partly in one of those modes and partly in another or others, or in any such other mode as the Court thinks fit.

§ 47. Payment of costs out of settled property.

§ 47.
Payment of costs out of settled property.

This section gives the Court a choice of various ways in which the costs, charges, or expenses may be raised when it has made an order under s. 46 (6), that they shall be paid out of property subject to the settlement: The following table contains the several alternatives:—

1. Capital money arising under the Act, which must be either in court, or in the hands of the trustees (s. 22).
2. Money liable to be invested in land, which may be in court under an Act of Parliament (s. 32), or in the hands of trustees under the powers of a settlement (s. 33).
3. Investments of *such* money. This seems to include the interim investment of money in court (s. 32), and the investment of capital moneys mentioned in s. 21 (i.).
4. Income of any such money or investments as are specified above.
5. Accumulations of income of *land*, money or investments.
6. Sale of part of the settled land; or
7. Mortgage or charge thereof.

It will be observed that the future income of money or investments may be impounded for this purpose, but that in the case of land, the section is expressly confined to accumulations; and it seems that there is no power to direct a charge or mortgage of the life estate for the purposes of this section.

Where the plaintiff failed to establish that he was a tenant for life, or a person entitled to exercise the powers of a tenant for life, his summons was dismissed with costs, to be paid out of the *rents;* but the order as to costs seems to have been made on the application of the plaintiff himself: *Re Atkinson*, 30 Ch. D. 605. The costs, charges, and expenses, of or incidental to the exercise of any of the powers, or the execution of any of the provisions of the Act (s. 21 (x.)) are, it would seem, payable only out of capital money, and do not come within the terms of this section.

§ 48.
Constitution of Land Commissioners; their powers, &c.

48.—(1.) The commissioners now bearing the three several styles of the Inclosure Commissioners for England and Wales, and the Copyhold Commissioners, and the Tithe Commissioners for England and Wales, shall by virtue of this Act, become and shall be styled the Land Commissioners for England.

(2.) The Land Commissioners shall cause one seal to be made with their style as given by this Act; and in the execution and discharge of any power or duty under any Act relating to the three several bodies of commissioners aforesaid, they shall adopt and use the seal and style of the Land Commissioners for England, and no other.

§ 48.

(3.) Nothing in the foregoing provisions of this section shall be construed as altering in any respect the powers, authorities, or duties of the Land Commissioners, or as affecting in respect of appointment, salary, pension, or otherwise, any of those commissioners, in office at the passing of this Act, or any assistant commissioner, secretary, or other officer or person then in office or employed under them.

(4.) All Acts of Parliament, judgments, decrees, or orders of any court, awards, deeds, and other documents, passed or made before the commencement of this Act, shall be read and have effect as if the Land Commissioners were therein mentioned instead of one or more of the three several bodies of commissioners aforesaid.

(5.) All acts, matters, and things commenced by or under the authority of any one or more of the three several bodies of commissioners aforesaid before the commencement of this Act, and not then completed, shall and may be carried on and completed by or under the authority of the Land Commissioners; and the Land Commissioners, for the purpose of prosecuting, or defending, and carrying on any action, suit, or proceeding pending at the commencement of this Act, shall come into the place of any one or more, as the case may require, of the three several bodies of commissioners aforesaid.

(6.) The Land Commissioners shall, by virtue of this Act, have, for the purposes of any Act, public, local, personal, or private, passed or to be passed, making provision for the execution of improvements on settled land, all such powers and authorities as they have for the purposes of the Improvement of Land Act, 1864; and the provisions of the last-mentioned Act relating to their proceedings and inquiries, and to authentication of instruments, and to declarations, statements, notices, applications, forms, security for expenses, inspections, and examinations, shall extend and apply, as far as the nature and circumstances of

27 & 28 Vict. c. 114.

§ 48. the case admit, to acts and proceedings done or taken by or in relation to the Land Commissioners under any Act making provision as last aforesaid; and the provisions of any Act relating to fees or to security for costs to be taken in respect of the business transacted under the Acts administered by the three several bodies of commissioners aforesaid shall extend and apply to the business transacted by or under the direction of the Land Commissioners under any Act, public, local, personal, or private, passed or to be passed, by which any power or duty is conferred or imposed on them.

Sect. 48. Land Commissioners.

The three bodies of commissioners here united into a single commission, long consisted of the same individuals, but acting under different styles, and using different seals. The powers and duties of the Land Commissioners under this and other Acts have now devolved upon the Board of Agriculture established by 52 & 53 Vict. c. 30.

This section was transferred to its present position from the Conveyancing Bill during the progress of the measures through Parliament, which accounts for the words "passed or to be passed" in sub-s. (6).

§ 49. Filing of certificates, &c., of commissioners.

49.—(1.) Every certificate and report approved and made by the Land Commissioners under this Act shall be filed in their office.

(2.) An office copy of any certificate or report so filed shall be delivered out of their office to any person requiring the same, on payment of the proper fee, and shall be sufficient evidence of the certificate or report whereof it purports to be a copy.

Filing certificates, &c.

See, as to certificates and reports of the commissioners, ss. 26, 28.

XII.—RESTRICTIONS, SAVINGS, AND GENERAL PROVISIONS.

§ 50. Powers not assignable; contract not to

50.—(1.) The powers under this Act of a tenant for life are not capable of assignment or release, and do not pass to a person as being, by operation of law or otherwise, an assignee of a tenant for life, and remain exerciseable by the tenant for life after and notwithstanding any assignment, by operation of law or otherwise, of his estate or interest under the settlement.

(2.) A contract by a tenant for life not to exercise any of his powers under this Act is void.

(3.) But this section shall operate without prejudice to the rights of any person being an assignee for value of the estate or interest of the tenant for life; and in that case the assignee's rights shall not be affected without his consent, except that, unless the assignee is actually in possession of the settled land or part thereof, his consent shall not be requisite for the making of leases thereof by the tenant for life, provided the leases are made at the best rent that can reasonably be obtained, without fine, and in other respects are in conformity with this Act.

(4.) This section extends to assignments made or coming into operation before or after and to acts done before or after the commencement of this Act; and in this section assignment includes assignment by way of mortgage, and any partial or qualified assignment, and any charge or incumbrance; and assignee has a meaning corresponding with that of assignment.

§ 50. exercise powers void.

This and the next two sections endeavour to prevent the powers of the Act from being assigned, suspended, or extinguished, or in any manner rendered incapable of being exercised, whether by the action of the tenant for life, or the caprice of the settlor.

Sect. 50. Powers not assignable.

An assignment or charge by the tenant for life made in consideration of marriage or by way of family arrangement, and not being a security for payment of money advanced is excepted from this section by the Act of 1890, s. 4.

So far as regards the suspension and extinguishment of the powers, the saving clause in sub-s. (3) renders the present section to a great extent an expression of the existing law on the subject, which rests on the principle that a man cannot derogate from his own grant. Thus, a mortgage by the tenant for life cannot be affected by a subsequent exercise of his power of sale : *Goodright* v. *Cator*, Dougl. 460 ; and "a total alienation of the estate must operate as an extinguishment of the power, where it cannot be exercised without defeating the interest granted : " Sugden on Powers, 57, 8th ed., and see p. 70. " If tenant for life who hath power to make leases depart with his

Suspension or extinguishment.

L 2

§ 50.

estate his power is gone:" *Berry* v. *White*, Bridg. 82, 91; *secus* if he conveys only by way of mortgage: *Ren* v. *Bulkeley*, Dougl. 292. It would seem, indeed, that, notwithstanding the passage cited from Lord St. Leonards' work, a total alienation does not legally extinguish *any* power; for it has been held that after bankruptcy (*Holdsworth* v. *Goose*, 29 Beav. 111; *Simpson* v. *Bathurst*, L. R. 5 Ch. 193), or a sale of the life interest by the assignees in bankruptcy (*Eisdale* v. *Hammersly*, 31 Beav. 255), or the absolute alienation of his estate by the tenant for life (*Warburton* v. *Farn*, 16 Sim. 625; *Alexander* v. *Mills*, L. R. 6 Ch. 125), powers of leasing or of sale could, with the concurrence of the assignees, be exercised by the tenant for life.

Release of powers.

The prohibition against a release of the powers, or a contract not to exercise them, introduces an exception to the well-established law expressed in the 52nd sect. of the Conv. Act, 1881. See *West* v. *Berney*, 1 R. & My. 431; *Hurst* v. *Hurst*, 16 Beav. 372; *Isaac* v. *Hughes*, L. R. 9 Eq. 191.

Sub-s. 2. Contract not to exercise powers.

This section does not in terms extend to the case of a contract by a person who is not, at the date of such contract, a tenant for life, but who subsequently comes into possession of the estate. There can be little doubt, however, that a contract of that kind, even by an expectant tenant for life would be void under this section. Where by a settlement the land was during the successive lives of A. and B. limited to trustees upon trust to sell and divide the proceeds between A. and B., a covenant by them not to claim their life estates *in specie* was treated as void; and it was held that the two together could make a title to the land under this Act: *Re Hale and Clark*, 34 W. R. 624.

Sub-s. 3. Assignee of life estate.

The Court, in the exercise of its discretion under s. 10 of the Act, of 1890, will not authorize the sale of the principal mansion-house without the consent of the mortgagees of the life estate: *Re Sebright's Settled Estates*, 33 Ch. D. 429.

The costs of obtaining the consent to a sale by a mortgagee of the life estate, are costs incidental to the exercise of the statutory power, and may under special circumstances be paid out of capital; but as a general rule the Court will not allow them to be so paid; and when the capital money is not in Court but in the hands of trustees, they should act upon the same rule: *Cardigan* v. *Curzon-Howe*, 41 Ch. D. 375.

Tenant for life bankrupt.

It would seem that where a tenant for life becomes bankrupt he cannot be called upon to exercise the powers of the Act for the benefit of his creditors; and it is observable that in some cases his estate would be directly benefited thereby, as in the case of mining leases (s. 11), and sales of timber (s. 35). See *Re Mansel's Settled Estates*, W. N. 1884, 209, and as to the exercise of powers by the trustee in bankruptcy, "The Bankruptcy Act, 1883," 46 & 47 Vict. c. 52,

s. 44. The trustee in bankruptcy, however, would seem to be an "assignee for value" within the meaning of this sub-section.

§ 50.

Under the Settled Estates Act, s. 23, the assignee of the tenant for life may apply to the Court to exercise the powers of the Act: *Re Hutchinson*, 14 L. T. 129; but the definition of "Settlement" in that Act contains the words, "including any such instruments affecting the estates of any *one* or more of such persons exclusively," which do not occur in "Settlement" as defined by this Act. An assignee, therefore, of the tenant for life, although beneficially entitled to possession, would not be so entitled *under the settlement*. See s. 2 (1), (5) *ante*, p. 25.

51.—(1.) If in a settlement, will, assurance, or other instrument executed or made before or after, or partly before and partly after, the commencement of this Act a provision is inserted purporting or attempting, by way of direction, declaration, or otherwise, to forbid a tenant for life to exercise any power under this Act, or attempting, or tending, or intended, by a limitation, gift, or disposition over of settled land, or by a limitation, gift, or disposition of other real or any personal property, or by the imposition of any condition, or by forfeiture, or in any other manner whatever, to prohibit or prevent him from exercising, or to induce him to abstain from exercising, or to put him into a position inconsistent with his exercising, any power under this Act, that provision, as far as it purports, or attempts, or tends, or is intended to have, or would or might have, the operation aforesaid, shall be deemed to be void.

§ 51.
Prohibition or limitation against exercise of powers, void.

(2.) For the purposes of this section an estate or interest limited to continue so long only as a person abstains from exercising any power shall be and take effect as an estate or interest to continue for the period for which it would continue if that person were to abstain from exercising the power, discharged from liability to determination or cesser by or on his exercising the same.

In *Re Hazle's Settled Estates* (29 Ch. D. 78), the Earl of Selborne, L. C., gives the following account of the object of this section:—" I have considered whether the 51st section of the statute, which is undoubtedly retrospective, and is conceived in extremely large terms, can properly be applied to this case. I think it cannot. I

Sect. 51.
Object of the section.

§ 51.

think the object of that section is to strike at and defeat (so far as they might control the powers given by the Act) all provisions, even if contained in existing settlements, which might be in their intention and substance prohibitory, obstructive, or penal, for the purpose of preventing alienations or other acts contemplated by the statute. I do not think it was intended to enlarge or alter the substance of any original limitation of a particular estate (not properly an estate for life) which might be lawfully in force when the statute came into operation, and as to which the author of the settlement had neither contemplated nor in any manner provided against any such acts as those in question, nor indeed could rationally have done so, as the law stood when the settlement was made," p. 84.

Private Act.

The comprehensive definition of "settlement" in s. 2, *ante*, does not seem to apply to the word in this section, but the words " or other instrument" include every form of instrument there enumerated, except an Act of Parliament, which cannot be said to be "executed or made". within the meaning of this section. An Act of Parliament passed subsequently to the Settled Land Act might of course repeal all or any of its provisions, and it was not the intention of the Legislature to override any previously existing prohibitions against alienation contained in Acts of Parliament. See s. 58 (1) i. A provision, however, in a private estate Act, passed before the Settled Land Act, imposing restrictions on the exercise of a power of sale thereby conferred, does not apply to the power of sale in this Act: *Re Chaytor's Settled Estate Act*, 25 Ch. D. 651.

Condition as to residence.

A limitation to the use of a person so long as he shall reside on the estate for three months in each year with a gift over in case of his not complying with the condition, does not prevent the tenant for life from selling the estate: *Re Paget's Settled Estates*, 30 Ch. D. 161; *Re Thompson's Will*, 21 L. R., Ir. 109. But such a condition so far as it does not hinder the tenant for life from disposing of the property is effectual; and if he fails to observe the condition, except for the purpose of exercising the statutory powers, he will incur a forfeiture : *Re Haynes*, 37 Ch. D. 306. See also *Re Moir*, 25 Ch. D. 605.

§ 52.

Provision against forfeiture.

52. Notwithstanding anything in a settlement, the exercise by the tenant for life of any power under this Act shall not occasion a forfeiture.

Forfeiture.

The last section relates to the prohibitory clause in the instrument, the present, *ex abundanti cauteld*, saves the tenant for life from the consequences of acting in contravention thereof.

It may also apply where the forfeiture is not of the interest under the settlement, but of some subsidiary benefit conferred, it may be, by a different instrument. For example, if a testator bequeaths an annuity of £1000 a-year to A., but if he sells any part of the family estate, then the same to be forfeited, it is clear that A. can sell the estate and keep the annuity. But some difficulty is not unlikely to arise in particular cases, as to the provision in the last section rendering certain gifts void, if they tend to induce the tenant for life to abstain from exercising his powers. A testator, for example, bequeaths £1000 a-year to A. so long as he resides in the principal mansion-house to enable him to keep up the same, but if he lets or sells the house the annuity to cease. It would seem that this gift, being an inducement not to exercise the powers of the Act, is void, and that A. in such a case forfeits his annuity.

§ 52.

A condition as to residence, or any other onerous condition imposed on the tenant for life, so far from being an inducement to him not to exercise the statutory powers, operates in quite the opposite manner, and in fact supplies a motive for selling the property, and thereby relieving himself from the condition. See *Re Haynes*, 37 Ch. D. 306.

53. A tenant for life shall, in exercising any power under this Act, have regard to the interests of all parties entitled under the settlement, and shall, in relation to the exercise thereof by him, be deemed to be in the position and to have the duties and liabilities of a trustee for those parties.

§ 53.
Tenant for life trustee for all parties interested.

The tenant for life, it will be observed, is to have regard to the interests of *all parties* entitled under the settlement, not of himself alone, nor of the remaindermen alone, he must hold the balance evenly and exercise his discretion *bonâ fide* as head of the family for the benefit of all concerned. It may be that in the exercise of his powers some one or more of the beneficiaries may be prejudicially affected, and even an indirect advantage may be secured by himself. Thus where heirlooms had been sold with the leave of the Court, the tenant for life was held to be justified in applying the proceeds of sale in the discharge of incumbrances affecting the inheritance of the settled land, although the tenant in tail in remainder was thereby deprived of the absolute interest which he would have taken in the chattels on attaining the age of twenty-one years, and in lieu thereof became entitled to a limited interest in the unincumbered estate: *Re Duke of Marlborough's Settlement*, 32 Ch. D. 1. Lopes, L. J., in the course of his judgment in that case made the following observations :—" It was said that the tenant for life, selling heirlooms and applying the proceeds in discharge of incumbrances, would not have a proper regard to the interests of all entitled under the settlement, and would not be doing his duty as trustee to the tenant in tail, as was intended, under s. 53. I do not take that view of the meaning

Sect. 53. How far a trustee.

§ 53.

of that section, I think that the meaning of that section is this: that the tenant for life is to be answerable for an improper or improvident exercise of the powers conferred upon him by the Act, in the same manner as if he were an actual trustee under the settlement exercising similar powers conferred upon him by that settlement. I believe that to be the true meaning of that section, and I think that its meaning cannot be carried further than that," p. 13.

The consequence of the tenant for life being placed, as regards the exercise of his powers, in the position of a trustee is that "if a purchaser knows the tenant for life is exercising the power improperly, and is aware that what the tenant for life is doing would amount to a breach of trust, he, the purchaser has a perfect right to say, 'I will not complete:'" *Hatten* v. *Russell*, 38 Ch. D. 334, at p. 345. Mr. Justice Stirling, after referring to this section, said "it is the duty of the tenant for life in exercising the discretion which is vested in him under the Act as to the application of capital moneys, to consider whether he is unduly prejudicing any of the parties by the proposed exercise of that discretion, and if he is then it would not be proper so to exercise the discretion; but where it is matter of doubt, in the absence of any reason for supposing that the discretion is unfairly exercised, then that discretion ought to prevail:" *Re Lord Stamford's Settled Estates*, 43 Ch. D. 84, 95. See also *Thomas* v. *Williams*, 24 Ch. D. 558.

Accumulation of rents. — Where there is a trust to accumulate the rents in order to pay off incumbrances, the tenant for life may it seems exercise his statutory power of sale, apply the proceeds in discharging the incumbrances, and enter into possession of the unsold part of the estate: *Norton* v. *Johnstone*, 30 Ch. D. 649; but if no estate or interest is given until the trust for accumulation has come to an end, there is no tenant for life capable of exercising the powers: *Re Strangways*, 34 Ch. D. 423.

The tenant for life by discharging incumbrances out of *corpus*, instead of allowing a trust for accumulation to continue for the purpose, clearly gains an advantage at the expense of the remainderman; and so also in the circumstances which occurred in *Clarke* v. *Thornton*, 35 Ch. D. 307, where it was held that, notwithstanding an express power vested in trustees to provide for "improvements" out of rents and profits, the tenant for life might require capital money to be so applied by virtue of his powers under this Act. See also *Re The Earl of Stamford*, 56 L. T. 484.

Effect of decree for administration of trusts. — After a decree has been made for the execution of the trusts of an instrument the trustees cannot exercise a discretionary power of sale without the sanction of the Court. But this Act gives an overriding power of sale to the tenant for life which remains unaffected by the institution of a suit and a decree for the execution of the trusts: *Cardigan* v. *Curzon-Howe*, 30 Ch. D. 531. In this case the decree

had been made before the Act came into operation, but Mr. Justice § 53.
Chitty intimated an opinion that this made no difference, and in the
course of his judgment said, " The object of the section is best seen
by reading it in connection with s. 54, and the result is that the
tenant for life must pursue his powers according to the Act. He
must sell for the best price, and if he does not, and there is any
corrupt or underhand bargain between him and the purchaser, then
neither is his sale good, nor does the purchaser obtain a good title.
But if the matter of sale is carried forward in good faith, and the
purchaser deals in good faith with the tenant for life, then his contract for sale and conveyance stand. S. 53 does not, to my mind,
make the tenant for life trustee of his power within the scope of
the declaration contained in the decree made before this Act came
into operation for the execution of the trusts under the settlement,"
p. 540.

This section seems rather to impose the responsibilities, than to Costs.
confer the rights of a trustee upon the tenant for life, and does not
entitle him as of right to all his costs, charges and expenses properly
incurred: *Re Llewellin*, 37 Ch. D. 317. The Court has a discretion
in the matter, and may, for example, refuse to allow the costs of
obtaining the concurrence in a sale of the mortgagees of the life
estate: *Cardigan* v. *Curzon-Howe*, 41 Ch. D. 375; and see *Sebright*
v. *Thornton*, 29 S. J. 682; *Re Beck*, 24 Ch. D. 608.

The tenant for life, being in the position of a trustee, cannot him- Purchase
self purchase or take a lease of any part of the property. This was by tenant
different when the power of sale was vested in trustees with the con- for life.
sent (*Howard* v. *Ducane*, T. & R. 81), or at the request (*Dicconson* v.
Talbot, L. R. 6 Ch. 32) of the tenant for life, who was, in these cases,
decided not to stand in a fiduciary position towards the remaindermen.

The Act of 1890, however, now provides that in dealings with the
tenant for life the trustees of the settlement shall stand in his place
and represent him, s. 12.

A further consequence of the tenant for life being declared a Statute of
trustee seems to be that the Statute of Limitations is thereby Limita-
excluded; and that an account, for example, of mining rents tions.
received by him under s. 11 may be carried back beyond six years.
See *Hickman* v. *Upsal*, 4 Ch. D. 144; and such a claim, or a claim
founded on a fraudulent or collusive exercise of the statutory powers,
is not affected by the Trustee Act, 1888, 51 & 52 Vict. c. 59, s. 8. It
is conceived that this Act has no application to a tenant for life in
his character of trustee.

It is to be remembered that, as between the tenant for life and the
remainderman, time will not run while the estate of the latter continues reversionary; and that even knowledge of a breach of trust

§ 53. will not import acquiescence. See *Life Association of Scotland* v. *Siddal*, 3 D. F. & J. 58 ; *Thomson* v. *Eastwood*, 2 App. Cas. 215.

§ 54.
General protection of purchasers, &c.

54. On a sale, exchange, partition, lease, mortgage, or charge, a purchaser, lessee, mortgagee, or other person dealing in good faith with a tenant for life shall, as against all parties entitled under the settlement, be conclusively taken to have given the best price, consideration, or rent, as the case may require, that could reasonably be obtained by the tenant for life, and to have complied with all the requisitions of this Act.

Sect. 54.
Payment of purchase-money.

It is to be observed that, as regards the payment of the purchase-money, or other capital money arising under this Act, the payer is protected by the receipt of the trustees (s. 40), or by payment into court (s. 46 (2)) ; and it is absolutely essential that he should obtain a discharge in one of these ways ; for if he pays to the tenant for life what should by s. 22 be paid to the trustees or into court, this section will not protect him. See *Hatten* v. *Russell*, 38 Ch. D. 334, 346.

Note that it is the purchaser and not the tenant for life who is to be "taken to have complied with all the requisitions of this Act," although it is upon the latter alone that any onus is thrown by the Act.

The useless provision in Lord Cranworth's Act (23 & 24 Vict. c. 145), s. 2 (repealed s. 64, *post*), saving a purchaser from inquiry as to re-investment, is not repeated here. See the remarks on that sect. in Dav. Conv. iii. 562, 3rd ed.

Notices to trustees.

By s. 45 (3) *ante*, the purchaser is specially protected from inquiry as to the giving of the prescribed notices by the tenant for life. See as to sale, exchange, and partition, ss. 3, 4 ; as to leases, ss. 6-11, and ss. 7, 8, & 9 of the Act of 1890 ; as to mortgages and charges, ss. 5, 18, 47, and s. 11 of the Act of 1890.

§ 55.
Exercise of powers ; limitation of provisions, &c.

55.—(1.) Powers and authorities conferred by this Act on a tenant for life or trustees or the Court or the Land Commissioners are exerciseable from time to time.

(2.) Where a power of sale, enfranchisement, exchange, partition, leasing, mortgaging, charging, or other power is exercised by a tenant for life, or by the trustees of a settlement, he and they may respectively execute, make, and do all deeds, instruments, and things necessary or proper in that behalf.

(3.) Where any provision in this Act refers to sale, purchase, exchange, partition, leasing, or other dealing, or to any power, consent, payment, receipt, deed, assurance, contract, expenses, act, or transaction, the same shall be construed to extend only (unless it is otherwise expressed) to sales, purchases, exchanges, partitions, leasings, dealings, powers, consents, payments, receipts, deeds, assurances, contracts, expenses, acts, and transactions under this Act.

§ 55.

The statutory powers might, without the express authority of this section, have been exercised from time to time, both as to different parcels, and as to the same parcel where the nature of the power admitted of repeated execution. See Sug. Powers, 272, 8th ed. ; Chance on Powers (440); *Sir Richard Lee's Case*, 1 And. 67 ; *Versturme v. Gardiner*, 17 Beav. 338.

Sect. 55. Exercise of powers.

"Enfranchisement" is in other parts of the Act treated as included in "sale," see ss. 3, 20, 45, 54.

Enfranchisement.

As a general rule, *all* the powers of the Act are exerciseable by the tenant for life; but where there is an infant owner they may be exercised on his behalf by the trustees of the settlement, or, if there are none, by a person appointed by the Court : s. 60, *post*. If this special authority to execute deeds were necessary in any case, it ought to have been extended to such persons as are appointed by the Court in the case of infants, and also to the committees of lunatics under s. 62.

56.—(1.) Nothing in this Act shall take away, abridge, or prejudicially affect any power for the time being subsisting under a settlement, or by statute or otherwise, exerciseable by a tenant for life, or by trustees with his consent, or on his request, or by his direction, or otherwise; and the powers given by this Act are cumulative.

§ 56. Saving for other powers.

(2.) But, in the case of conflict between the provisions of a settlement, and the provisions of this Act, relative to any matter in respect whereof the tenant for life exercises or contracts or intends to exercise any power under this Act, the provisions of this Act shall prevail ; and, accordingly, notwithstanding anything in the settlement, the consent of the tenant for life, shall, by virtue of this Act, be necessary to the exercise by the trustees of the settlement or other person of any power conferred by the settlement exerciseable for any purpose provided for in this Act.

§ 56.

(3.) If a question arises, or a doubt is entertained, respecting any matter within this section, the Court may, on the application of the trustees of the settlement, or of the tenant for life, or of any other person interested, give its decision, opinion, advice, or direction thereon.

Sub-s. 1.
Cumulative powers.

The meaning of the first sub-section has been declared to be "that it is not intended to take away from the trustees named in any settlement powers given to them by that settlement, and that if all parties are contented to exercise those powers, those powers may still be exercised ; but if the powers in the settlement are more restricted than the power in the Act, then the Act says that the provisions of the Act or the powers given by the Act are cumulative, that is to say that the powers in the Act, so far as they give larger authority than is given by the trusts of the settlement, may be exercised in the manner prescribed by the Act:" Per Pearson, J., *Re Duke of Newcastle's Estates*, 24 Ch. D. 129, 138.

Saving of other powers.

Although powers conferred upon trustees and others are saved by this section, yet they can never be exercised without the consent of the tenant for life, or of some person on his behalf where he is an infant or a lunatic, ss. 60, 62.

The same object, viz., the sale, exchange, lease, &c., of the settled land, may in some cases be effected either under the powers of the settlement, or under this Act; but it should be carefully borne in mind that the procedure of one or other must be consistently pursued.

Thus, if the power of sale by trustees is to be exercised with the consent of both the husband and wife, those consents must be obtained if the sale is made by the trustees under the power in the settlement, but not if the tenant for life sells under this Act.

A restriction imposed on the exercise of the power of sale in a settlement, even when it is contained in a Private Act of Parliament, does not attach to the statutory power of the tenant for life. *Re Chaytor's Settled Estate Act*, 25 Ch. D. 651. Where, however, an order for sale had been made by the Court under the Settled Estates Act, it was held that although six years had elapsed since the order had been made, and no sale had been effected, the tenant for life could not exercise the powers of this Act over the land comprised in the order until proceedings had been stayed thereunder, which the Court under the circumstances declined to do. *Re Barrs-Haden's Settled Estates*, 32 W. R. 194. Followed, as to leasing powers, in *Re Poole's Settled Estates*, 32 W. R. 956.

Sub-s. 2.
Consent of the tenant for life.

The effect of the second sub-section is that "the consent of the tenant for life must now be added to the exercise of any power for leasing or sale" [or exerciseable for any purpose provided for in this

Act] by the trustees of the settlement although not required by the settlement :" per Pearson, J., in *Re Duke of Newcastle's Estates*, 24 Ch. D. 129, 139. And the power of giving this consent where the tenant for life is an infant is exerciseable under s. 60 by the trustees of the settlement on behalf of the infant. *Ibid.*

§ 56.

The question was raised in several cases where land was vested in trustees upon trust for sale, whether the concurrence of the persons entitled to the income of the proceeds of sale could be required by the purchaser under this section. *Re Earle and Webster's Contract*, 24 Ch. D. 144; *Taylor* v. *Poncia*, 25 Ch. D. 646. But no such question can now arise, for by the Act of 1884 it is enacted that in the case of a settlement within the meaning of s. 63 of the Act of 1882, any consent not required by the terms of the settlement is not by force of anything contained in that Act to be deemed necessary to enable the trustees of the settlement or any other person to execute any of the trusts or powers created by the settlement s. 6 (1).

Trust for sale.

' The result of this enactment is that when land is vested in trustees upon trust for sale they can make a title without the concurrence of the beneficiaries, and without disclosing the trusts declared of the proceeds of sale, unless an order has been made under s. 7 of the Act of 1884 authorising the tenant for life to exercise the powers of the Act. See *Re Harding's Settled Estate* [1891], 1 Ch. 60.

A further qualification of this sub-section has been introduced by the Act of 1884, which in effect provides that when two or more persons together constitute the tenant for life, the consent of any one of such persons shall be sufficient to satisfy this sub-section. Act of 1884 s. 6 (2).

Several tenants for life.

Where a will charges real estate with the payment of debts or legacies, the devisees in trust (if any), or failing them the executors, have power to sell or mortgage the land in order to raise the amount of such charges. In former times this power was held to arise by implication of law, but it now depends on the express provisions of Lord St. Leonards' Act (22 & 23 Vict. c. 35), ss. 14, 16. It is conceived, therefore, that it is not a " power conferred by the settlement " within the meaning of this sub-section, and that the consent of the tenant for life is not necessary. The power of raising the money by mortgage is, at all events, unaffected by this sub-section ; for that is not a "power exerciseable for any purpose provided for in this Act." See *Re Wilson*, 34 W. R. 512.

Sale for payment of debts or legacies.

The power of executors to deal with leaseholds for years is, it is submitted, unaffected by this Act, as their title as executors is paramount to any settlement of the leaseholds made by the will. See *Re Whistler*, 35 Ch. D. 561.

A case of "conflict" arises under this section where the trustees, alleging that there is no " tenant for life," intend to exercise the

Conflict.

§ 56.

powers conferred by the settlement; and the person who claims to be tenant for life also intends to exercise the statutory powers: *Re Clitheroe Estate*, 28 Ch. D. 378, affirmed, 31 Ch. D. 135. It is clear from this case that the consent of a person who, though not tenant for life, has the powers of a tenant for life under s. 58, is necessary to the exercise by the trustees of the powers conferred by the settlement.

Sub-s. 3. Procedure.

The procedure under this sub-section will be analogous to that under s. 30 of Lord St. Leonards' Act (22 & 23 Vict. c. 35), whereby trustees were authorised to apply by petition or summons for the opinion or direction of the judge.

This sub-section, which, however, is extended to "any other person interested," is analogous to s. 44, *ante*, providing for the adjustment by the Court of "differences" between the trustees and the tenant for life. The application is to be made either by petition or summons at chambers: s. 46 (3), but if a petition is presented without the direction of the judge, no further costs are to be allowed than would be allowed upon a summons: Rule 2, and see Form XXI.

§ 57.
Additional or larger powers by settlement.

57.—(1.) Nothing in this Act shall preclude a settlor from conferring on the tenant for life, or the trustees of the settlement, any powers additional to or larger than those conferred by this Act.

(2.) Any additional or larger powers so conferred shall, as far as may be, notwithstanding anything in this Act, operate and be exerciseable in the like manner, and with all the like incidents, effects, and consequences, as if they were conferred by this Act, unless a contrary intention is expressed in the settlement.

Sect. 57. Special powers.

The effect of this section will be to make special powers in the settlement, *e.g.*, powers of granting building leases for 999 years, operate as if they were conferred by this Act, "unless a contrary intention is expressed in the settlement." It is conceived that, in the absence of any such expression of intention, all powers conferred on the trustees of the settlement, will now operate as statutory powers, and not by way of revocation of use as formerly. A settlor who confers larger powers on the tenant for life than those conferred by the Act, may, it is presumed, attach restrictions to their exercise, which would have been void if imposed on the statutory powers. For example, if the consent of the trustees were required to the grant by the tenant for life of a lease for 999 years, although such an attempted limitation of the powers of the tenant for life under this Act would be void (s. 51), yet the consent must be obtained if the special power is to be exercised.

§ 57.

The "additional or larger powers" may possibly be inconsistent with the policy of this Act, in which event they will no doubt be held to be inoperative. If, for example, power is given to the trustees to sell without the consent of the tenant for life, or to the tenant for life on exercising the power of sale to receive the purchase-money, it is presumed that such powers would be controlled by ss. 56 and 22 respectively. Compare the analogous provision in the Conv. Act, 1881, s. 18 (14).

XIII.—Limited Owners generally.

58.—(1.) Each person as follows shall, when the estate or interest of each of them is in possession, have the powers of a tenant for life under this Act, as if each of them were a tenant for life as defined in this Act (namely) :

§ 58.

Enumeration of other limited owners, to have powers of tenant for life.

    (i.) A tenant in tail, including a tenant in tail who is by Act of Parliament restrained from barring or defeating his estate tail, and although the reversion is in the Crown, and so that the exercise by him of his powers under this Act shall bind the Crown, but not including such a tenant in tail where the land in respect whereof he is so restrained was purchased with money provided by Parliament in consideration of public services :

    (ii.) A tenant in fee simple, with an executory limitation, gift, or disposition over, on failure of his issue, or in any other event:

    (iii.) A person entitled to a base fee, although the reversion is in the Crown, and so that the exercise by him of his powers under this Act shall bind the Crown.

    (iv.) A tenant for years determinable on life, not holding merely under a lease at a rent :

    (v.) A tenant for the life of another, not holding merely under a lease at a rent :

    (vi.) A tenant for his own or any other life, or for years determinable on life, whose estate is

§ 58.

liable to cease in any event during that life, whether by expiration of the estate, or by conditional limitation, or otherwise, or to be defeated by an executory limitation, gift, or disposition over, or is subject to a trust for accumulation of income for payment of debts or other purpose:

(vii.) A tenant in tail after possibility of issue extinct:

(viii.) A tenant by the curtesy:

(ix.) A person entitled to the income of land under a trust or direction for payment thereof to him during his own or any other life, whether subject to expenses of management or not, or until sale of the land, or until forfeiture of his interest therein on bankruptcy or other event.

(2.) In every such case, the provisions of this Act referring to a tenant for life, either as conferring powers on him or otherwise, and to a settlement, and to settled land, shall extend to each of the persons aforesaid, and to the instrument under which his estate or interest arises, and to the land therein comprised.

(3.) In any such case any reference in this Act to death as regards a tenant for life shall, where necessary, be deemed to refer to the determination by death or otherwise of such estate or interest as last aforesaid.

Sect. 58. Estate or interest in possession.

The words "when the estate or interest of each of them is in possession" mean that the right is immediate, and not in reversion or expectancy: per Baggallay, L.J., *Re Jones*, 26 Ch. D. 736, 741. As, moreover, "possession" includes receipt of income, s. 2 (10) i.; a person may be in possession within the meaning of this section although the property is in the occupation of tenants. *Re Morgan*, 24 Ch. D. 114; see also *Re Atkinson*, 31 Ch. D. 577.

The estate or interest of a limited owner may, it is conceived, be "in possession," although his mortgagee may have entered into possession of the land; and the limited owner with the consent of the mortgagee may exercise the powers of a tenant for life under the Act.

Various additional powers are conferred by the Act of 1890 upon the tenant for life, but not in express terms upon "persons having the powers of a tenant for life under the Act of 1882." Section 2, however, of the later Act, directs the Settled Land Acts 1882 to 1890 to be read and construed together as one Act, and s. 3 declares that expressions used in the Act of 1890 are to have the same meanings as they bear in the previous Acts. Having regard, therefore, to the wide terms of sub-s. (2) of this section, there can be no doubt that the limited owners here enumerated can exercise all powers conferred upon the tenant for life by subsequent Acts.

§ 58.

Act of 1890.

A tenant in tail in possession can under the Fines and Recoveries Act (3 & 4 Will. 4, c. 74), ss. 15, 40, 41, by a deed inrolled bar the entail and acquire an estate in fee simple; but his power of disposition without inrolment was limited under that Act to the granting of leases for not more than twenty-one years. This formality of inrolment is unnecessary in exercising the powers of the present Act, but it must be remembered that if the tenant in tail assumes its powers he must comply with its provisions, and cannot require payment of the purchase-money into his own hands, or otherwise act as if he were an absolute owner.

i. Tenant in tail.

"With the exception of alienation, including leases, unless according to the statute, a tenant in tail is at this day to be considered as much the absolute owner of the estate as a tenant in fee simple, and as such, may do what he pleases with the buildings and timber on the estate:" *Att.-Gen.* v. *Duke of Marlborough*, 3 Mad. 498, 532. If all the provisions of the present Act apply to a tenant in tail he will be bound to set aside one-fourth of the mining rent (s. 11), and to get the consent of the trustees to a lease of the mansion-house although he is entitled if he pleases to work out the mines for his own benefit, and to pull down the mansion-house: Co. Litt. 224, a.

It has been held that where a baronetcy was created by a Patent which limited the dignity to the heirs male of the body, the baronet was a tenant in tail so as to be able to dispose of heirlooms under s. 37 of this Act: *Re Sir J. Rivett-Carnac's Will*, 30 Ch. D. 136.

As to estates tail where the reversion is in the Crown, see 34 & 35 Hen. 8, c. 20, the Fines and Recoveries Act (3 & 4 Will. 4, c. 74), s. 18; and the Settled Estates Act, 1877 (40 & 41 Vict. c. 18), s. 55.

And as to the inalienable estates purchased with money provided by Parliament in consideration of public services, see 3 & 4 Anne, c. 6; 5 Anne, c. 3 (Marlborough Estates); 46 Geo. 3, c. 146; 53 Geo. 3, c. 134; 55 Geo. 3, c. 96 (Nelson Estates); and 55 Geo. 3, c. 186, and other Acts mentioned in 2 & 3 Vict. c. 4 (Wellington Estates).

On the application of a tenant in tail restrained by Act of Parliament from barring or defeating his estate tail, a sum of Consols in Court representing the purchase-money of part of the settled estates,

§ 58.

ii. Fee simple defeasible.

which had been sold under a Private Act, was ordered to be transferred to the trustees for the purpose of being more advantageously invested under s. 21 : *Re The Bolton Estates Act*, 1863, 52 L. T. 728.

A devise of land unto and to the use of the testator's wife and another in trust to pay the income to the wife for the maintenance, education, and benefit of the testator's infant son until he should attain the age of twenty-one years, without being liable to account, and upon his attaining that age upon trust for him absolutely, with a gift over in case he should die under that age without leaving issue —was held to come within clause ii. of this sub-section, and the infant was declared to be a person who had the powers of a tenant for life: *Re Morgan*, 24 Ch. D. 114.

There is a large class of cases in which the question arises on the construction of a will whether an infant takes a vested interest subject to its being devested on his death under twenty-one, or whether the gift is contingent upon his attaining that age. If the case falls under the former category the infant has the powers of a tenant for life under this clause. See *Re James*, 32 W. R. 898. If, on the other hand, the gift is contingent, the persons in whom the land is in the meantime vested, seem to have the powers of a tenant for life, being persons entitled in fee simple with a gift over in the event of the infant attaining twenty-one.

iii. Base fee.

The expression "base fee" is defined by the Fines and Recoveries Act (3 & 4 Will. 4, c. 74), s. 1, to mean "that estate in fee simple into which an estate tail is converted where the issue in tail are barred, but persons claiming estates by way of remainder or otherwise are not barred." Such an estate is created by a disposition of the lands entailed without the consent of the protector (Fines and Recoveries Act, s. 34). See as to the enlargement of base fees, *ibid.* ss. 19, 35 ; where there is no provision as to barring the rights of the Crown, *secus* in the corresponding Irish Statute, 4 & 5 Will. c. 92, s. 16.

iv. Years determinable on life.

A testator having granted a lease of a public-house for 31 years at a rent of £50 a year, devised it to trustees upon trust to permit his wife to receive the rent thereof during the rest of the term, if she should so long live, and if she died before the end of the term, then he devised the house and premises to the children of his brother in fee ; but if his wife should live beyond the expiration of the term, then the trustees were directed to sell the house and premises and invest a sufficient sum to provide £50 a year for his wife during the rest of her life, and subject thereto he gave the proceeds of sale to the children of his brother. Under these circumstances it was held that the testator's widow was not a tenant for years determinable on life, and that she could not accept a surrender and grant a new lease of the house : *Re Hazle's Settled Estates*, 29 Ch. D. 78.

A devise to A. for 99 years if he should so long live gives him only a chattel interest: *Harris* v. *Barnes*, 4 Burr. 2157. It is to be observed that however short the term may be, this clause confers the powers of a tenant for life on the termor.

§ 58.

The ordinary form of mortgage by a tenant for life vests in his mortgagee an interest of this description (Dav. Conv. ii. pt. 2, 510, 4th ed.); but having regard to s. 50, *ante*, it cannot be supposed that the powers of the Act may be exercised by the mortgagee.

For a similar reason clause v. cannot be read as including the assignee of a tenant for life, but must be confined to a grant or devise to A. to hold during the life of B.

v. Tenant *pur autre vie*.

Where renewable leaseholds for lives are settled, the tenant for life has of course the powers of the Act without reference to this clause. See *Allen* v. *Allen*, 2 Dru. & W. 307; *Re Barber's S. E.*, 18 Ch. D. 624.

Examples illustrating clause vi. are furnished by a gift to a woman during widowhood: *Williams* v. *Williams*, 9 W. R. 888; to a spinster until marriage: *Eaton* v. *Hewitt*, 2 Dr. & Sm. 184; to a man until he becomes bankrupt, &c.: *Etches* v. *Etches*, 3 Drew. 441; in fact, wherever the prior gift is determinable in any manner, the donee is to rank as tenant for life until it is actually determined. Thus where the first tenant for life had forfeited his estate by non-compliance with a name and arms clause, and had no son to take the estate in tail male limited to his first and other sons, the second tenant for life was held to have the powers of a tenant for life under this clause, his estate being subject to determination on the birth of a son of the first tenant for life: *Re Parry*, W. N. 1884, 43. So a life estate which is subject to a conditional limitation over on non-residence, comes within the terms of this clause: *Re Paget's Settled Estates*, 30 Ch. D. 161.

vi. Life estate subject to determination.

Where a testator directed his trustees to accumulate the rents of his residuary real estate during twenty years after his death, and to invest the accumulations in the purchase of land to be settled "after the determination of the said term of twenty years" upon the trusts of an existing settlement, under which the son of the testator was tenant for life, it was held that during the term of twenty years the testator's son had not an estate or interest in possession, and could not exercise the powers of a tenant for life under this Act: *Re Strangways*, 34 Ch. D. 423. In his judgment in this case Cotton, L.J., after referring to the words of this clause—"is subject to a trust for accumulation"—said that "in order to bring himself within that the person claiming to be tenant for life must show that he has an immediate estate—a present estate for life, but that present estate is only subject to a trust for accumulation. That is a very different thing from there being a disposition of the entire rent for a given

Accumulation of income.

§ 58.

period, and a postponement until the expiration of that period of any interest whatever in the tenant for life," p. 431.

In another case a devise in strict settlement was followed by a direction to the trustees of the will to receive the rents and accumulate them until the amount should be sufficient to discharge the mortgages on the estate. Pearson, J., seems to have considered it clear that the tenant for life might sell under his statutory power, discharge the mortgages and enter into possession of the property. *Norton* v. *Johnstone*, 30 Ch. D. 649. See also *Re Clitheroe Estate*, 31 Ch. D. 135.

If the debts for payment of which accumulation is directed are not a charge upon the settled land, the tenant for life cannot, of course, apply corpus in discharging them; but he may exercise his power of sale and re-invest the proceeds either in land or in authorized securities, the income of which will be subject to the direction for accumulation contained in the will. It seems doubtful, however, whether in such a case the purchase money could be applied in payment for improvements.

vii. Tenant in tail after possibility of issue extinct.

As to "tenant in tail after possibility of issue extinct," see Littleton's Tenures, ss. 32—34; Tudor's L. C. in Conv. 58, 3rd ed. This estate arises where lands are limited in tail to a man and the heirs of his body by a particular wife, and the wife dies without issue. Such a tenant is for most purposes to be regarded merely as a tenant for life, unimpeachable however in respect of waste, unless it be wilful and malicious : Tudor's L. C. in Conv. 115, 3rd ed.

viii. Tenant by curtesy.

The life estate which a husband takes in the freehold land of inheritance belonging to his wife is here placed on the same footing as life estates under a settlement.

The Act of 1884, s. 8, gets rid of an obvious difficulty in the way of giving practical effect to this clause by enacting that for the purposes of the Act of 1882 the estate of a tenant by the curtesy is to be deemed an estate arising under a settlement made by his wife.

ix. Person entitled to income.

This last clause of the section is certainly a startling extension of the powers of the Act, but one which is absolutely necessary in order to prevent an evasion of its policy. It enables a person who has no legal estate, no right to actual possession, and no voice in the management of the estate, to exercise all the powers of an absolute owner. The person entitled to receive the net rents may, without the concurrence of the managing trustees, convey the estate to a purchaser, or grant leases, or deal with it in any of the modes authorized by the Act ; and this he may do although the estates are so heavily encumbered that after payment of outgoings there is no income for him to receive : *Re Jones*, 26 Ch. D. 736 ; *Re Cooke's Settled Estates*, W. N. 1885, 177.

In *Re Clitheroe Estate*, 31 Ch. D. 135, the testator devised the estate to the use of trustees for a long term of years, and subject thereto to the use of his second son for life, with remainders over. The trusts of the term were, (1) to raise portions for other children; (2) to raise the interest upon certain sums charged on other estates; (3) in certain events to pay an annuity to the second son; and (4) to accumulate the surplus rents and profits for the purpose of discharging incumbrances amounting to so large a sum that many years should elapse before the estate would be cleared, and the tenant for life be entitled to receive the rents. It was held, nevertheless, by the Court of Appeal, affirming the decision of Vice-Chancellor Bacon, that the second son was a person having by virtue of this clause the powers of a tenant for life, and that the power of sale vested in the trustees could not be exercised without his consent.

§ 58.

In *Re Horne's Settled Estate*, 39 Ch. D. 84, a testator devised his estate to trustees upon trust to sell at the expiration of twenty-one years from the date of his will (a time which had not arrived at the date of the application), and directed the rents and profits until sale to be applied in the same manner as the income of the proceeds of sale. In the events that happened the proceeds of sale were to be held in trust for the testator's children who, being sons, should attain twenty-five years, or being daughters, should attain that age or marry, in equal shares. The testator empowered his trustees to apply "the whole or such part as might be required of the annual income of the share or interest to which any child might be entitled in expectancy" for or towards his or her maintenance or education, with a direction that the unapplied surplus should be accumulated in augmentation of the share whence such income should have proceeded, and should eventually devolve in the same manner. All the six children being under twenty-five, and four of them being infants, it was held that neither under this clause, nor ss. 59 and 63, were the children entitled to exercise the powers of a tenant for life. The discretion as to the amount to be applied in maintenance excluded the case from this clause of s. 58; the interests of the children in the land not being "in possession," prevented the operation of s. 59; and the trust for sale being postponed, s. 63 was inapplicable.

This sub-section extends the provisions of the Act referring to a tenant for life to the limited owners enumerated in sub-s. (1); those referring to a settlement to "the instrument under which the estate or interest arises;" and those referring to settled land, to the land comprised in such last-mentioned instrument. It will be noticed that no mention is made of trustees of the settlement, the powers of the Court, the provisions as to investment, or to capital money arising under the Act. If these matters are not provided for, as they do not seem to be, the Act must remain a dead letter as regard

Sub-s. 2. Application of other provisions of the Act.

§ 58.

Sub-s. 3. Reference to death.

these limited owners: see, however, ss. 61 (4), 63 (2), and notes thereon.

There is no reference in the Act to " death as regards a tenant for life." The clause to which it originally applied, relating to "Improvements with money of tenant for life," was struck out of the Bill at a late stage.

XIV.—INFANTS; MARRIED WOMEN; LUNATICS.

§ 59.

Infant absolutely entitled to be as tenant for life. Sect. 59.

59. Where a person, who is in his own right seised of or entitled in possession to land, is an infant, then for purposes of this Act the land is settled land, and the infant shall be deemed tenant for life thereof.

The general intention of this part of the Act, which it will be remembered, is entitled "An Act for facilitating Sales, Leases, and other Dispositions of Settled Land, and for promoting the Execution of Improvements thereon," is to make the land to which a person under disability is entitled in possession, whatever may be his or her estate or interest therein, capable of alienation, notwithstanding such disability. The present section deals with land to which an infant is absolutely entitled, and brings it within the provisions of the Act by making the infant a constructive tenant for life. The next section proceeds to define the persons who are to exercise the statutory powers on behalf of the infant.

Land.

" Land " includes incorporeal hereditaments, and also an individual share in land : s. 2 (10) i.; and probably a term of years as well as an estate in fee simple is within the section, although s. 41 of the Conv. Act, 1881, which is superseded by it, contained express mention of "*any leasehold interest at a rent.*"

Possession.

The expression " entitled in possession " means not that the infant must be in the actual occupation of the land, which he seldom can be, but that his interest is not to be reversionary : *Re Morgan*, 24 Ch. D. 114.

A contingent interest is clearly not within the section : *Re Horne's Settled Estates*, 39 Ch. D. 84.

Partnership land.

The interest of an infant as next of kin of his father, who had died intestate, in land which had belonged to a firm of which the father had been a member, and which had been retained *in specie* by the administratrix, although personalty, may be treated as settled land within the meaning of this section : *Re Wells*, 31 W. R. 764.

Where an infant is absolutely entitled, since there is no " settlement," the provisions of s. 24, *ante*, do not apply ; and capital money cannot therefore be re-invested in land.

60. Where a tenant for life, or a person having the powers of a tenant for life under this Act, is an infant, or an infant would, if he were of full age, be a tenant for life, or have the powers of a tenant for life under this Act, the powers of a tenant for life under this Act may be exercised on his behalf by the trustees of the settlement, and if there are none, then by such person and in such manner as the Court, on the application of a testamentary or other guardian or next friend of the infant, either generally or in a particular instance, orders.

§ 60.
Tenant for life, infant.

The trustees of the settlement may under this section exercise on behalf of an infant the various powers of the Act; and they need not go through the "idle ceremony" of giving notices to each other or to their solicitor under s. 45 : *Re Countess of Dudley's Contract*, 35 Ch. D. 338.

Sect. 60. Tenant for life an infant.

The union of the two characters of tenant for life and trustees in the same persons gives rise to some curious results. They possess an absolute discretion as to sale and investment, ss. 3, 22; they may submit for their own approval a scheme for the improvement of the estate, and on the certificate of an engineer or surveyor nominated by themselves (who, however, must be approved by the Board of Agriculture or by the Court), may apply any capital money in their hands in payment for the works (s. 26). It is also important to observe that they possess an uncontrolled discretion as to selling or letting the principal mansion-house and park (s. 15); and as to the cutting and sale of timber (s. 35).

The infant need not be a consenting party to the exercise of the statutory powers by the trustees; for s. 56 (2) applies only to powers conferred by the settlement, and in this case they are conferred not by the settlement but by the Act. Where the trustees are exercising powers conferred upon them by the settlement the power of consenting to such exercise is by this section vested in the trustees of the settlement, and cannot be given by the infant in person : *Re Duke of Newcastle's Estates*, 24 Ch. D. 129 : and see *Re D'Angibau*, 15 Ch. D. 228.

The present section empowers the Court to appoint persons who, although not "trustees of the settlement," may exercise such of their powers as the Court sees fit to confer; but if, under s. 38, persons are properly appointed "trustees under the settlement for purposes of this Act," they will, without any further authority from the Court, be able to exercise *all* the powers of the Act: *Re Countess of Dudley's Contract*, 35 Ch. D. 338; the effect of s. 38 being to enlarge the definition

§ 60.

of "trustees of the settlement" contained in s. 2 (8) by the addition of the persons appointed by the Court. Where persons are appointed to exercise the powers of the Act on behalf of an infant, it is unnecessary also to appoint "trustees of the settlement" for the purpose of receiving notices under s. 45, and "there is good ground for saying that if trustees were appointed under s. 38, the powers of such trustees would, under the first part of s. 60, override or supersede the powers conferred on the guardians:" per Chitty, J., *Re Countess of Dudley's Contract*, 35 Ch. D. 338. The order made under this section ought to direct the purchase-money to be brought into Court: *Ibid.* But the sale may be allowed to take place out of Court: *Re Price*, 27 Ch. D. 552. Rule 8, *post*, (regulating the manner of sales), seems to refer to a sale of the principal mansion-house, timber, or heirlooms, and not to the appointment of persons with certain defined powers under this section.

The Court will not appoint the owner of one undivided share to exercise the powers of the infant over another, but will appoint independent persons: *Re Greenville Estate*, 11 L. R. Ir. 138.

Where property was held by trustees upon trust for sale and investment, with power "to use so much of the annual income arising therefrom as should be required for the maintenance and education of two infants," the remainder of such income being accumulated for their benefit, and upon trust to divide the whole of the principal and interest between the infants on their respectively attaining twenty-one, it was held that the infants were persons entitled concurrently to the income for a limited period subject to a trust for accumulation so as to be tenants for life within the meaning of s. 63, and that the trustees of the settlement could exercise on their behalf the powers of the Act under this section: *Re Powell*, W. N. 1884, 67. This case appears to be distinguishable from *Re Horne's Settled Estate*, 39 Ch. D. 84, on the ground that in the latter there was no immediate power of sale, and s. 63 did not therefore apply.

Infants' Settlements Act.

Where the settlement whose powers are being exercised has been made upon the marriage of an infant under the Infants' Settlements Act (18 & 19 Vict. c. 43, extended to Ireland by 23 & 24 Vict. c. 83), it should be remembered that, if the infant dies under twenty-one, "any appointment under a power of appointment, or any disentailing assurance" executed by the infant under the provisions of the Act becomes absolutely void. The settlement, therefore, if dependent on an appointment, or disentailing assurance, would also in the event of the infant's death become void; and a purchaser under the powers either of the settlement or of this Act, would have no title to the property.

The section applies not only where the tenant for life is an infant, but also where "an infant would if he were of full age be a tenant for life." There is some obscurity as to the meaning of these latter words, as it seems impossible to read them literally. For example, a devise "to A. during the minority of B., then to B. for life, with remainders over," would bring B. within the words, and yet it could not be intended to vest the statutory powers in the trustees during the minority of B., whose interest is contingent and reversionary. Compare the words in s. 61 (2), "if she had not been a married woman would have been a tenant for life," which are followed by provisions applicable only to married women. It is conceived that the hypothetical words in both cases, "if he were of full age," and "if she had not been a married woman," were introduced to meet the requirements of the Act as to "possession," neither an infant, nor, at the passing of this Act, a married woman, being capable of being "beneficially entitled to the possession of land."

§ 60.

61.—(1.) The foregoing provisions of this Act do not apply in the case of a married woman.

(2.) Where a married woman who, if she had not been a married woman, would have been a tenant for life or would have had the powers of a tenant for life under the foregoing provisions of this Act, is entitled for her separate use, or is entitled under any statute, passed or to be passed, for her separate property, or as a *feme sole*, then she, without her husband, shall have the powers of a tenant for life under this Act.

(3.) Where she is entitled otherwise than as aforesaid, then she and her husband together shall have the powers of a tenant for life under this Act.

(4.) The provisions of this Act referring to a tenant for life and a settlement and settled land shall extend to the married woman without her husband, or to her and her husband together, as the case may require, and to the instrument under which her estate or interest arises, and to the land therein comprised.

(5.) The married woman may execute, make, and do all deeds, instruments, and things necessary or proper for giving effect to the provisions of this section.

(6.) A restraint on anticipation in the settlement shall not prevent the exercise by her of any power under this Act.

§ 61. Married woman, how to be affected.

Marriage does not remove the disability of infancy: *Re D'Angibau*,

Infant married woman.

§ 61.

15 Ch. D. 228 ; *Shipway* v. *Ball*, 16 Ch. D. 376 ; and therefore a married woman cannot while she is an infant herself exercise the powers of the Act. Whether the trustees of the settlement can do so on her behalf is a question of some difficulty ; for sub-s. (1) excludes all "the foregoing provisions of this Act" (ss. 59 and 60 among the rest). And sub-s. (4) seems scarcely wide enough in its terms to re-enact those sections with the necessary modifications in the case of a married woman.

Sub-s. 2. Separate use.

The words "if she had not been a married woman" (as to which see note to s. 60, *ante*), would seem to be applicable rather to the case where there is no separate use, than to that in which there is. For, when a married woman is entitled to land for her separate use, or as her separate property, although the legal estate may be in the husband or in trustees, she would be now regarded as equitable tenant for life (see *Wade* v. *Wilson*, 33 W. R. 610), and at all events would have the powers of a tenant for life as "a person entitled to the income of land under a trust, &c. :" s. 58, ix. ; and see the Married Women's Property Act, 1882 (45 & 46 Vict. c. 75), s. 1.

Sub-s. 3. Entitled otherwise than aforesaid.

The previous sub-section having provided for the cases in which a married woman is entitled for her separate use, or for her separate property, or as a *feme sole*, the present clause deals with the case "where she is entitled otherwise than as aforesaid," *i.e.*, where she is not entitled for her separate use, separate property, or as a *feme sole*. It does not include her separate property held in fee simple, or any estate which from her infancy or lunacy is not comprised in sub-s. 2.

By the Settled Estates Act, 1877 (40 & 41 Vict. c. 18), s. 46, powers of granting leases for twenty-one years are conferred upon any person entitled to the possession, or to the receipt of the rents and profits of settled estates, for an estate for life, or for any greater estate, either in his own right, or in right of his wife; and also in the case of unsettled estates where such person is entitled as tenant by the curtesy, or in dower, or in right of a wife who is seised in fee.

When a married woman is seised in fee simple of land not settled to her separate use the powers of this Act are not applicable.

Sub-s. 4. Certain provisions applied.

The limited terms in which the provisions of the Act are here incorporated, excludes the supposition that, subject to the modifications introduced by this section, the entire body of the Act is to be applicable in the case of married women. It will be observed that provisions relating to only three subjects, viz., a tenant for life, a settlement, and settled land, are here referred to. What the effect of this section may be upon the trustees of the settlement, the Court, the Land Commissioners, and purchasers, is extremely doubtful ; but it is submitted that, since the powers would be unworkable without the ancillary provisions of the Act (*e.g.*, Trustees of the settlement, powers to give receipts, &c.), some interpretation must be put either upon sub-s. (1) or sub-s. (4), so as to authorize the adoption of those provisions.

§ 61.

A married woman may exercise the powers of this Act without a deed acknowledged; as to which see the Conv. Act, 1882, s. 7.

Sub-s. 5. Execution of deeds, &c.

A married woman seised of land in fee simple as her separate property with a restraint on anticipation, cannot make use of the powers of this Act; but if she wishes to dispose of it must make a case under s. 39 of the Conv. Act, 1881 : *Re Currey*, 35 W. R. 326.

Sub-s. 6. Restraint on anticipation.

62. Where a tenant for life, or a person having the powers of a tenant for life under this Act, is a lunatic, so found by inquisition, the committee of his estate may, in his name and on his behalf, under an order of the Lord Chancellor, or other person intrusted by virtue of the Queen's Sign Manual with the care and commitment of the custody of the persons and estates of lunatics, exercise the powers of a tenant for life under this Act; and the order may be made on the petition of any person interested in the settled land, or of the committee of the estate.

§ 62.

Tenant for life, lunatic.

This section does not apply to persons of unsound mind not so found by inquisition, nor as regards persons under such disability is there any provision in the Act authorizing the trustees of the settlement or any other persons to exercise the statutory powers on behalf of a tenant for life. At the time when the Settled Land Act was passed there was no jurisdiction either in Chancery or in Lunacy enabling the Court to authorize the exercise of powers vested in a lunatic not so found by inquisition. Now, however, under the Lunacy Act, 1890 (53 Vict. c. 5), the Judge in Lunacy has administrative powers not only over lunatics so found by inquisition, but also over some classes of those not so found; the powers of the Act in such cases being exerciseable by some person to be appointed for the purpose instead of by the committee (see s. 116). By the combined operation of ss. 116 and 120, the judge may by order authorize and direct the person so to be appointed to "exercise any power or give any consent required for the exercise of any power where the power is vested in the lunatic for his own benefit, or the power of consent is in the nature of a beneficial interest in the lunatic," s. 120 (1).

Sect. 62. Lunatic not so found.

Where the power is vested in the lunatic in the character of trustee or guardian, or the consent of a lunatic to the exercise of a power is necessary in the like character, or as a check upon the undue exercise

§ 62. of the power, there is jurisdiction to make a similar order under s. 128.

Now it may be argued that the powers conferred by the Settled Land Act are not vested in the tenant for life wholly for his own benefit, or wholly in the character of trustee, but partly in one character and partly in the other, and therefore that they do not fall within either of the provisions which have been cited. It is conceived that as regards the powers of dealing with the settled land by way of sale, exchange, partition, lease, mortgage or charge, this objection is well founded; and that the statutory powers cannot be apportioned so as to fall within the combined operation of the two sections of the Lunacy Act; but that as regards the power of consent required by s. 56 (2), *ante*, which is wholly for the benefit of the tenant for life (see *Dicconson* v. *Talbot*, L. R. 6 Ch. 32), a person may be appointed by the Judge in Lunacy to give such consent on behalf of a lunatic not so found by inquisition.

Infant. If the person of unsound mind is an infant, ss. 59 and 60 are applicable, and the powers of the Act may be exercised on his behalf by trustees of the settlement or the persons appointed for the purpose by the Court. An infant is rarely, if ever, found lunatic by inquisition. See *Re Edwards*, 10 Ch. D. 605.

Married woman. Where a married woman is entitled to land for her separate use, or as her separate property, this section seems to apply in case of her being found lunatic; but where she is not so entitled, then, as she is not tenant for life, but only would have been tenant for life if she had not been a married woman (s. 61 (2)), this section is not strictly applicable. The lunacy of her husband also, when his concurrence is required, seems to render the exercise of the powers impossible.

Practice. An order under this section may now be obtained on summons at Chambers before a Master in Lunacy, and a petition is not to be presented, unless the judge directs it, in any particular case. Rules in Lunacy, 1890, r. 16, Form 10.

Notice of the application should be served on the trustees of the settlement, and if there are none they should be appointed under s. 38: *Re Taylor*, 31 W. R. 596.

Before giving notice under s. 45 of the intention to exercise the powers of the Act, the committee should obtain the sanction of the Judge in Lunacy: *Re Ray's Settled Estates*, 25 Ch. D. 464.

The Court can authorize the committee under this section to take proceedings for the purpose of selling an undivided share in respect of which the lunatic is tenant for life, or a person having the powers of a tenant for life, to the owner of the other shares: *Re Gaitskell*, 40 Ch. D. 416.

XV.—Settlement by way of Trusts for Sale.

63.—(1.) Any land, or any estate or interest in land, which under or by virtue of any deed, will, or agreement, covenant to surrender, copy of court roll, Act of Parliament, or other instrument or any number of instruments, whether made or passed before or after, or partly before and partly after, the commencement of this Act, is subject to a trust or direction for sale of that land, estate, or interest, and for the application or disposal of the money to arise from the sale, or the income of that money, or the income of the land until sale, or any part of that money or income, for the benefit of any person for his life, or any other limited period, or for the benefit of two or more persons concurrently for any limited period, and whether absolutely, or subject to a trust for accumulation of income for payment of debts or other purpose, or to any other restriction, shall be deemed to be settled land, and the instrument or instruments under which the trust arises shall be deemed to be a settlement; and the person for the time being beneficially entitled to the income of the land, estate, or interest aforesaid until sale, whether absolutely or subject as aforesaid, shall be deemed to be tenant for life thereof; or if two or more persons are so entitled concurrently, then those persons shall be deemed to constitute together the tenant for life thereof; and the persons, if any, who are for the time being under the settlement trustees for sale of the settled land, or having power of consent to, or approval of, or control over the sale, or if under the settlement there are no such trustees, then the persons, if any, for the time being, who are by the settlement declared to be trustees thereof for purposes of this Act are for purposes of this Act trustees of the settlement.

Provision for case of trust to sell and re-invest in land.

(2.) In every such case the provisions of this Act referring to a tenant for life, and to a settlement, and to settled land, shall extend to the person or persons aforesaid, and to the instrument or instruments under which his or their estate or interest arises, and to the land therein comprised,

§ 63. subject and except as in this section provided (that is to say):

(i.) Any reference in this Act to the predecessors or successors in title of the tenant for life, or to the remaindermen, or reversioners, or other persons interested in the settled land, shall be deemed to refer to the persons interested in succession or otherwise in the money to arise from sale of the land, or the income of that money, or the income of the land, until sale (as the case may require).

(ii.) Capital money arising under this Act from the settled land shall not be applied in the purchase of land unless such application is authorized by the settlement in the case of capital money arising thereunder from sales or other dispositions of the settled land, but may, in addition to any other mode of application authorized by this Act, be applied in any mode in which capital money arising under the settlement from any such sale or other disposition is applicable thereunder, subject to any consent required or direction given by the settlement with respect to the application of trust money of the settlement.

(iii.) Capital money arising under this Act from the settled land and the securities in which the same is invested, shall not for any purpose of disposition, transmission, or devolution, be considered as land unless the same would, if arising under the settlement from a sale or disposition of the settled land, have been so considered, and the same shall be held in trust for and shall go to the same persons successively in the same manner, and for and on the same estates, interests, and trusts as the same would have gone and been held if arising under the settlement from a sale or disposition of the settled land, and the income of such capital money and securities shall be paid or applied accordingly.

(iv.) Land of whatever tenure acquired under this Act, by purchase, or in exchange, or on partition, shall be conveyed to and vested in the trustees of the settlement, on the trusts, and subject to the powers and provisions which, under the settlement or by reason of the exercise of any power of appointment or charging therein contained, are subsisting with respect to the settled land, or would be so subsisting if the same had not been sold, or as near thereto as circumstances permit, but so as not to increase or multiply charges or powers of charging.

§ 63.

The marginal note is misleading, as the section is not confined to cases where there is a trust for re-investment in land. See sub-s. (2) ii.

This section, which was introduced during the progress of the Bill through Parliament, and which has "given rise to much controversy" (31 Ch. D. 509), has been paralysed by the Act of 1884, which enacts that the powers conferred by this section shall not be exercised without the leave of the Court, and that the consent of the tenant for life shall not be required for a valid execution by the trustees of the trust for sale under the settlement (Act of 1884, ss. 6, 7). The necessity for this amendment appears from the following observations of Mr. Justice North in a recent case. "Upon that part of the Act (s. 63) difficulties arose in some cases (not simple cases) in respect of land subject to a trust for sale, and so coming within that section. Very often the land was to be sold and the proceeds to be applied in a number of different ways—for instance in the payment of funeral expenses, or of debts, or of legacies. Then subject to making provisions for all those objects, there was a trust for investment of the surplus. In such cases difficulties arose as to the exact application of the Act to land brought within its terms by s. 63; as, for instance, whether having regard to the 56th section, the trustees for sale could sell without the consent of the tenant for life of the proceeds. In the case of *Taylor* v. *Poncia* (25 Ch. D. 646), Mr. Justice Pearson took the view that trustees for sale were not precluded by the 56th section from selling without such consent, at any rate in that particular case. That

Sect. 63.
Settlement by way of trust for sale.

§ 63.

solved the difficulty to a limited extent. To get rid of the difficulty more completely the legislature passed the 6th and 7th sections of the Act of 1884. Section 6 seems to me a recognition of the decision in *Taylor* v. *Poncia*, as applicable not only to cases of a complex character but to every case. In fact the right of the trustees for sale to sell without the consent of the tenant for life is made clear. The tenant for life is not to be the person to direct how the land subject to the trust for sale is to be put on the market. Then to prevent the Acts conflicting the legislature went on to provide by s. 7, that the powers conferred by s. 63, were not to be exercised without the leave of the Court, &c. The effect of the two sections is that the trustees for sale and not the tenant for life are the persons who are to have the conduct of a sale ; but the Court is to have power to allow the tenant for life to exercise the power:" *Re Harding's Estate* (1891), 1 Ch. 60, 63.

Tenant for life.

The definition of the "tenant for life" contained in this section, viz., " the person for the time being beneficially entitled to the income of the land, estate, or interest until sale, whether absolutely or subject as aforesaid," refers solely to the income of the unsold land, not to that of the proceeds of sale ; and if it had been held that the tenant for life must be a person entitled to the income of the land by the express terms of the settlement, much of the difficulty experienced in the earlier cases would have disappeared.

Cases, however, in which there was no power to postpone the sale, and no direction that the rents until sale should go in the same way as the income of the proceeds of sale, have been held to fall within the section : *Taylor* v. *Poncia*, 25 Ch. D. 646 ; *Re Ridge*, 31 Ch. D. 504 ; *Re Harding's Estate* (1891), 1 Ch. 60.

Settlement.

Where the limitations of the original settlement were exhausted, and the right to the proceeds of sale had vested absolutely in the beneficiaries it was held that sub-settlements of certain undivided shares thereof did not form part of the "Settlement" under this section, and that the trustees for sale could accordingly make a title without the concurrence of the beneficiaries : *Re Earle and Webster's Contract*, 24 Ch. D. 144.

This decision, however, seems to be inconsistent with *Re Ridge*, 31 Ch. D. 504, where a testator, who was absolutely entitled to a share of the proceeds of sale of land under a settlement by way of trust for sale, bequeathed his personal estate to his executors upon trust for payment of his debts and funeral and testamentary expenses, and subject thereto upon trust for conversion and investment and payment of the annual produce to Mrs. M., for her life and after her death in trust for other persons. A mineral lease having been granted of part of the settled property the question arose whether Mrs. M. was a tenant for life impeachable for waste in respect of minerals so that three-fourths of the rents and royalties reserved by the lease should be set aside as capital money, and it was so decided by the Court of Appeal reversing the decision of Bacon, V.-C.

§ 63.

In order to create a settlement within this section the trust or direction for sale must be capable of being immediately carried into effect : *Re Hornes' Settled Estate,* 39 Ch. D. 84, see *ante,* p. 165, where the facts of this case are stated. The ground on which the Court of Appeal rested their decision was that the discretionary trust for the maintenance of the children did not make them "beneficially entitled to the land or the income until sale," as if they all died under 25, the accumulations would go to other persons. If the accumulations had been given to them or any of them absolutely, this point would have been differently decided. See *Re Powell,* W. N. 1884, 67.

It is conceived that where there is a trust to sell in consideration of a fee farm rent this section does not apply, inasmuch as the rent is not "income of the money to arise from the sale."

Fee farm rent.

This form of incorporating the provisions of the Act is similar to that employed in ss. 58 (2), 61 (4) ; and as an exception often enlarges the scope of an ambiguous gift, by showing what would have been included but for the exception ; so, here, valuable aid is furnished in the interpretation of this clause, by the matters which are excepted from its operation. These sub-clauses show at once that the provisions relating to "remaindermen," "capital money arising under the Act," and "the trustees of the settlement," although not referred to, must be intended to be included in the preceding provision. See *Re Ridge,* 31 Ch. D. 504.

Sub-s. 2. Application of other provisions.

For references in the Act to "predecessors in title," see ss. 12, 20 ; to "successors in title," see ss. 20, 28, 29, 31 ; and to "remaindermen or reversioners, or other persons interested in the settled land," see ss. 28, 38, 53, 54.

Clause i.

As to the re-investment of capital money in the purchase of land, see ss. 21, 24 ; and as to the modes of application of capital money authorized by the Act, see s. 21.

Clause ii.

The saving in this clause as to "any consent required or direction given by the settlement with respect to the application of trust money of the settlement," seems to refer not to applications of the money in accordance with this Act, but only to the additional modes of application authorized by the settlement.

The land being by "the trust or direction for sale" equitably converted into personalty, the provision in s. 22 (5) has to be excluded, in order that the purchase-money may not be reconverted contrary to the intentions of the parties.

Clause iii.

The form of conveyance of freeholds directed in s. 24 would be of

Clause iv.

§ 63.

course inapplicable to a case where the interests of the beneficiaries are declared by trusts of the purchase-money, and not by limitations of the freehold.

XVI.—Repeals.

§ 64.

Repeal of enactments in schedule.

64.—(1.) The enactments described in the schedule to this Act are hereby repealed.

(2.) The repeal by this Act of any enactment shall not affect any right accrued or obligation incurred thereunder before the commencement of this Act; nor shall the same affect the validity or invalidity, or any operation, effect, or consequence, of any instrument executed or made, or of anything done or suffered, or of any order made, before the commencement of this Act; nor shall the same affect any action, proceeding, or thing then pending or uncompleted; and every such action, proceeding, and thing may be carried on and completed as if there had been no such repeal in this Act.

Repeal.

The Acts hereby repealed are Lord Cranworth's Act (23 & 24 Vict. c. 145), so far as it had not been already repealed; certain provisions of the Improvement of Land Act, 1864, relating to preliminary advertisements and notices, and to the dissent by persons interested in the property; and s. 17 of the Settled Estates Act, which relates to proceedings for the protection of the settled estate, and which is replaced by the more extensive provisions of s. 36, *ante*, p. 125.

It should be noticed that ss. 8 and 9 of Lord Cranworth's Act, relating to the power of trustees to renew leases, and authorizing them to raise money by mortgage for the purpose of paying for equality of exchange or renewal of leases, were not replaced by any other similar enactments. These sections, however, so far as they relate to leases, have been re-enacted by the Trustee Act, 1888 (51 & 52 Vict. c. 59), ss. 10, 11.

XVII.—Ireland.

§ 65.

Modifications respecting Ireland.

65.—(1.) In the application of this Act to Ireland the foregoing provisions shall be modified as in this section provided.

(2.) The Court shall be Her Majesty's High Court of Justice in Ireland.

§ 65.

(3.) All matters within the jurisdiction of that Court shall, subject to the Acts regulating that Court, be assigned to the Chancery Division of that Court; but General Rules under this Act for Ireland may direct that those matters or any of them be assigned to the Land Judges of that Division.

(4.) Any deed inrolled under this Act shall be inrolled in the Record and Writ Office of that Division.

(5.) General Rules for purposes of this Act for Ireland shall be deemed Rules of Court within the Supreme Court of Judicature Act (Ireland), 1877, and may be made accordingly, at any time after the passing of this Act, to take effect on or after the commencement of this Act. 40 & 41 Vict. c. 57.

(6.) The several Civil Bill Courts in Ireland shall, in addition to the jurisdiction possessed by them independently of this Act, have and exercise the power and authority exerciseable by the Court under this Act, in all proceedings where the property, the subject of the proceedings, does not exceed in capital value five hundred pounds, or in annual value thirty pounds.

(7.) The provisions of Part II. of the County Officers and Courts (Ireland) Act, 1877, relative to the equitable jurisdiction of the Civil Bill Courts, shall apply to the jurisdiction exerciseable by those Courts under this Act. 40 & 41 Vict. c. 56.

(8.) Rules and Orders for purposes of this Act, as far as it relates to the Civil Bill Courts, may be made at any time after the passing of this Act, to take effect on or after the commencement of this Act, in manner prescribed by section seventy-nine of the County Officers and Courts (Ireland) Act, 1877.

(9.) The Commissioners of Public Works in Ireland shall be substituted for the Land Commissioners.

(10.) The term for which a lease other than a building or mining lease may be granted shall be not exceeding thirty-five years.

Leases in Ireland. — Under the Land Law Ireland Act, 1881 (44 & 45 Vict. c. 49), a lease in order to be binding on the tenant, except where he has power to contract himself out of the Act (s. 22), must be either a

§ 65. judicial lease (s. 10) or a fixed tenancy (s. 11); and save as aforesaid any lease inconsistent with the provisions as to those statutory tenancies is by s. 22 declared to be void. It seems clear, therefore, that a lease made under the Settled Land Act must, in order to be binding on the tenant, conform to the requirements of a judicial lease; for a fixed tenancy, *i. e.*, a perpetuity, is not within the powers thereby conferred.

The characteristics of a judicial lease which it is necessary here to notice are, that it must be for thirty-one years or upwards, that it must be sanctioned by the Court (*i.e.*, the Civil Bill Court or the Land Commission), and that upon its expiration the lessee is to be deemed the tenant of a "present ordinary tenancy" at the rent and subject to the conditions of the lease.

Having regard to the last mentioned provision it seems open to question whether the grant of a judicial lease is within the powers conferred on a tenant for life by this Act; but it must be admitted that if it were so held the operation of the Act as regards leases would be confined to the exceptional cases where a tenant has power to contract himself out of the Act (s. 22), or where the tenancies are excluded from the operation of the Act (s. 58).

The Settled Land Act is applied with modifications to sales by limited owners under the Purchase of Land (Ireland) Act, 1885 (48 & 49 Vict. c. 73), ss. 5, 6; and see the Land Law (Ireland) Act, 1887 (50 & 51 Vict. c. 33), s. 14.

By s. 8 of the last mentioned Act a middleman is empowered in certain events to surrender his term; and where he is a limited owner the surrender is to be regarded as a sale within the meaning of the Settled Land Act.

THE SCHEDULE.

Sect. 64.

REPEALS.

23 & 24 Vict. c. 145 . in part.	An Act to give to trustees, mortgagees, and others, certain powers now commonly inserted in settlements, mortgages, and wills . . . . } in part; namely,— PARTS I. AND IV. (being so much of the Act as is not repealed by the Conveyancing and Law of Property Act, 1881).
27 & 28 Vict. c. 114 . in part.	The Improvement of Land Act, 1864, in part; namely,— Sections seventeen and eighteen: Sections twenty-one, from "either by a party" to "benefice) or" (inclusive); and from "or if the land owner" to "minor or minors" (inclusive); and "or circumstance" (twice): Except as regards Scotland.
40 & 41 Vict. c. 18 . in part.	The Settled Estates Act, 1877 . in part; namely,— Section seventeen.

THE
SETTLED LAND ACT. 1884.

47 & 48 VICT. c. 18.

An Act to amend the Settled Land Act, 1882.

[3rd July, 1884.]

BE it enacted by the Queen's most Excellent Majesty, by and with the advice and consent of the Lords Spiritual and Temporal, and Commons, in this present Parliament assembled, and by the authority of the same, as follows :

§ 1.
Short title.

1. This Act may be cited as the Settled Land Act, 1884.

§ 2.
Interpretation.

2. The expression "the Act of 1882" used in this Act means the Settled Land Act, 1882.

§ 3.
Construction of Act.

3. The Act of 1882 and this Act are to be read and construed together as one Act, and expressions used in this Act are to have the same meanings as those attached by the Act of 1882 to similar expressions used therein.

§ 4.
Fine on a lease to be capital money.

4. A fine received on the grant of a lease under any power conferred by the Act of 1882 is to be deemed capital money arising under that Act.

As to leasing powers, see ss. 4, 6—12 of the Act of 1882 ; and as to the sources whence capital money may arise, *ante*, p. 14.

Capital money must be paid either to the trustees of the settlement or into Court, s. 22 (1) of the Act of 1882.

§ 5.
Notice under 45 & 46 Vict. c. 38, s. 45, may, as to a sale, exchange,

5.—(1.) The notice required by section forty-five of the Act of 1882 of intention to make a sale, exchange, partition, or lease may be notice of a general intention in that behalf.

(2.) The tenant for life is, upon request by a trustee of the settlement, to furnish to him such particulars and information as may reasonably be required by him from time to time with reference to sales, exchanges, partitions, or leases effected, or in progress, or immediately intended.

§ 5. partition, or lease, be general.

(3.) Any trustee, by writing under his hand, may waive notice either in any particular case, or generally, and may accept less than one month's notice.

(4.) This section applies to a notice given before, as well as to a notice given after, the passing of this Act.

(5.) Provided that a notice, to the sufficiency of which objection has been taken before the passing of this Act, is not made sufficient by virtue of this Act.

This section has been fully considered in connection with s. 45 of the Act of 1882, see *ante*, p. 138.

6.—(1.) In the case of a settlement within the meaning of section sixty-three of the Act of 1882, any consent not required by the terms of the settlement is not by force of anything contained in that Act to be deemed necessary to enable the trustees of the settlement, or any other person, to execute any of the trusts or powers created by the settlement.

§ 6. As to consents of tenants for life.

(2.) In the case of every other settlement, not within the meaning of section sixty-three of the Act of 1882, where two or more persons together constitute the tenant for life for the purposes of that Act, then, notwithstanding anything contained in subsection (2.) of section fifty-six of that Act, requiring the consent of all those persons, the consent of one only of those persons is by force of that section to be deemed necessary to the exercise by the trustees of the settlement, or by any other person, of any power conferred by the settlement exerciseable for any purpose provided for in that Act.

(3.) This section applies to dealings before, as well as after, the passing of this Act.

The first sub-section gets rid of the difficulties raised in *Re Earle and Webster's Contract*, 24 Ch. D. 144, and *Taylor v. Poncia*, 25 Ch. D. 646. See also the observations of Mr. Justice North in *Re Harding's Estate* [1891], 1 Ch. 60 ; and note to s. 63, *ante*.

Sub-s. 1.

By s. 2 (6) of the Act of 1882 it is declared that all persons

Sub-s. 2.

§ 6. entitled concurrently for their lives shall together constitute the tenant for life for the purposes of the Act; and accordingly the consent of all such persons would have been necessary, but for this section, in order to enable the trustees to exercise any of the powers conferred upon them by the settlement.

§ 7.

Powers given by s. 63 to be exercised only with leave of the Court.

7. With respect to the powers conferred by section sixty-three of the Act of 1882, the following provisions are to have effect:—

(i.) Those powers are not to be exercised without the leave of the Court.

(ii.) The Court may by order, in any case in which it thinks fit, give leave to exercise all or any of those powers, and the order is to name the person or persons to whom leave is given.

(iii.) The Court may from time to time rescind, or vary, any order made under this section, or may make any new or further order.

(iv.) So long as an order under this section is in force, neither the trustees of the settlement, nor any person other than a person having the leave, shall execute any trust or power created by the settlement, for any purpose for which leave is by the order given, to exercise a power conferred by the Act of 1882.

(v.) An order under this section may be registered and re-registered, as a lis pendens, against the trustees of the settlement named in the order, describing them on the register as "Trustees for the purposes of the Settled Land Act, 1882."

(vi.) Any person dealing with the trustees from time to time, or with any other person acting under the trusts or powers of the settlement, is not to be affected by an order under this section, unless and until the order is duly registered, and when necessary re-registered as a lis pendens.

(vii.) An application to the Court under this section may be made by the tenant for life, or by the persons who together constitute the tenant for life, within the meaning of section sixty-three of the Act of 1882.

(viii.) An application to rescind or vary an order, or to make any new or further order under this section, may be made also by the trustees of the settlement, or by any person beneficially interested under the settlement.

(ix.) The person or persons to whom leave is given by an order under this section, shall be deemed the proper person or persons to exercise the powers conferred by section sixty-three of the Act of 1882, and shall have, and may exercise those powers accordingly.

(x.) This section is not to affect any dealing which has taken place before the passing of this Act, under any trust or power to which this section applies.

The effect of this section coupled with the first sub-section of the preceding section is to restore to the trustees for sale the unfettered exercise of the powers conferred upon them by the settlement, unless an order is obtained giving the tenant for life or some other person leave to exercise the statutory powers, and unless such order is registered, and if necessary re-registered as a *lis pendens*.

The Court has a discretion as to making an order under this section, but in simple cases, where there are no interests subsisting prior to the interest of the tenant for life, he is the proper person to be entrusted with the conduct of a sale : *Re Harding's Estate* [1891], 1 Ch. 60.

A *lis pendens* does not bind a purchaser or mortgagee unless re-registered every five years, 2 & 3 Vict. c. 11. s. 7 ; and accordingly the search need only be carried back for five years prior to a purchase.

The fifth sub-section enables the order to be registered only against the trustees of the settlement named in the order. If, therefore, new trustees are appointed a fresh order should be obtained and registered against them.

§ 7.

In the case of land within the jurisdiction of the Counties Palatine, the registration of *lis pendens* may be effected in the local registries, 18 & 19 Vict. c. 15, s. 3 ; and a search should therefore be made there when such land is sold by trustees for sale.

§ 8.

Curtesy to be deemed to arise under settlement.

8. For the purposes of the Act of 1882, the estate of a tenant by the curtesy is to be deemed an estate arising under a settlement made by his wife.

See s. 58 (1) viii. of the Act of 1882, which confers on a tenant by the curtesy the powers of a tenant for life.

THE

SETTLED LAND ACT, 1887.

50 & 51 VICT. c. 30.

An Act to amend the Settled Land Act (1882).

[23rd August, 1887.]

WHEREAS by the twenty-first section of the Settled Land Act, 1882 (in this Act referred to as the Act of 1882), it is provided that capital money arising under that Act may be applied in payment for any improvement by that Act authorised.

45 & 46 Vict. c. 38.

Be it therefore enacted by the Queen's most Excellent Majesty, by and with the advice and consent of the Lords Spiritual and Temporal, and the Commons, in this present Parliament assembled, and by the authority of the same, as follows :

1. Where any improvement of a kind authorised by the Act of 1882, has been or may be made either before or after the passing of this Act, and a rentcharge, whether temporary or perpetual, has been or may be created in pursuance of any Act of Parliament, with the object of paying off any moneys advanced for the purpose of defraying the expenses of such improvement, any capital money expended in redeeming such rentcharge, or otherwise providing for the payment thereof, shall be deemed to be applied in payment for an improvement authorised by the Act of 1882.

§ 1.
Amendment of s. 21 of the Settled Land Act, 1882.

See note to s. 21 of the Act of 1882 where the effect of this section is considered.

2. An improvement in payment for which capital money is applied or deemed to be applied under the pro-

§ 2.
Section 23

§ 2.
of Settled Land Act, 1882, to apply to improvements within preceding section.

visions of the preceding section shall be deemed to be an improvement within the meaning of section twenty-eight of the Act of 1882, and the provisions of such last-mentioned section shall, so far as applicable, be deemed to apply to such improvement.

See note to s. 28, of the Act of 1882.—Drainage is the improvement most frequently effected by the creation of such a rent-charge as is mentioned in the first section ; and the provisions of s. 28 of the Act of 1882 relating to maintenance repairs and insurance seems scarcely applicable to such a case. See *Re Lord Sudeley's Settled Estates*, 37 Ch. D. 123.

§ 3.
Short title.

3. This Act shall be construed as one with the Settled Land Act, 1882, and the Settled Land Act, 1884, and may be cited together with those Acts as the Settled Land Acts, 1882 to 1887, and separately as the Settled Land Acts (Amendment) Act, 1887.

THE

SETTLED LAND ACT, 1889.

52 & 53 Vict. c. 36.

An Act to amend the Settled Land Act, 1882.

[12th August, 1889.]

BE it enacted by the Queen's most Excellent Majesty, by and with the advice and consent of the Lords Spiritual and Temporal, and Commons, in this present Parliament assembled, and by the authority of the same, as follows :

1. This Act shall be construed as one with the Settled Land Acts, 1882 to 1887, and may be cited together with those Acts as the Settled Land Acts, 1882 to 1889, and separately as the Settled Land Act, 1889.

§ 1.
Construction and short title.

2. Any building lease, and any agreement for granting building leases, under the Settled Land Act, 1882, may contain an option, to be exercised at any time within an agreed number of years not exceeding ten, for the lessee to purchase the land leased at a price fixed at the time of the making of the lease or agreement for the lease, such price to be the best which having regard to the rent reserved can reasonably be obtained, and to be either a fixed sum of money or such a sum of money as shall be equal to a stated number of years purchase of the highest rent reserved by the lease or agreement.

§ 2.
Option of purchase in building lease.
45 & 46 Vict. c. 38.

The general power of leasing is conferred by s. 6 of the Act of 1882, and the special regulations as to building leases are contained in s. 8 of the same Act. If and when the lessee exercises the option of purchase, the transaction is, it is conceived, for all purposes a sale under the powers of the Acts; and accordingly the tenant for life can convey the land by virtue of s. 20 of the principal Act. A successor

§ 2. in title of the tenant for life who granted the lease can execute such a conveyance under s. 6 of the Act of 1890. The expression "the highest rent reserved by the lease or agreement" refers to the power of reserving in a building lease a peppercorn or nominal or other rent less than the rent ultimately payable for the first five years or any less part of the term. Act of 1882, s. 8 (2).

§ 3.
Price to be capital money.

3. Such price when received shall for all purposes be capital money arising under the Settled Land Act, 1882.

The price must accordingly be paid either to the trustees of the settlement or into Court. Act of 1882, s. 22 (1).

THE

SETTLED LAND ACT, 1890.

53 & 54 VICT. c. 69.

An Act to amend the Settled Land Acts, 1882 to 1889.

[18th August, 1890.]

BE it enacted by the Queen's most Excellent Majesty, by and with the advice and consent of the Lords Spiritual and Temporal, and Commons, in this present Parliament assembled, and by the authority of the same, as follows:

Preliminary.

1. This Act may be cited as the Settled Land Act, 1890.

2. The Settled Land Acts, 1882 to 1889, and this Act are to be read and construed together as one Act, and may be cited as the Settled Land Acts, 1882 to 1890.

3. Expressions used in this Act are to have the same meanings as those attached by the Settled Land Acts, 1882 to 1889, to similar expressions used therein.

§ 1.
Short title.

§ 2.
Acts to be construed together.

§ 3.
Interpretation.

Definitions.

4.—(1.) Every instrument whereby a tenant for life, in consideration of marriage or as part or by way of any family arrangement, not being a security for payment of money advanced, makes an assignment of or creates a charge upon his estate or interest under the settlement is to be deemed one of the instruments creating the settlement, and not an instrument vesting in any person any right as assignee for value within the meaning or operation of section fifty of the Act of 1882.

§ 4.
Instrument in consideration of marriage, &c., to be part of the settlement.
45 & 46 Vict. c. 38.

§ 4.

(2.) This section is to apply and have effect with respect to every disposition before as well as after the passing of this Act, unless inconsistent with the nature or terms of the disposition.

This section includes both "assignments" and "charges" of the estate or interest of the tenant for life. As regards the latter, the effect of considering the instrument which creates the charge as part of the settlement, is to enable the tenant for life to convey the settled land freed from the charge under s. 20 (2) of the Act of 1882, and without the consent mentioned in s. 50 (3); but if there is an absolute assignment of the life interest the effect of the section is to confer on the assignee the powers of the Act. The main object of the section seems to be to enable a tenant for life on his marriage to charge his estate with pin money for his wife, without clogging the subsequent exercise of his statutory powers by imposing on him the necessity of obtaining her consent. See Key & Elphinstone's Precedents, ii. 674, 3rd ed.

It will be observed that the section applies only to tenants for life and does not extend to "persons having the powers of a tenant for life."

Exchanges.

§ 5.

Creation of easements on exchange or partition.

5. On an exchange or partition any easement, right, or privilege of any kind may be reserved or may be granted over or in relation to the settled land or any part thereof, or other land or an easement, right, or privilege of any kind may be given or taken in exchange or on partition for land or for any other easement, right, or privilege of any kind.

See note to s. 20 of the Act of 1882 where this section is considered.

Completion of Contracts.

§ 6.

Power to complete predecessor's contract.

6. A tenant for life may make any conveyance which is necessary or proper for giving effect to a contract entered into by a predecessor in title, and which if made by such predecessor would have been valid as against his successors in title.

Where a lessee exercises an option of purchase conferred upon him in pursuance of the Act of 1889, after the death of the original tenant for life, any successor in title can by virtue of this section convey the settled land to the lessee. It seems open to question whether he could have done so without this express power. As to the powers of the principal Act there can be little doubt that, having regard to s. 31 (2), this enactment was unnecessary.

§ 6.

Leases.

7. A lease for a term not exceeding twenty-one years at the best rent that can be reasonably obtained without fine, and whereby the lessee is not exempted from punishment for waste, may be made by a tenant for life—

(i.) Without any notice of an intention to make the same having been given under section forty-five of the Act of 1882; and

(ii.) Notwithstanding that there are no trustees of the settlement for the purposes of the Settled Land Acts, 1882 to 1890; and

(iii.) By any writing under hand only containing an agreement instead of a covenant by the lessee for payment of rent in cases where the term does not extend beyond three years from the date of the writing.

§ 7. Provision as to leases for 21 years.

45 & 46 Vict. c. 38.

The words "whereby the lessee is not exempted from punishment for waste" introduce a very important qualification of the power conferred by this section, and render clause iii. almost if not wholly inoperative. If the proviso had been that the lessee should not be *expressly* exempted &c. or that he should not be exempted from punishment for *committing* waste, permissive waste would not have been included in the prohibition: see *Doe* v. *Bettison*, 12 East, 305; *Doe* v. *Stephens*, 6 Q. B. 208. But there appears to be nothing to limit the generality of the words: see *Yellowly* v. *Gower*, 11 Ex. 274. The lessee therefore must in all cases where this power is exercised covenant or agree to keep the premises in repair and no provision can be inserted whereby the commission or permission of waste is expressly or impliedly authorised. See Sugden on Powers, 788; 3 Dav. 504.

Waste.

8. In a mining lease—

(i.) The rent may be made to vary according to the price of the minerals or substances gotten, or any of them:

(ii.) Such price may be the saleable value, or the price

§ 8. Provision as to mining leases.

§ 8.

or value appearing in any trade or market or other price list or return from time to time, or may be the marketable value as ascertained in any manner prescribed by the lease (including a reference to arbitration), or may be an average of any such prices or values taken during a specified period.

See note to s. 9 of the Act of 1882, *ante*, p. 57.

§ 9.

Power to reserve a rentcharge on a grant in fee simple.

44 & 45 Vict. c. 41.

9. Where, on a grant for building purposes by a tenant for life, the land is expressed to be conveyed in fee simple with or subject to a reservation thereout of a perpetual rent or rentcharge, the reservation shall operate to create a rentcharge in fee simple issuing out of the land conveyed, and having incidental thereto all powers and remedies for recovery thereof conferred by section forty-four of the Conveyancing and Law of Property Act, 1881, and the rentcharge so created shall go and remain to the uses on the trusts and subject to the powers and provisions which, immediately before the conveyance, were subsisting with respect to the land out of which it is reserved.

This section does not confer on the tenant for life any power which he did not previously possess, it merely attaches the statutory powers and remedies to the rent-charge when it is reserved, and settles it by reference to the limitations of the settlement. See s. 10 of the Act of 1882, which provides that the Court may in special cases sanction such a grant. It will be observed that the section does not extend to a grant by a "person having the powers of a tenant for life," which seems to be a serious omission.

The better course would seem to be to reserve the rent-charge generally, as in the case of an ordinary lease, and thereupon by force of this statute the person entitled for the time being under the settlement to the receipt of the rent-charge will have all the remedies conferred by s. 44 of the Conveyancing Act. Those remedies are :—

(1.) If the rent-charge is in arrear for twenty-one days, to distrain.

(2.) If it is in arrear for forty days, to enter on the land and receive the profits thereof.

(3.) In the like case to limit a term to trustees upon trust by sale, mortgage or demise to raise and pay the rent-charge and all arrears thereof. §9.

It is usual in a grant of this description to insert a covenant by the purchaser to pay the rent-charge. There is nothing in this section to give the benefit of this covenant to the persons entitled from time to time to the rent-charge, and it should therefore be expressed to be entered into with " the tenant for life and his successors in title." The liability on such a covenant runs with the land so as to bind successive owners so long as they are in possession. *Thomas* v. *Sylvester,* L. R. 8 Q. B. 368; *Re Blackburn and District Benefit Building Society,* 42 Ch. D. 343; *Searle* v. *Cooke,* 43 Ch. D. 519.

Covenant for payment.

Mansion and Park.

10.—(1.) From and after the passing of this Act section fifteen of the Act of 1882, relating to the sale or leasing of the principal mansion house, shall be and the same is hereby repealed.

§ 10. Restriction on sale of mansion.

(2.) Notwithstanding anything contained in the Act of 1882, the principal mansion house (if any) on any settled land, and the pleasure grounds and park and lands (if any) usually occupied therewith, shall not be sold, exchanged, or leased by the tenant for life without the consent of the trustees of the settlement or an order of the Court.

(3.) Where a house is usually occupied as a farmhouse, or where the site of any house and the pleasure grounds and park and lands (if any) usually occupied therewith do not together exceed twenty-five acres in extent, the house is not to be deemed a principal mansion house within the meaning of this section.

See note to s. 15 of the Act of 1882, *ante,* p. 69.

The Raising of Money.

11.—(1.) Where money is required for the purpose of discharging an incumbrance on the settled land or part thereof, the tenant for life may raise the money so required, and also the amount properly required for payment of the

§ 11. Power to raise money by mortgage.

§ 11. costs of the transaction on mortgage of the settled land, or of any part thereof, by conveyance of the fee-simple or other estate or interest the subject of the settlement, or by creation of a term of years in the settled land, or any part thereof, or otherwise, and the money so raised shall be capital money for that purpose, and may be paid or applied accordingly.

(2.) Incumbrance in this section does not include any annual sum payable only during a life or lives or during a term of years absolute or determinable.

Incumbrance on the settled land.

"Settled land" is defined by s. 2 (3) of the Act of 1882 to be "land and any estate or interest therein which is the subject of settlement," and it would, therefore, seem reasonably clear that the words "incumbrance on the settled land" do not include a mortgage or charge having priority to the settlement. In other words, when an equity of redemption is the subject of a settlement, there is no power under this section to raise money for the discharge of the paramount mortgage. The terms of s. 20 of the Act of 1882, which defines the effect and operation of the mortgage deed, support this view; for the deed is only effectual to pass the land conveyed subject to and with the exception of all estates, interests, and charges having priority to the settlement.

Power of mortgaging.

The tenant for life has, under the Act of 1882, power to raise money on mortgage only for enfranchisement, or for equality of exchange or partition, s. 18. Compare with this section the provisions of s. 5 of the Act of 1882, enabling the tenant for life to transfer an incumbrance from one part of the settled land to another. As all the Settled Land Acts are to be "read and construed together as one Act" (Act of 1890, s. 2), it seems that the power here conferred on the tenant for life may be exercised by any of the persons having the powers of a tenant for life under s. 58 of the Act of 1882; and that the protection afforded to mortgagees by s. 40 of that Act extends to a mortgagee advancing money under this section.

Capital money.

The money raised being capital money must be paid either to the trustees of the settlement or into Court (Act of 1882, s. 22 (1)); and subject to its application for the special purpose hereby authorized may be invested or applied in any of the modes specified in s. 21 of the same Act.

Form of mortgage.

The tenant for life will, in general, have to enter into a personal covenant for the payment of the money to be raised; and in such a case a clause should be inserted in the mortgage providing that as between the tenant for life and his estate on the one hand, and the settled land on the other, the latter should be primarily liable for the payment of the mortgage debt. §11.

Dealings as between Tenant for Life and the Estate.

12. Where a sale of settled land is to be made to the tenant for life, or a purchase is to be made from him of land to be made subject to the limitations of the settlement, or an exchange is to be made with him of settled land for other land, or a partition is to be made with him of land an undivided share whereof is subject to the limitations of the settlement, the trustees of the settlement shall stand in the place of and represent the tenant for life, and shall, in addition to their powers as trustees, have all the powers of the tenant for life in reference to negotiating and completing the transaction. §12. Provision enabling dealings with tenant for life.

Before the Settled Land Act came into operation the powers thereby conferred upon the tenant for life were generally vested in trustees, who were free to deal with the tenant for life as if he were a stranger. Such express powers are now seldom given to trustees, and inconvenience was in some cases caused by the absence of any power to carry out transactions between the tenant for life and the estate. This is now rectified by putting the trustees of the settlement in the place of the tenant for life when the transaction takes place between him in the character of tenant for life, and him as a party outside the settlement. Tenant for life and trustees.

The trustees take the powers of the tenant for life so far as they may be required for negotiating and completing the transaction. Thus, for example, if a sale of a piece of the settled land is to be made to the tenant for life, the trustees will be able to convey the land and to receive the purchase-money, but when it has been received the powers of the tenant for life again vest in him, and he can prescribe the manner in which the money is to be invested or applied by the trustees.

This section has not been extended to any other limited owners besides the tenant for life; and as it does not confer any power upon him, s. 58 of the Act of 1882 has no application. Other limited owners.

Application of Capital Money.

13. Improvements authorized by the Act of 1882 shall include the following; namely, §13. Application

§ 13.
of capital money.

(i.) Bridges;
(ii.) Making any additions to or alterations in buildings reasonably necessary or proper to enable the same to be let;
(iii.) Erection of buildings in substitution for buildings within an urban sanitary district taken by a local or other public authority, or for buildings taken under compulsory powers, but so that no more money be expended than the amount received for the buildings taken and the site thereof;
(iv.) The rebuilding of the principal mansion house on the settled land : Provided that the sum to be applied under this sub-section shall not exceed one-half of the annual rental of the settled land.

See note to s. 25 of the Act of 1882, where this section is considered.

§ 14.
Capital money in Court may be paid out to trustees.

14. All or any part of any capital money paid into Court may, if the Court thinks fit, be at any time paid out to the trustees of the settlement for the purposes of the Settled Land Acts, 1882 to 1890.

This section reverses the decision in *Cookes* v. *Cookes*, 34 Ch. D. 498. See s. 32 of the Act of 1882, which relates to money in Court under the Lands Clauses Consolidation Acts, and the note thereto.

§ 15.
Court may order payment for improvements executed.

15. The Court may, in any case where it appears proper, make an order directing or authorizing capital money to be applied in or towards payment for any improvement authorized by the Settled Land Acts, 1882 to 1890, notwithstanding that a scheme was not, before the execution of the improvement, submitted for approval, as required by the Act of 1882, to the trustees of the settlement or to the Court.

Like the preceding section, this is the legislative reversal of a judicial decision. See *Re Hotchkin's Settled Estates*, 35 Ch. D. 41. See also note 26 of the Act of 1882, where it is pointed out that the present section does not authorize the trustees of the settlement to apply capital money without having a scheme submitted for the execution of the improvement before the work was commenced.

§ 15.

Trustees.

16. Where there are for the time being no trustees of the settlement within the meaning and for the purposes of the Act of 1882, then the following persons shall, for the purposes of the Settled Land Acts, 1882 to 1890, be trustees of the settlement; namely,

§ 16.

Trustees for the purposes of the Act.

> (i.) The persons (if any) who are for the time being under the settlement trustees, with power of or upon trust for sale of any other land comprised in the settlement and subject to the same limitations as the land to be sold, or with power of consent to or approval of the exercise of such a power of sale, or, if there be no such persons, then
>
> (ii.) The persons (if any) who are for the time being under the settlement trustees with future power of sale, or under a future trust for sale of the land to be sold, or with power of consent to or approval of the exercise of such a future power of sale, and whether the power or trust takes effect in all events or not.

It is difficult to see how two pieces of land, one held upon trust for sale, the other not so held, can be subject to the same limitations, yet this is implied in sub-s. i. There is, however, no similar difficulty in the case of a *power* of sale. The whole estate may be settled together, but part of it may be excluded from the power of sale; and in that case, which but rarely occurs, the trustees are by this section trustees of the settlement for the whole, and not merely for that part subject to the power.

Trust for sale of other land.

The second sub-section deals with a much more common case, viz., where there is a future power of, or trust for sale, as, for example, a devise to trustees upon trust for the testator's widow during her life, and on her death upon trust to sell and divide the proceeds between his children. In such a case the trustees would be under this section trustees of the settlement during the lifetime of the widow.

Future power of sale.

§ 16.

The position of the trustees referred to in this section depends on whether there are other trustees of the settlement in existence or not; and it is clear that they may at any time be displaced by an appointment of trustees under s. 38 of the Act of 1882, or under the next succeeding section of this Act where it is applicable.

The personal representatives of the last surviving or continuing trustees appointed by the Court are, under s. 38 (2) of the Act of 1882, declared to be trustees of the settlement "until the appointment of new trustees;" and it is conceived that the existence of such personal representatives in the case that has been put excludes the operation of the present section.

"Land to be sold."

The words in this section "the land to be sold" create a difficulty, and it has been suggested that they limit the section to cases of contemplated sale. See 34 Sol. Journ., p. 812. It is submitted, however, that this is not so, for the trustees of the settlement if they are appointed at all exist for all the purposes of the Act, and it would be unreasonable to construe the words "to be sold" as importing a condition precedent to the appointment of the trustees, when they may be read as words of mere description, to indicate the land which may require to be sold, but which is not saleable under the powers of the settlement.

§ 17.

Application of provisions of 44 & 45 Vict. c. 41, as to appointment of trustees.

17.—(1.) All the powers and provisions contained in the Conveyancing and Law of Property Act, 1881, with reference to the appointment of new trustees, and the discharge and retirement of trustees, are to apply to and include trustees for the purposes of the Settled Land Acts, 1882 to 1890, whether appointed by the Court or by the settlement, or under provisions contained in the settlement.

(2.) This section applies and is to have effect with respect to an appointment or a discharge and retirement of trustees taking place before as well as after the passing of this Act.

(3.) This section is not to render invalid or prejudice any appointment or any discharge and retirement of trustees effected before the passing of this Act otherwise than under the provisions of the Conveyancing and Law of Property Act, 1881.

See note to s. 38 of the Act of 1882, p. 130, where this section is discussed.

18. The provisions of section eleven of the Housing of the Working Classes Act, 1885, and of any enactment which may be substituted therefor, shall have effect as if the expression "working classes" included all classes of persons who earn their livelihood by wages or salaries: Provided that this section shall apply only to buildings of a rateable value not exceeding one hundred pounds per annum.

§ 18.

Extension of meaning of "working classes" in 48 & 49 Vict. c. 72.

By the Housing of the Working Classes Act, 1890 (53 & 54 Vict. c. 70), which received the royal assent on the same day as the Settled Land Act of that year, the Housing of the Working Classes Act, 1885, was repealed, and s. 74 of the later Act was in effect substituted for s. 11 of the previous Act, and was thus amended by this section from the first moment of its existence. Section 74 of the Housing of the Working Classes Act, 1890, so far as it relates to the Settled Land Act, is in the following terms:—

"74. (1). The Settled Land Act, 1882, shall be amended as follows:—

(*a.*) Any sale, exchange, or lease of land in pursuance of the said Act when made for the purpose of the erection on such land of dwellings for the working classes may be made at such price, or for such consideration, or for such rent, as, having regard to the said purpose, and to all the circumstances of the case, is the best that can be reasonably obtained, notwithstanding that a higher price, consideration, or rent might have been obtained if the land were sold, exchanged or leased for another purpose.

(*b.*) The improvements on which capital money may be expended, enumerated in section twenty-five of the said Act, and referred to in section thirty of the said Act, shall, in addition to cottages for labourers, farm servants and artizans, whether employed on the settled land or not, include any dwellings available for the working classes the building of which in the opinion of the Court is not injurious to the estate."

It is conceived that the "rateable value" mentioned in s. 18, *supra*, is that of the land with the buildings thereon; and that the proviso fixes the limit of £100 rateable value only with reference to the better class of workers introduced by this section. As regards the "working classes" properly so called there is no such limit.

19. The registration of a writ or order affecting land

Power to vacate

§ 19.
registration of writ.

may be vacated pursuant to an order of the High Court or any judge thereof.

This section is an Amendment of the Land Charges Registration and Searches Act, 1888 (51 & 52 Vict. c. 51), and provides for the difficulty experienced in *Cook* v. *Cook*, 38 W. R. 656.

RULES.

RULES UNDER THE SETTLED LAND ACT, 1882.

1. The expression "the Act" used in these rules means the Settled Land Act, 1882.

Words defined by the Act when used in these rules have the same meanings as in the Act.

The expression "the tenant for life" includes the tenant for life as defined by the Act, and any person having the powers of a tenant for life under the Act.

2. All applications to the Court under the Act may be made by summons in chambers; and if in any case a petition shall be presented without the direction of the judge, no further costs shall be allowed than would be allowed upon a summons.

3. The forms in the Appendix to these Rules are to be followed as far as possible, with such modification as the circumstances require. All summonses, petitions, affidavits, and other proceedings under the Act are to be entitled according to Form I. in the Appendix.

See the Practice Master's Rules (4) and the Appendix of Titles of Petitions, Summons, &c., annexed thereto, Example 9. Annual Practice, Part V.

The application need not be entitled in a suit for the administration of the trusts of the settlement, or in a suit concerning the interests of the parties, if the objects of such suit have been effected, and it is to be regarded as spent. *Re Parry*, W. N. 1884, 43.

4. The persons to be served with notice of applications to the Court shall, in the first instance, be as follows:—

In the case of applications by the tenant for life under sections 15 and 34, the trustees.

In the case of applications under section 38, the trustees (if any), and the tenant for life if not the applicant.

In the case of applications under section 44, the tenant for life, or the trustees, as the case may be.

No other person shall in the first instance be served. Except as hereinbefore provided where an application under the Act is made by any person other than the tenant for life, the tenant for life alone shall be served in the first instance.

For s. 15, referred to in this rule, must now be read s. 10 of the Act of 1890.

Section 46 (4) provides that on an application by the trustees of a settlement notice shall be served in the first instance on the tenant for life.

The result of this enactment and of the above rule is that:

(1.) The tenant for life must always be before the Court. If he is not the applicant he should be served.

(2.) The trustees of the settlement, who are, it is conceived, referred to as "the trustees," must be served in the case of applications by the tenant for life, under ss. 34, and 44, or s. 10 of the Act of 1890; and in the case of all applications under s. 38, whether by the tenant for life or others, if there are any trustees of the settlement.

(3.) No other person is to be served except by the direction of the Court under s. 46 (5).

. The terms of this rule indicate that if there are no trustees of a settlement, new trustees must be appointed before an application can be made under s. 34 or s. 10 of the Act of 1890. It will be noticed however that applications by the tenant for life under s. 35, for the cutting and sale of timber, which may be made either to the trustees or the Court, are not referred to in this rule.

Applications under s. 62 are governed by the Rules in Lunacy, 1890, and should be made by summons at chambers before a master (r. 16). See as to summonses rr. 93—100, and schedule thereto, Form X.

On an application by the committee of a lunatic under s. 62, where there were no trustees of the settlement, the Court directed them to be appointed and notice of the application to be served upon them: *Re Taylor*, 31 W. R. 596.

5. Except in the cases mentioned in the last rule, applications by a tenant for life shall not in the first instance be served on any person.

For a list of the applications which may be made to the Court, see *ante*, p. 12. Where the tenant for life is an infant, the persons authorized to exercise the powers of the Act on his behalf (s. 60) constitute the tenant for life within the meaning of this rule. Notice of any application by them should therefore not be served on the infant, although in all other cases this should be done.

6. The judge may require notice of any application under the Act to be served upon such persons as he thinks fit, and may give all necessary directions as to the persons (if any) to be served, and such directions may be added to or varied from time to time as the case may require. Where a petition is presented, the petitioner may, after the petition has been filed, apply by summons in chambers (Appendix, Form XXIII.) for directions with regard to the persons on whom the petition ought to be served. If any person not already served is directed to be served with notice of an application, the application shall stand over generally, or until such time as the judge directs. The judge may in any particular case, upon such terms (if any) as he thinks fit, dispense with service upon any person upon whom, under these rules, or under any direction of the judge, any application is to be served.

This rule repeats the statutory provision, s. 46 (5), that on any application notice shall be served on such persons, if any, as the Court thinks fit.

7. It shall be sufficient upon any application under the Act to verify by affidavit the title of the tenant for life and trustees or other persons interested in the application unless the judge in any particular case requires further evidence. Such affidavit may be in the form or to the effect of Form No. VIII. in the Appendix.

This rule and Form VIII. seem to imply that the evidence should be confined to an affidavit, which may be made by the tenant for life, stating that A. B. is tenant for life, and that C. D. and E. F. are trustees of the settlement, without noticing intermediate events on which the devolution of title may depend. Deaths of previous limited owners, marriages, births of children, and other facts may thus be ignored. Where however there are no trustees of the settlement, it should be so stated in the affidavit.

8. Any sale authorised or directed by the Court under the Act, shall be carried into effect out of Court, unless the judge shall otherwise order, and generally in such manner as the judge may direct.

<small>The cases in which the Court may authorize or direct a sale under the Act are : (1) The sale of the principal Mansion House, Act of 1890, s. 10; (2) The sale of timber, s. 35; (3) The sale of heirlooms, s. 37; and (4) A sale for payment of costs, s. 47.

On an application in an action for the appointment of trustees of the settlement with a view to a sale of an infant's land under ss. 59, 60, the Court authorized the trustees to sell out of Court : *Re Price*, 27 Ch. D. 552. Compare R. S. C. 1883, Ord. LI. r. 1 A.</small>

9. Where the Court authorises generally the tenant for life to make from time to time leases or grants for building or mining purposes under section 10 of the Act, the order shall not direct any particular lease or grant to be settled or approved by the judge unless the judge shall consider that there is some special reason why such lease or grant should be settled or approved by him. Where the Court authorises any such lease or grant in any particular case, or where the Court authorises a lease under section 15 of the Act, the order may either approve a lease or grant already prepared or may direct that the lease or grant shall contain conditions specified in the order or such conditions as may be approved by the judge at chambers without directing the lease or grant to be settled by the judge.

10. Any person directed by the tenant for life to pay into Court any capital money arising under the Act may apply by summons at chambers for leave to pay the money into Court. (Appendix, Forms IX., X., XI.)

11. The summons shall be supported by an affidavit setting forth—

1. The name and address of the person desiring to make the payment.
2. The place where he is to be served with notice of any proceeding relating to the money.
3. The amount of money to be paid into Court and the account to the credit of which it is to be placed.

4. The name and address of the tenant for life under the settlement by whose direction the money is to be paid into Court.

5. The short particulars of the transaction in respect of which the money is payable.

Section 22 of the Act confers upon the tenant for life an option as to whether capital money shall be paid to the trustees or into Court. If he adopt the latter alternative, the purchaser must take out a summons for leave to obey that direction.

12. The order made upon the summons for payment into Court, may contain directions for investment of the money on any securities authorised by section 21, sub-section 1 of the Act, and for payment of the dividends to the tenant for life, either forthwith or upon production of the consent in writing of the applicant; the signature to such consent to be verified by the affidavit of a solicitor. But if the transaction in respect of which the money arises, is not completed at the date of payment into Court, the money shall not, without the consent of the applicant, be ordered to be invested in any securities other than those upon which cash under the control of the Court may be invested.

This rule seems to ignore s. 22 (3), *ante*, p. 92, which enacts that "the investment or other application under the direction of the Court shall be made on the application of the tenant for life or of the trustees." It may also be observed that, so far as the rule authorises any delay in the investment of the money, or any withholding of the dividends from the tenant for life, it contradicts the provisions of the same section, which require that capital money "*shall* be invested," sub-s. (1), and that the income of the securities *shall* be paid or applied as the income of the land, if not disposed of, would have been payable and applicable under the settlement: sub-s. (6).

Until the transaction is completed, there is no "capital money" which can be paid into Court, and once the capital money arises under the Act, it replaces the land to all intents and purposes.

13. Money paid into Court under the Act shall be paid to an account, to be entitled in the matter of the settlement, with a short description of the mode in which the money arises if it is necessary or desirable to identify it, and in the matter of the Act. (Appendix, Forms IX., X., and XI.)

The cases in which it is "necessary or desirable" to identify the money paid into Court are those in which the nature of the property affects the interests of the successive beneficiaries. Thus money arising from the sale of a lease or reversion (s. 34), or from the sale of personal chattels (s. 37), ought to be paid to an account indicating the source whence it arises.

14. Any person paying into Court any capital money arising under the Act shall be entitled first to deduct the costs of paying the money into Court.

The tenant for life can require the purchaser to pay his purchase money to the trustees and not into Court (s. 22); and if the purchaser unreasonably insists upon paying the money into Court he ought not to be allowed the costs occasioned thereby. A person, however, who is *not* directed by the tenant for life to pay the money into Court, would seem to have no right under r. 10 to apply for an order; and without an order it is presumed that the money will not be received.

15. In all cases not provided for by the Act or these rules, the existing practice of the Court as to costs and otherwise, so far as the same may be applicable, shall apply to proceedings under the Act.

16. The fees and allowances to Solicitors of the Court in respect to proceedings under the Act shall be those provided by the Rules of the Supreme Court as to costs for the time being in force, so far as they are applicable to such proceedings.

17. The fees to be taken by the officers of the Court in respect to proceedings under the Act shall be those provided by the Rules of the Supreme Court as to Court fees for the time being in force, so far as they are applicable to such proceedings.

18. These rules shall come into operation from and after the 31st December, 1882.

19. These rules may be cited as the Settled Land Act Rules, 1882.

(Signed) SELBORNE, C.   NATH. LINDLEY, L.J.
COLERIDGE, L.C.J.   H. MANISTY, J.
G. JESSEL, M.R.   E. FRY, J.

APPENDIX.

Form I.*

Title of Proceedings.

In the High Court of Justice,
    Chancery Division,
        Vice-Chancellor Bacon,
            or
        Mr. Justice Chitty,
[*or other judge before whom the application is to be heard.*]

In the matter of the   estate [*or*, of the timber upon the estate], situate at   in the county of   [*or*, of the chattels], settled by a settlement made by an indenture dated the   day of   , and made between [*or*, by the Will of   dated   *or, as the case may be*].
And in the matter of the Settled Land Act, 1882.

Form II.

Formal part of Summons.

Title as in Form I.

Let all parties concerned attend at my chambers at the Royal Courts of Justice on   day, the   day of   18 , at   o'clock in the forenoon, on the hearing of an application—

(*a.*) On the part of *A.B.*, the tenant for life [*or*, tenant in tail, [*or as the case may be, describing the nature of the applicant's estate*] under the above-mentioned settlement.

Or, (*b.*) On the part of *A.B.*, the tenant for life (*or as the case*

---

* See r. 3, p. 201, and the note thereto. For additional Forms under the Acts, see Marcy and Dodd on Originating Summons, p. 418 *et seq.*

may be) under the above-mentioned settlement an infant, by *X.Y.*, his testamentary guardian [*or*, guardian appointed by order dated the   , or, next friend].

Or, (*c.*) On the part of *C.D.*, and *E.F.*, the trustees of the above-mentioned settlement for the purposes of the above-mentioned Act.

Or, (*d.*) On the part of *G.H.*, the tenant for life in remainder [*or*, tenant in tail in remainder, *or as the case may be, describing the applicant's interest*] under the above-mentioned settlement subject to the life interest of *A.B.*, [*or as the case may be*].

Or, (*e.*) On the part of *I.J.*, the purchaser of the lands [*or*, the timber upon the lands *or* chattels, *or as the case may be*] settled by the above-mentioned settlement.

Or, (*f.*) On the part of *I.J.*, the lessee under a mining lease dated the   18   , granted under the powers of the above-mentioned Act of the mines and minerals under the lands settled by the above-mentioned settlement.

Or, (*g.*) On the part of *I.J.*, the mortgagee under a mortgage intended to be created under section 18 of the above-mentioned Act of the lands settled by the above-mentioned settlement.

Or, (*h.*) On the part of *K.L.*, interested under the contract hereinafter mentioned.

Dated the   day of   18 .

This summons was taken out by   of   , solicitor for the applicant.

To

(*Add the names of the persons (if any) on whom the summons is to be served.*)

Form III.

Summons under Section 10 for General Leasing Powers.

Title and formal parts as in Forms I. and II. *a.* or *b.*

1. That the applicant [*or in the case of an infant* that the said *X.Y.*, during the infancy of the said *A.B.*], and each of his successors in title [*or in the case of an infant*, each of the successors in title of the said *A.B.*,], being a tenant for life or having the powers of a tenant for life under the above-mentioned Act, may pursuant to section 10 of the said Act be authorised from time to time to make building [*or* mining] leases of the lands comprised in the said settlement for the term of   years [*or* in

perpetuity] on the conditions specified in the said Act [*or* on other conditions than those specified in sections 7 to 9 of the said Act].

2. That the costs of this application may be directed to be taxed as between solicitor and client, and that the same when taxed may be paid out of the property subject to the said settlement, and that for that purpose all necessary directions may be given.

Note.—The proposed conditions ought not, except in simple cases, to be set forth in the summons.

Form IV.

Summons under Sections 10 *or* 15 *for Authority to grant a particular lease where the Tenant for Life has entered into a contract.*

Title as in Form I.

Formal parts as in Form II. *a* or *b*.

1. That the conditional contract, dated the   18   , and made between the applicant [*or* the said *X.Y.*] of the one part and   of the other part, for a [building *or* mining] lease to the said   of the hereditaments therein mentioned for the term, and upon the conditions therein stated, may, pursuant to section 10 [*or* 15] of the above-mentioned Act be approved, and that the said *A.B.* [*or X.Y.*] may be authorised to execute a lease in pursuance of the said contract.

2. (*Add application for costs as in Form III.* 2.)

Form V.

Summons under Sections 10 *or* 15 *for Authority to grant a particular Lease when no Contract has been entered into.*

Title as in Form I.

Formal parts as in Form II. *a* or *b*.

1. That the [building *or* mining] lease intended to be granted to   of the lands [*or* of the mansion house, &c.] settled by

p 2

the said settlement may, pursuant to section 10 [*or* 15] of the above-mentioned Act be approved, and that the applicant [*or* the said *X.Y*] may be authorised to execute the same.

2. (*Add application for costs as in Form III*. 2.)

Form VI.*

Summons under Sections 15, 35, *or* 37 *for a Sale out of Court of the principal Mansion House, and Demesnes, or of Timber or Chattels.*

Title as in Form I.

Formal parts as in Form II. *a* or *b*.

1. That the applicant [*or in the case of an infant* the said *X.Y.*] may be authorised to sell the principal mansion house [*or* the timber ripe and fit for cutting] on the land [*or* the furniture and chattels] settled by the above-mentioned settlement in such manner and subject to such particulars, conditions, and provisions as he may think fit.

2. That the costs of this application may be taxed as between solicitor and client, and that *C.D.* and *E.F.*, the trustees of the said settlement, may be at liberty to pay the costs when taxed out of the proceeds of the said sale [*or, in case of timber*, out of the three-fourths of the proceeds of the said sale to be set aside as capital money arising under the said Act], *or if this form is not applicable as in Form III*. 2.

Form VII.

Summons under Sections 15, 35, *or* 37 *for Sale by the Court* † *of the principal Mansion House, and Demesnes, or of Timber or Chattels.*

Title as in Form I.

Formal parts as in Form II. *a* or *b*.

1. That the principal mansion house [*or* the timber ripe and fit for cutting] on the land [*or* the furniture and chattels], settled by

---

* The Forms relating to s. 15 of the Act of 1882 should be adapted, if necessary, to suit the slightly altered language of s. 10 of the Act of 1890.

† See r. 8, *ante*, p. 206.

the above-mentioned settlement, may be sold under the direction of the Court.

2. (*Application for costs as in Form III. 2.*)

Form VIII.

*Affidavit verifying Title.**

Title as in Form I.

I   of   make oath and say as follows :

1. By the above-mentioned settlement the above-mentioned lands [*or* certain chattels, *shortly describing them*] stand limited to uses [*or* upon trusts] under which *A.B.* is [*or* I am] beneficially entitled in possession as tenant for life [*or* tenant in tail *or* tenant in fee simple, with an executory gift over, *or as the case may be*].

2. (*If it is the fact.*) The said *A.B.* is an infant of the age of   years or thereabouts.

3. *C.D.* of   and *E.F.* of   are Trustees under the said settlement, with a power of sale of the said lands [*or* with power of consent to or approval of the exercise of a power of sale of the said lands contained in the said settlement, *or* are the persons by the said settlement declared to be Trustees thereof for purposes of the above-mentioned Act].

Form IX.

Summons under Section 22 by Purchaser for Payment into Court of Purchase Money of Settled Land, Timber, or Chattels.†

Title as in Form I.

Formal parts as in Form II. *e.*

1. That the applicant may be at liberty to pay into court to the credit of " In the matter of the settlement, dated the   and " made between   [*or* will, &c.] proceeds of sale of the " A. estate [*or as the case may be*], and in the matter of the Settled " Land Act, 1882," the sum of £   on account of the purchase money of the said A. estate (*or as the case may be*) settled by the said settlement [*or* will, &c.]

---

* See r. 7, p. 205.
† See r. 10, p. 206, and r. 13, p. 207.

2. That such directions may be given for the investment of the said sums when paid into Court, and the accumulation or payment of the dividends of the securities, representing the same as the Court may think proper.

Form X.

Summons under Section 22 for Payment into Court by Lessee under a Mining Lease (see Section 11).*

Title as in Form I.

Formal parts as in Form II. *f.*

1. That the applicant may be at liberty to pay into Court to the credit of " In the matter of the settlement dated the " and made between   [*or* the will, &c.] mineral rents " under lease dated the   and in the matter of the Settled " Land Act, 1882," the sum of £   being three-fourths [*or* one-fourth] of the rents payable by him under the said lease for the half-year ending the   less £   the costs of payment into Court.

2. That the applicant may be at liberty on or before the   day of   and the   day of   in every year during the term created by the said lease,† to pay into Court to the credit aforesaid, so much of the rents payable by him under the said lease as is by section 11 of the above-mentioned Act directed to be set aside as capital money arising under the said Act after deducting therefrom the costs of payment in, the amount paid in to be verified by affidavit.

3. That the said sum of £   and all other sums to be paid into Court to the credit aforesaid may be invested in the purchase of (*name the investment*) to the like credit, and that the dividends on the said   when purchased may be paid to A. B., the tenant for life under the above-mentioned settlement, during his life or until further order.

---

* See r. 10, p. 206, and r. 13, p. 207.

† Each periodical payment is capital money, and must be paid to the trustees or into Court at the option of the tenant for life for the time being. The order as to future payments should therefore be qualified by the insertion of the words, "during the life of the said A. B."

Form XI.

Summons under Section 22 for payment into Court by Mortgagee (see Section 18).*

Title as in Form I.

Formal parts as in Form II. *g*.

1. That the applicant may be at liberty to pay into Court to the credit of " Money advanced on mortgage of lands settled by " the settlement dated the   and made between "[*or* the will, &c.] and in the matter of the Settled Land Act, " 1882," the sum of £   being the amount agreed to be advanced by him on mortgage of the lands comprised in the above-mentioned settlement less the costs of payment in.

2. (*Add directions for investment as in Form VIII. 2.*) †

Form XII.

Summons under Section 26 (1).

Title as in Form I.

Formal parts as in Form II. *a* or *b*.

1. That the scheme left at my chambers this day for the execution of improvements on the lands settled by the above-mentioned settlement may be approved.

2. (*Add application for costs as in Form III. 2.*)

Form XIII.

Summons under Section 26, Sub-section (2) (ii.) for Appointment of an Engineer or Surveyor.

Title as in Form I.

Formal parts as in Form II. *a* or *b*.

1. That *M. N.* of   Engineer [*or* surveyor] may be

---

* See r. 10, p. 206, and r. 13, p. 207.

† For VIII. read IX. As money can be raised on mortgage under s. 18 only for special purposes, the directions for investment seem to be scarcely necessary.

approved as engineer [*or* surveyor] for the purposes of section 26, sub-section (2) (ii.) of the above-mentioned Act.

2. (*Add application for costs as in Form III. 2.*)

Form XIV.

Nomination of an Engineer or Surveyor by the Trustees.

Title as in Form I.

We *C. D.* of   , and *E. F.* of   the trustees of the above-mentioned settlement for the purposes of the above-mentioned Act, hereby nominate   of   Engineer, [*or* surveyor], for the purposes of section 26, sub-section (2) (ii.) of the said Act.

(Signed)   *C. D.*
           E. F.

Form XV.

Summons under Section 26, Sub-section (2) (iii.).

Title as in Form I.

Formal parts as in Form II. *a* or *b.*

1. That *C. D.* and *E. F.* the trustees of the above-mentioned settlement, for the purposes of the above-mentioned Act may be directed to apply the sum of £   out of the capital money arising under the said Act in their hands subject to the said settlement in payment for [*describe the work or operation*] being [*part of*] an improvement executed upon the lands subject to the said settlement pursuant to a scheme approved by the said *C. D.* and *E. F.* under the said Act.

2. (*Add application for costs as in Form III. 2.*)

Form XVI.

Summons under Section 26, Sub-section 3.

Title as in Form I.

Formal parts as in Form II. *a* or *b*.

1. That the sum of £   may be ordered to be raised out of the   in Court to the credit of   and that the same when raised may be paid to   upon his undertaking to apply the same in payment for [*describe the works or operation*] being part of an improvement executed upon the land settled by the above-mentioned settlement pursuant to the scheme approved by Order dated the

2. (*Add application for costs as in Form III. 2.*)

Form XVII.

Summons under Section 31.

Title as in Form I.

Formal parts as in Form II. *a* or *b*.

1. That the applicant may be at liberty to enforce [*or* carry into effect *or* vary *or* rescind *as the case may be*] the contract entered into between the applicant of the one part, and   of the other part.

2. Or that such directions may be given relating to the said contract as the judge may think fit.

3. (*Add application for costs as in Form III. 2.*)

Form XVIII.

Summons under Section 34 for application of Money paid for a Lease or Reversion.

Title as in Form I.

Formal parts as in Form II., *a*, *b*, or *d*.

1. That the sum of £   being the proceeds of sale of a lease for years [*or* life *or* a reversion *or other interest describ-*

ing it] settled by the above-mentioned settlement, may, pursuant to section 34 of the above-mentioned Act, be directed to be applied for the benefit of the parties interested under the said settlement in such manner as the Court may think fit.

2. (*Add application for costs as in Form III. 2.*)

Form XIX.

Summons under Section 38 for the Appointment of New Trustees.

Title as in Form I.

Formal parts as in Form II. *a, b, c,* or *d*.

1. That *G. H.* and *I. J.* may be appointed trustees under the above-mentioned settlement for the purposes of the above-mentioned Act.

2. (*Add application for costs as in Form III. 2.*)

Form XX.

Summons under Section 44.

Title as in Form I.

Formal parts as in Form II. *a, b,* or *c*.

1. That it may be declared that (*set out the declaration required*).

2. (*Add application for costs as in Form III. 2, or as the circumstances require.*)

Form XXI.

Summons under Section 56 for Advice and Direction.

Title as in Form I.

Formal parts in Form II., *a* to *h*.

For the opinion, advice, and direction of the Judge on the following questions :—

1. Whether
2. Whether
3. Whether
(*or if the questions involve complicated facts*)
for the opinion, advice, and direction of the Judge on the facts and questions submitted by the statement left in my chambers this day.

(*Add application for costs as in Form III. 2.*)

Form XXII.

Summons under Section 60 for Appointment of Persons to exercise Powers on behalf of Infant.

Title as in Form I.

Formal parts as in Form II. *b.*

1. That the powers conferred upon a tenant for life by sections 6 to 13, both inclusive, and sections 16 to 20, both inclusive, of the above-mentioned Act (*or such other powers as it is desired to exercise*) may be exercised by the said   on behalf of the said   during his minority.

2. (*Add application for costs as in Form III. 2.*)

Form XXIII.

Summons for Directions as to Service of a Petition.*

Title as in Form I.

Formal parts as in Form II.

That directions may be given as to the persons to be served with the petition presented in the above matter on the   day of   18 .

* See r. 6, *ante*, p. 205.

INDEX.

ACCUMULATION
  of income, trust for, does not prevent exercise of powers, 32, 41, 163
  for payment of debts, 152

ACKNOWLEDGMENT,
  exercise of powers by married women without, 171

ACREAGE,
  mining rent may vary with, 56

ACTION
  for protection or recovery of settled land, 125

ACTS AND DEFAULTS,
  each trustee liable only for his own, 134

ADDITIONAL OR LARGER POWERS
  may be conferred by the settlement, 158

ADMINISTRATORS
  of last surviving trustee "trustees of the settlement," 120

ADMITTANCE,
  right to, under statutory conveyance, 78
  fines and fees payable on, 81

ADVICE OF THE COURT
  as to powers in settlement, 156
  form of summons for, 218

AFFIDAVIT
  verifying title, form of, 213
      See EVIDENCE.

AGRICULTURAL HOLDINGS ACT, 1883
  effect of, on rent to be reserved, 53
  improvements authorized by, 101

AGRICULTURE, BOARD OF,
  functions of, 13
      See LAND COMMISSIONERS.

ALIENATION
  of mansion-house and park restricted, 8, 69, 195
  of heirlooms under an order of the Court, 127

AMENDMENTS
  of principal Act, 3

ANTICIPATION, RESTRAINT ON,
  not to prevent exercise of powers, 169

APPLICATION OF CAPITAL MONEY,
  tenant for life can in general direct, 15, 92
  various modes of, 15, 83, 86—91
  money in Court under other Acts, 118
  money in the hands of trustees liable to be invested in land, 120
  when arising from sale of lease or reversion, 122

APPLICATION TO THE COURT,
  summary of rules, 11
  when to be made, 11
  tabular list, 12
  costs of, 140
  notice of, on whom to be served, 140
  for advice or direction, 156
  for leave to exercise powers of s. 63, 184
        by whom to be made, 185
  service of, rules as to, 203, 204
  notice of, order as to, 205
  evidence on, 205

APPOINTMENT
  of trustees of the settlement by the Court, 10, 129
              under the Conv. Act, 130, 200
              summons for, 130, 218
  of persons to exercise powers on behalf of an infant, 107
              summons for, 219

APPORTIONMENT
  of rents,
     where land is contracted to be leased in lots, 54
     on surrender of part of the land leased, 66
  of conditions
     under the Conv. Act, 1881, 67
  of money paid for lease or reversion, 122
     form of summons for, 217

APPROVAL
  of scheme by trustees, or by the Court, 103
     form of summons for, 215
  of proceedings for protection or recovery of land, 125

INDEX.

ASSIGNEE
    cannot exercise powers of tenant for life, 146
    consent of, when required, 147

ASSIGNMENT OF LIFE INTEREST,
    when deemed part of settlement, 27, 190
    grant of leases by tenant for life after, 147
    powers exerciseable after, 147

AUCTION,
    tenant for life may sell by, 44
                         fix reserve biddings and buy in at, 44

BANKER,
    trustee not liable for default of, 134

BARONETCY
    is "land" for purposes of the Act, 5, 127
    heirlooms attached to, 127

BASE FEE,
    person entitled to, a "limited owner," 159
    definition of, 162

"BEST PRICE,"
    sale to be made at, 44
    how determined, 45
    on sale for working-classes' dwellings, 46, 201
    purchaser to be deemed to have given, 154

"BEST RENT"
    to be reserved on lease, 51
    whether reserved a question for the jury, 52
    value of surrendered lease may be taken into account, 53
    in lease under Agricultural Holdings Act, 53
    in lease for working-classes' dwellings, 53, 0
    lessee to be deemed to have given, 154

BIDDINGS,
    tenant for life may fix reserve, 44

BREACH OF TRUST,
    Act applies to land retained in, 36, 166
    sale amounting to, restrained, 40

BROKER,
    trustee not liable for default of, 134

BUILDING LEASE,
    definition of, 26
    void if no covenant to build, 52
    includes repairing lease, 55

BUILDING LEASE—*continued.*
    power to grant, 50
    regulations respecting, 54
    peppercorn may be reserved for first five years, 54
    in pursuance of building contract, 54
        apportionment of rent in, 56
    extent of ground which may be included in, 55
    stamp duty on, 55
    option of purchase in, 55, 189
    on special conditions under an order of the Court, 59
    dedication of land for streets and open spaces in connection with, 76

BUILDING PURPOSES,
    definition of, 26
    grant for, in consideration of fee farm rent, 194
        when to be settled by judge, 206

BUILDINGS,
    for farm purposes, an "authorized improvement," 99
    capital money not to be expended in repair of, 100

CALCULATION,
    matter of, statement in lease concerning, 51, 54

"CAPITAL MONEY ARISING UNDER THE ACT,"
    tabular statement of sources whence it arises, 14
    investment or application of, 14, 83—92, 197
        regulations respecting, 92
    definition of, 26
    summary of provisions of Act, as to, 35
    produced by sale of settled land, 40
            enfranchisement, 42
            equality money on exchange or partition, 43
            fines on leases, 53, 182
            setting aside part of mining rent, 60
            payment for licence, 68
            mortgage of settled land, 75, 196
            conversion of securities, 93
            consideration for varying contract, 114
            sale of timber, 124
                heirlooms, 126, 128
            price paid under option of purchase, 190
    payment of, to the trustees, or into Court, 92
    to be considered as land, 92
    improvements effected with, 98—103
    money in Court to be applied as, 118
    money in the hands of trustees to be applied as, 120
    sole trustee not to receive, 132
    payment of costs out of, 143

INDEX.

"CAPITAL MONEY ARISING UNDER THE ACT"—*continued.*
  special provisions as to, where settlement is by way of trust for sale, 174
  application of, in redemption of rentcharge, 187
  may be raised by mortgage, 196
  payment of, out of Court to trustees, 198
  application of, by Court without scheme, 198
  payment of, into Court, 206
  summons for application of, 216, 217

CERTIFICATE
  of Land Commissioners,
      of proper execution of improvements, 103
      as to maintenance and insurance of improvements, 106
      variation of, 107, 110
      to be filed in their office, 146
      office copies of, evidence, 146
  of steward, evidence of licence, 68
  of engineer or surveyor, authorizing payment for improvement, 106

CHARGES,
  transfer of, on sale, &c., 48, 97
  creation of, by deed, 77
  settled land conveyed subject to, 78
  may affect part only of settled land, 95
  conveyance to uses of settlement not to increase or multiply, 95
  purchased land, a substituted security for, 95, 97

CHATTELS
  cannot be entailed, 97
  sale of personal, under an order of the Court, 126

CHECKS UPON THE TENANT FOR LIFE
  for security of remainderman, 7
  as to alienation of principal mansion house, 69
  sale of timber, 124
    heirlooms, 126
        And see POWERS OF TENANT FOR LIFE.

CHIEF RENT,
  redemption of, with capital money, 84
        under Conv. Act, 1881, 88

COMMENCEMENT OF ACT, 24

COMMITTEE OF LUNATIC,
  exercise of powers by, 171

COMMON, RIGHTS OF,
  regrant of, on enfranchisement, 45
    whether necessary to secure, 48
  conveyance subject to, 78

C.S.L.A.

CONDITION,
   attempted imposition of, upon exercise of powers, void, 149
   as to residence, how far valid, 150

CONDITION OF RE-ENTRY,
   lease by tenant for life to contain, 51
   apportioned on surrender of part, 67

CONFIRMATION
   of void or voidable lease by tenant for life, 63, 65
      by acceptance of rent, 66
      by acts of remainderman, 65

CONFIRMATION OF SALES ACT,
   sale of land and minerals separately under, 74

CONFLICT
   between Settlement and Act, the latter to prevail, 155
   application to Court in cases of, 156

CONSENT
   of the trustees,
      to the alienation of the principal mansion house, 69, 195
         or pleasure grounds and park, 69, 195
      to the cutting and sale of timber, 124 *impeachable*
      indemnity in respect of giving, 135
   of tenant for life,
      to leases by trustees, 50
      to change of investment, 92
      to exercise of all powers, 155
      except under settlement by way of trust for sale, 183
      may be given by one of several, 183
      by trustees on behalf of infant, 157
   of assignee,
      to exercise of powers, 147

CONSIDERATION
   to be obtained on exchange or partition, 44
   for a building lease, 46, 54
   for a mining lease, 57
   payable on surrender of a lease, 66
   trustees indemnified as to, 135
   may be a fee farm rent, 194

CONSTRUCTIVE CONVERSION
   of capital money, 92
   except when it arises from sale of chattels, 128

CONTRACT,
   by tenant for life not to exercise powers, void, 22, 147
   defective lease operates as, 52

CONTRACT—*continued.*
    for lease, when equivalent to lease, 52
    leasing powers to give effect to, 63
    two classes of, binding on tenant for life, 64
    under power considered defective execution, 64
    power of tenant for life to enter into, 114
                      to vary or rescind, 114
    by tenant for life, binding on settled land, 115
                  enforceable against his successors, 115
                  directions of the Court as to, 115, 217
    preliminary, not part of title to lease, 115
    completion of, by tenant for life, 117, 192
    trustees not liable for adopting, 135
    notice of, to be given to the trustees, 137
    form of summons as to enforcing, 217

CONVERSION,
    constructive, of capital money into land, 92
    of investments into money, 93

CONVEYANCE,
    completion of sale, &c., by, 77
    of copyholds, 77, 81
        leaseholds, 77, 79
    operation of, under express power, 78
                    the statute, 79
    subject to charges, 78
    covenants for title in, 83
    how far trustees liable for form of, 135

CONVEYANCING ACTS, 1881, 1882. *See* TABLE OF STATUTES.

COPYHOLDS
    may be enfranchised by tenant for life, 38
    may be exchanged for freeholds and *vice versâ*, 43
    licences to grant leases of, 68
    forfeiture of, by unauthorized lease, 68
    vested in trustees may be conveyed by tenant for life, 77
    deed relating to, entry of, on court rolls, 78
    surrender of unnecessary, on statutory conveyance, 81
        fines and fees payable on, 81
    enfranchisement of, by means of capital money, 84
    investment of capital money in purchase of, 84
    purchased, how to be settled, 93

CORPUS,
    when costs payable out of, 143, 144

COSTS
    of mortgagees of tenant for life, 91, 153
    of defending action, 91

COSTS—continued.
    payable by company on re-investment, 120
    of "reference of differences to the Court," 137
    position of tenant for life as to, 153

COSTS, CHARGES AND EXPENSES,
    capital money may be applied in payment of, 85, 90
    of scheme for improvements, 91
    of elaborate survey disallowed, 91
    of proceedings for protection or recovery of settled land, 125
    discretion of Court as to, 140, 142
    how to be raised out of settled property, 143

COTTAGES
    for labourers and artizans, an "authorized improvement," 99

COUNTERPART OF LEASE
    to be executed by lessee, 51
    evidence against lessee, 53

COUNTY COUNCILS,
    investment on securities of, 86

COUNTY COURTS,
    jurisdiction of, under Settled Land Act, 11, 141
    actions in, against tenant for life, 110
    equitable jurisdiction of, 142
    powers of, in respect of capital money, 143
                    improvements, 143

COURT,
    applications to, when to be made, 12
    definition of, 27
    powers of, may be exercised by Palatine and County Courts, 38
    may authorize leases for any term or in perpetuity, 59
                alienation of principal mansion house, 69, 195
    delivery of title deeds, under order of, 82
    capital money may be paid into, 92
    approval of "scheme" by, 103
    payment for "improvements" when money is in, 104
    may give directions respecting contracts, 115, 117
    money in, under L. C. C. Acts, 118
    application by, of purchase-money paid for lease or reversion, 122
    cutting and sale of timber under order of, 124
    proceedings for protection or recovery of settled land, sanction of, 125
    sale of heirlooms under an order of, 127
                discretion as to, how exercised, 128
    appointment of trustees by, 129
    reference to, of differences between tenant for life and trustees, 137
                of question as to powers of settlement, 156

COURT—*continued.*
    matters to be assigned to Chancery Division of, 140
    payment into, exonerates payer, 140
    applications to, by petition or summons, 140
    may direct notice of application to be served on any person, 140
    discretion of, as to costs, 140
    directions by, as to raising costs, 143
    applications to, in cases of conflict, 156
    appointment by, of persons to exercise powers on behalf of infants, 167
    may give leave to exercise powers under s. 63, 185
    may order payment for improvements without scheme, 198

COURT ROLLS,
    licence to be entered on, 68
    statutory conveyance to be entered on, 78

COVENANT,
    restrictive, on sale, &c., 45, 47
        constructive notice of, binds assignee, 47
    by lessee for payment of rent, 51, 53
    to renew, lease to give effect to, 63
    for production, when to be inserted, 82

CROWN RENT,
    redemption of, with capital money, 84

CUMULATIVE,
    powers of the Act are, 155

CURTESY,
    tenant by the, a "limited owner," 160
    deemed an estate settled by the wife, 164

CUSTOMARY FREEHOLDS.—*See* COPYHOLDS.

CUSTOM OF THE COUNTRY,
    variation of building or mining lease to suit, 59

DAMAGES
    for default of tenant for life in maintaining improvements, 107
    for permissive waste, 108
    measure of, in action for non-repair, 111

DEBENTURES AND DEBENTURE STOCK
    of railway companies, investment in, 84

DEDICATION
    of settled land for squares, open spaces, &c., 71
    of roads must be gratuitous, 72
    of open space to the public is a charity, 73

DEED,
    leases to be by, 51
    except for terms not exceeding three years, 193
    conveyance by, under the Act, 77
        operation of, 77, 79
    relating to copyholds, to be entered on Court Rolls, 78

DEFECTIVE EXECUTION
    of leases aided by statute, 52

DEFENCE OF SETTLED LAND,
    proceedings for, 125

DEFINITIONS
    of terms in Settled Land Act, 1882, 24-27 35-38

DEPOSIT,
    whether capital money may be applied in paying,
    forfeited, is capital money, 115

DIFFERENCES
    may be referred to the Court, 137

DILAPIDATIONS,
    liability of tenant for life for, 107
    right of action in respect of, 110
    measure of damages in action for, 111

DISCHARGE FOR PURCHASE-MONEY,
    power of trustees to give, 133
    by payment into Court, 140

DOWER,
    leasing powers of tenant in, 50

DRAINAGE,
    redemption of rent-charge for, 87
    capital money may be expended in, 98

DURHAM, COUNTY PALATINE OF,
    concurrent jurisdiction of Courts in, 11, 38, 142

DUTY
    included in definition of "rent," 26
    is the proportion of ore delivered to lessor, 36
    no distress can be levied for, 58

EASEMENTS

included in definition of "land," 42
over settled land may be granted by tenant for life, 38, 42
creation of, on exchange or partition, 43, 80, 192
lease of, by tenant for life, 49
grant or reservation of, on separate dealings with mines and surface, 73
conveyance or creation of by deed, 77, 79
how to be made subject to settlement, 96

ENFRANCHISEMENT,

power of tenant for life, as to, 38, 42
money received for is capital money, 42
under power, how it operates, 42
general regulations as to, 45
effect of, upon commonable rights, 48
money required for, may be raised by mortgage, 75

ENGLAND,

settled land in, not to be exchanged for land out of, 45
includes Wales and Berwick-upon-Tweed, 94
purchase of land out of, restricted, 94

EQUALITY OF EXCHANGE OR PARTITION,

money for, may be paid or received, 38
    may be raised by mortgage, 75
capital money may be applied in payment for, 84

EVIDENCE,

lease is, of due execution of counterpart, 51
when counterpart of lease is, 53
furnished by statement in lease, 51, 54
of licence being entered on Court Rolls, 68
as to proper execution of works, 103, 104
office copies of certificates and reports to be, 146
to be adduced on application to the Court, 205
    on payment of money into Court, 20
form of affidavit, 213

EXCEPTION,

of mines on sale, &c., of surface, 73

EXCHANGE,

power of tenant for life as to, 38
money for equality of, how raised, 43
what may be given and taken in, 43
of freeholds for leaseholds, 43
creation of easements on, 43, 80, 192
general regulations as to, 44
of land in England for land out of England, prohibited, 45
transfer of incumbrances on, 48

EXCHANGE—continued.
of principal mansion house restricted, 69, 195
of surface and minerals separately, 73
money for equality of, may be raised by mortgage, 75
completion of, by conveyance, 77
land acquired in, how to be settled, 93
contracts for, 114
notice by tenant for life of intention to make, 137
protection of parties making, 154
for erection of dwellings for working classes, 201

EXCLUSION OF ACT
prohibited, 22, 149

EXECUTORS,
of tenant for life, whether answerable for dilapidations, 111
of last surviving trustee, "trustees of the settlement," 129
power of, to sell real estate charged with debts, 157
can sell leaseholds without consent of tenant for life, 157

EXECUTORY GIFT OVER,
persons "limited owners" notwithstanding, 159, 160

EXERCISE OF POWERS,
"differences" as to, may be referred to the Court, 137
notice of intended, to be given to trustees, 137
        may be general notice, 182
        may be waived by trustees, 183
by tenant for life after assignment, 147
prohibition or limitation against, void, 149
not to cause forfeiture, 150
tenant for life a trustee as to, 151
from time to time, 154
consent of tenant for life always necessary to, 155
on behalf of infants, 167
in the case of a married woman, 169
on behalf of lunatics, 171
under s. 63, only with leave of the Court, 184
by the trustees in dealings with tenant for life, 197

EXONERATION,
of part of settled land, from charge or mortgage, 48
of person paying money into Court, 140

EXPENSES,
of laying out streets, how to be raised, 72
capital money applicable for payment of, 85
trustees may reimburse themselves for, 136
discretion of Court as to, 140
how to be raised out of settled property, 143

INDEX. 233

EXTINGUISHMENT,
    of rights of common, 48
    of powers, 147

FACT,
    conclusive statement of, in lease, 51, 54

FARM HOUSE,
    not a principal mansion house, 69, 195

FEE FARM RENT,
    leases at, may be authorized by the Court, 59
    conveyance subject to, 78
    grant for building purposes in consideration of, 194

FEE SIMPLE,
    tenant in, subject to executory limitation, a "limited owner," 159

FENCING,
    capital money may be expended in, 98

FINE,
    definition of, 26
    may be taken on grant of a lease, 51
        except when tenant for life has assigned, 147
        and in leases without notice to trustees, 193
    is capital money, 53, 182
    surrender of beneficial lease equivalent to, 68
    indemnity of trustees in respect of, 135

FINES,
    amount of, may be fixed by licence, 68
        not altered by S. L. Act, 78, 81
    admittance of purchaser on payment of, 78

FORECLOSURE,
    costs of protecting settled land from, 126

FORFEITURE,
    lease by copyholder, when a cause of, 68
    meliorating waste not a ground of, 69
    clause as to, of estate on exercise of powers, void, 140
    exercise of powers not to occasion, 150

FORMS, 209
    See TABLE OF CONTENTS.

FREEHOLD LAND,
    in a manor, seignory of, may be sold by tenant for life, 38
    purchased with capital money, 84
    how made subject to settlement, 95

GARDENS,
dedication of land for, by tenant for life, 71
vesting of, in trustees, 71

GENERAL RULES,
how to be made, 140
under the Act, 203

GIFT
over of settled land on exercise of powers, void, 149
of other property to induce tenant for life not to exercise powers, void, 149

GLEBE LAND,
sale of, by incumbent, 41

GOVERNMENT SECURITIES,
capital money may be invested in, 83

GUARDIANS OF INFANTS
may apply to Court to appoint trustees of the settlement, 129
or persons to exercise powers, 167

HEIRLOOMS,
power of tenant for life to sell, under an order of the Court, 8, 126
when to be sold with mansion-house, 70
proceeds of sale of, how applied, 86
continue personalty while uninvested, 94
Court had formerly no power to sanction sale of, 127
may be attached to a title of honour, 127
discretion of Court as to sale of, 128
form of summons for leave to sell, 212

HIGH COURT OF JUSTICE.—*See* COURT.

HOUSING OF THE WORKING CLASSES ACT, 1890
improvements authorized by, 102
sale, &c., of settled land for erection of dwellings, 46, 53, 201
amendment of, by S. L. Act, 1890, 201

HUSBAND
entitled to curtesy, a "limited owner," 160, 164
deemed to take under settlement made by wife, 186
when to concur with wife in exercise of powers, 169

IMPEACHABLE FOR WASTE,
whether lessee should be made, 50
tenant for life, must set aside three-fourths of mining rent, 60
tenant for life under settlement by way of trust for sale, 61
open mines may be worked even when tenant for life is, 61
cutting of timber, where tenant for life is, 124

IMPROVEMENT OF LAND ACT,
   extended list of authorized works, 100
   upholding and insurance of improvements under, 109
   extension of its application, 112
   summary of its provisions, 113
   priority of charges under, 113
   amendment of, by subsequent Acts, 113
   powers of, to be exercised by Land Commissioners, 145
   And see TABLE OF STATUTES.

IMPROVEMENTS,
   application of capital money in payment for, 16, 84
   building lease may be granted in consideration of, 54
   description of works authorized as, 98–103
   repair of buildings not included in, 100
   payment for, how obtained, 103
   authorized by Agricultural Holdings Act, 101
   scheme for, 103
   payment for, though scheme not submitted, 105, 198
   concurrence in joint, 106
   maintenance, repair and insurance of, 107
   execution and repair of, 111
   provisions as to, in Improvement of Land Act, 113
   tenant for life may enter into contracts as to, 114
   redemption of rent-charge for, 187
   authorized by Act of 1890, 198

INCOME
   includes rents and profits, 26
   of investments, application of, 92
   payment of costs out of, 143
   of land, person entitled to, when a "limited owner,' 160, 164
   accumulation of, effect of, 163

INCORPOREAL HEREDITAMENTS
   included in definition of "land," 26

INCUMBRANCES,
   provision for, under S. L. Act, 17
   person to be deemed tenant for life notwithstanding, 25
      even if they exhaust the whole income, 32
   may be transferred by tenant for life to other parts of settled land, 48
   conveyance, subject to, 78, 80
   on reversion, powers of the Act exerciseable, 81
   on life estate, costs occasioned by, 91
   capital money may be applied in discharge of, 84, 86
   purchased land, how to be made subject to, 95
   money may be raised on mortgage for discharge of, 195

INDEMNITY OF TRUSTEES,
   individually and generally, 10, 134, 135

INFANT,
    exercise of powers on behalf of, 19, 167
    tenant in tail, leaseholds not to vest in absolutely, 97
    application by guardian or next friend of, for appointment of trustees, 129
    land of, deemed to be settled land, 166
    absolutely entitled, deemed to be tenant for life, 166
    trustees of the settlement may exercise powers on behalf of, 167
    appointment of persons to exercise powers on behalf of, 167
    capacity of, to execute a power, 167
    married woman, 169
    lunatic, 172
    Form of Summons to appoint persons to exercise powers of, 219

INFANTS' SETTLEMENT ACT,
    effect of, upon powers of Settled Land Act, 168

INJUNCTION
    to restrain sale by tenant for life, 39

INROLMENT
    of deed dedicating open space to the public, 72, 73

INSURANCE
    of improvements, 107

INVESTMENT OF CAPITAL MONEY
    to be made by direction of tenant for life, 15, 92
    in various forms, 14, 83
    not to be altered without consent of tenant for life, 92
    in Court under other Acts, 118
        And see APPLICATION, IMPROVEMENTS, CAPITAL MONEY ARISING UNDER THE ACT.

INVESTMENTS
    authorized by the Act, 15, 83

IRELAND,
    modifications of the Act as to, 178
    difficulty as to leases in, 180
    whether "judicial lease" may be granted, 180

JOINT IMPROVEMENTS
    by several landowners, 106
    provisions as to, in Land Improvement Act, 106

JOINT TENANTS,
    together, constitute "tenant for life," 25, 31
    must all concur in exercise of powers, 31
    consent of one sufficient, 183

LANCASTER, COUNTY PALATINE OF,
    concurrent jurisdiction of Courts in, 11, 38, 141
    rules of Court for, how to be made, 141
    registration of lis pendens in, 186

LAND,
    definition of, 5, 26
    includes incorporeal hereditaments, 26, 35
    investment of capital money in purchase of, 84, 94
    capital money considered as, 92
    settlement of purchased, 95
    costs of re-investment in, payable by company, 120
    of an infant to be deemed "settled land," 166

LAND COMMISSIONERS,
    replaced by Board of Agriculture, 12
    powers of, as regards improvements, 103
    may require tenant for life to maintain and insure improvements, 107
    incorporation of, 144
    filing of certificates and reports in office of, 146

LANDS CLAUSES CONSOLIDATION ACTS,
    money in Court under, to be applied as capital money, 118
                               payment out to trustees, 118
                                 application of, petition or summons, 119
                                 costs of investment, 120

LAND TAX,
    redemption of, with capital money, 84
    statutes relating to, 88

LEASEHOLDS,
    whether they may be taken in exchange, 43
    vested in trustees may be conveyed by tenant for life, 77
    reversion of settled, may be purchased with capital money, 84, 89
    application of capital money in purchase of, 84
    purchased, how to be settled, 95
    not to vest in tenant in tail by purchase, who dies under age, 95, 97
    purchase-money of, application of, 122
    sale of, by executors, 157
    of an infant, whether "settled land," 166

LEASES,
    power of tenant for life to grant, 49
    consent of tenant for life to grant of, by trustees, 50
    general regulations respecting, 51
    when to be under seal, 51, 52
    contracts for, when equivalent to leases, 52
    defective execution of, relief against, 52, 66
    tenant for life may covenant for renewal of, 53

LEASES—*continued.*
    building, regulations respecting, 54
    mining, regulations respecting, 56
    on special conditions under an order of the Court, 59
    to give effect to contracts and covenants, 63
    renewal of, 63, 65
    confirmation of void or voidable, 63, 65
    for lives, when tenant for life may grant, 65
    surrender of, 66
    of copyholds, licences to grant, 68
    of principal mansion house, restricted, 69
    grant of, by deed, 77
    conveyance under Settled Land Act to be subject to, 78
    contracts for, powers of tenant for life in respect of, 114, 116
    application of money paid for, 122
    notices to trustees previous to granting, 137
    consent of assignee of tenant for life, when requisite, 147
    protection of lessees in taking, 154
    for 21 years, modifications as to, 193
    for erection of dwellings for working classes, 201
    Form of Summons for leave to grant, 210, 211

LESSEE,
    covenant by, for payment of rent, 51, 53
    statement conclusive in favour of, 51
    execution of counterpart by, 51
    improvements by, may be regarded in fixing rent, 51
    to whom mining rent is payable by, 62
    protection of, as to requisitions of the Act, 154

LICENCE
    for mining purposes included in "mining lease," 27
        rights conferred by, 37
    to lease copyholds may be given by tenant for life, 68
        operation of, 68
        terms of, depend on custom, 68

LIFE ESTATE CHARGES,
    effect of, upon statutory powers, 81

LIMITATIONS, STATUTE OF,
    in action for dilapidations, 111
    tenant for life cannot plead, 153
    effect of Trustee Act, 1888, 153

LIMITED OWNERS,
    who may exercise powers of the Act, 19, 159
    erection of residences by, 102
    obligation on, to maintain, repair, and insure improvements, 106
    may execute and repair works without impeachment of waste, 111

LIMITED OWNERS—*continued.*
    loans to, under Improvement of Land Act, 113
    enumeration of, 159
    application of Act to, 160
    exercise of powers on behalf of, being infants, 167
    married women being, how powers are to be exercised, 169
    lunatics being, how powers are to be exercised, 171

LIMITED OWNERS RESIDENCES ACTS, 102, 113

LIS PENDENS,
    registration of order as, 184
        effect of, 185

LOCAL CUSTOMS,
    leases may be sanctioned in accordance with, 59

LOCAL LOANS ACT,
    power of investment under, 86

LOSS,
    indemnity of trustees against, 134, 135

LOTS,
    tenant for life may sell in one, or several, 44
    contract to grant leases in, apportionment of rent, 54, 56

LUNATIC,
    exercise of powers on behalf of, 19, 171
    undivided share, sale to co-owner, 77
    not so found, whether powers exerciseable, 171
    exercise of powers on behalf of infant, 172
        on behalf of married woman, 172

MAINTENANCE OF IMPROVEMENTS
    by limited owners, 107

MANOR,
    definition of, 27
    by reputation, meaning of the expression, 37
    tenant for life of, may enfranchise, 38, 42

MANSION HOUSE,
    alienation of, restricted, 8, 69, 195
    rebuilding of, 102, 198
    erection, completion, or improvement of, under the Limited Owners Residences Act, 102, 113
    personalty not spent in rebuilding, 103

MARRIED WOMEN,
 powers of the Act when exerciseable by, 19, 169
 convey without deed acknowledged, 83, 171
 modification of the Act as to, 169
 exercise of the powers of the Act over separate property, 169
 when their husbands must concur, 169
 restrained from anticipation may exercise powers, 169
 infant, cannot exercise powers, 170

MINERALS,
 in general part of the inheritance of the land, 36
 what substances are, 37
 mining rent may be determined by quantity of, 56
 dealt with apart from surface, 73

MINES,
 open, the working of, not waste, 36
 metalliferous, rent generally reserved in kind, 57
 right of tenant for life to work, 61
 works connected with an "authorized improvement," 100, 101

MINES AND MINERALS,
 definition of, 26
 exception or reservation of, on enfranchisement, 44
 restrictions or reservations as to, on sale, &c., 44
 may be excepted from surrender of lease, 66
 application of capital money in purchase of, 84
 conveyance of, to uses of settlement, on purchase, 96

MINIMUM RENT
 may be reserved in mining lease, 57
 payable though working stopped, 58

MINING LEASE,
 definition of, 26
 tenant for life may grant, 50
 regulations respecting, 56
 variable rent may be reserved in, 56, 57
 on special conditions under an order of the Court, 59
 part of rent under, to be set aside, 60
  to whom payable, 62
 surrender and new grant of, 66
 grant or reservation of rights in, 73
 determination of rent in, 193

MONEY
 in Court,
  application of, 118
  payment of, to trustees, 118
 in the hands of trustees,
  application of, 120

MORTGAGE,
    transfer of, to other part of settled land 48
    money may be raised on, for special purposes, 75
    completion of, by deed, 77
    on life estate, 81
    on reversion, 81
    application of capital money in discharge of, 84, 88
    tenant for life to give notice of his intention to, 137
    for costs, 143
    capital money may be raised by, for incumbrances, 196

MORTGAGEES
    not bound to see that money is wanted for any purposes of the Act, 133
    general protection of, 154
    of life estate, costs of obtaining concurrence, 91

MUNICIPAL CORPORATION,
    investment on securities of, 86

NEW TRUSTEES,
    appointment of, by the Court, 10, 129
                under the Conv. Act, 1881, 200

NEXT FRIEND OF INFANT,
    application by, for the appointment of trustees, 120
        of persons to exercise powers, 167

NOTICE
    by tenant for life to trustees of intended exercise of powers, 40, 137
        also to their solicitor, 138
    not effectual unless there are at least two trustees, 138
    bonâ fide purchaser not concerned to inquire as to, 138
    trustees can waive, 138, 183
    may be general, 138, 182
    none required of short leases, 138, 193
    absence of, not a defect of title, 138
    of application to the Court, on whom to be served, 140, 203

OFFICE COPIES
    of certificates and reports, 146

OPEN MINES,
    tenant for life may work, although impeachable for waste, 61

OPEN SPACES.—*See* STREETS.

OPINION OF COURT
    may be given as to powers in settlement, 156

C.S.L.A.   R

242 INDEX.

OPTION OF PURCHASE,
    tenant for life cannot in general give, at fixed price, 45
    may be given by building lease, 46, 55, 189

ORDER
    of the Court,
        sanctioning leases on special terms, 59
            alienation of Mansion House, 69
            cutting and sale of timber, 124
            proceedings for protection, &c., of settled land, 125
            sale of heirlooms, 126
        authorizing trustees to pay for works, 104
        giving leave to exercise powers of s. 63, 184
    affecting land,
        registration may be vacated, 201

OUTSTROKE ROYALTY,
    in what cases payable, 58

PALATINE COURTS.—*See* DURHAM, LANCASTER.

PARK,
    restrictions on alienation of, 8, 69, 193

PARLIAMENT,
    proceedings in, for defence of settled land, 104

PARTITION,
    power of tenant for life as to, 38, 43
    general regulations as to, 44
    transfer of incumbrances on, 48
    mines and minerals may be separately dealt with on, 73
    money required for equality of, may be raised by mortgage, 75
    completion of, by conveyance, 77
    creation of easements on, 80, 192
    land acquired on, how to be settled, 93
    contracts for, power to make, 114
    notice to trustees before making, 137
    protection of parties making, 154

PAYMENT
    to person absolutely entitled, 85, 90
    to trustees of the settlement, 90
    for improvements, how obtained, 103
    to sole trustee, when permitted, 132
    of trustees' expenses out of trust property, 136
    of money into Court exonerates payer, 140,
        rules as to, 203
        forms of summons for, 212, 213, 214

PAYMENT—*continued.*
    out of Court, procedure as to, 119
        to the trustees, 198
    of costs out of settled property, 140, 143
    of debts, sale for, consent of tenant for life to, 157

PEPPERCORN RENT
    may be reserved for first five years of building lease, 54

PERMISSIVE WASTE,
    lessee not liable for, 51
    liabilities of tenant for life in respect of, 108

PERPETUITY
    leases in, may be authorized by the Court, 59

PERSONAL REPRESENTATIVES OF LAST SURVIVING TRUSTEE
    to be trustees of the settlement, 129
    power of, to give receipts, 133

PETITION
    not to be presented without direction of judge, 203
    directions as to service of, 205
        summons for, 219

PLANTING,
    an authorized improvement, 99, 101

PLEASURE GROUNDS
    sale, exchange or lease of, restricted, 69, 195

POSSESSION
    estate of tenant for life must be in, 25, 33
    includes receipt of income, 26
    cestui que trust when entitled to, 30
    lease to take effect in, 51
    of title deeds, right to, 82
    estate of "limited owner" must be in, 159, 160

POST,
    service of notice by, 138

POWERS,
    defectively executed, when aided, 52
    contracts for value treated as executions, 64
        Conferred by the Act,
            cannot be assigned or released, 146
            contract not to exercise, void, 147
            prohibition against exercise of, void, 149

POWERS—*continued.*
    Conferred by the Act—continued.
        inducements not to exercise, void, 149
        forfeiture not caused by exercise of, 150
        may be exercised from time to time, 154
        construction of, 155
    Conferred by a Settlement,
        general saving as to, 155
        conflict of with those of the Act, 155
        consent of tenant for life to exercise of, 155
        additional or larger, operation of, 158
  suspension or extinguishment of, 147
  capacity of an infant as to, 167

POWERS OF TENANT FOR LIFE,
  tabular statement of, 6
    sale, enfranchisement, exchange, partition, 41
      general regulations as to, 44
    transfer of incumbrances, 48
    grant of leases, 49, 59, 63
    acceptance of surrenders, 66
    licences to copyholders, 68
    land for streets and open spaces, 71
    to deal separately with surface and minerals, 73
    mortgages for special purposes, 75
    conveyance of settled land by deed, 77
    choice of investments, 92
    execution of improvements, 111
    to make binding contracts, 114
    cutting of timber, 124
    sale of heirlooms, 126
    to complete contracts, 192
    to raise money for discharge of incumbrances, 195
  checks imposed upon, 7, 40
    as to amount of consideration, 7, 45
      preservation of property, 8, 106
      alienation of mansion house, 8, 69, 195
      cutting of timber, 124
      sale of heirlooms, 126
  may be exercised by other limited owners, 19, 159
    trustees on behalf of infant, 167
    married women as to separate property, 169
    husband and wife as to property not separate, 169
    committee on behalf of lunatic, 171
  assignment or release of, prohibited, 22, 146
  cumulative, 40, 155
  unaffected by decree for administration, 41
  reference of differences as to, to Court 137, 152
  notice to trustees of intended exercise, 137, 182
  continue after assignment of life interest, 147

POWERS OF TENANT FOR LIFE—*continued.*
    tenant for life a trustee in exercise of, 151
    cannot be excluded by contrary intention, 149
    when exerciseable by the trustees, 187

PREDECESSORS IN TITLE,
    lease to give effect to contract or covenant of, 63
    tenant for life may complete contract of, 192

PRELIMINARY CONTRACTS
    not part of title to lease, 115

PRESERVATION
    of property, checks imposed on tenant for life for, 8

PRINCIPAL MANSION HOUSE,
    sale, exchange or lease of, restricted, 8, 69, 195
    meaning of the expression, 69, 71, 195
    expenditure of capital money in rebuilding, 102, 198
    form of summons for leave to sell, 212

PRIVATE CONTRACT,
    tenant for life may sell by, 44

PROHIBITION
    against exercise of powers, void, 22, 149

PROTECTION
    of each trustee individually, 134
    of trustees generally, 135
    of mortgagees, 133, 154
    of purchasers, 154

PROTECTION OF SETTLED LAND,
    proceedings for, sanction of by Court, 125

PURCHASE,
    land acquired by, how to be settled, 95
    of land, money liable to be laid out in, may be applied as capital money, 121

PURCHASE MONEY
    cannot be received by tenant for life, 8, 40
    must be paid to the trustees or into Court, 92
    of lease or reversion, how apportioned, 122
    discharge for, 133, 140
    payment of, into Court, rules as to, 206
        summons for, 213, 214

PURCHASER,
    position of, under Settled Land Act, 17
    protection of, dealing in good faith, 154

QUIT RENT,
  redemption of, with capital money, 84
    under the Conv. Act, 1881, 88

RAILWAY COMPANY,
  investment of capital money on bonds, mortgages, or debentures of, 84
    rent-charge, guaranteed or preference stock, 85

RECEIPT
  of capital money by one trustee, prohibited, 132
  given for conformity, 134

RECEIPTS, POWER TO GIVE,
  trustees of the settlement have, 133
  under the Conv. Act, 1881, 133

RECOVERY OF SETTLED LAND,
  proceedings for, sanction of by Court, 125

RE-ENTRY.
  condition of, lease to contain, 51
    apportioned on surrender, 67

REGISTERED LETTERS,
  notices to be sent by, 138

REGISTRATION
  of writ or order affecting land may be vacated, 201

REIMBURSEMENT
  of trustees in respect of their proper expenses 136

RELEASE,
  powers of tenant for life not capable of, 146

REMAINDER
  not disposed of by settlement to be deemed to be included therein, 25, 29
  included in definition of "land," 35

REMAINDER-MEN,
  checks for security of, 7
  have right of action for dilapidations, 107, 110
  when bound by contracts of tenant for life, 117
  time does not run against, 153

RENEWAL
  lease by tenant for life in pursuance of covenant for 65
  effect of covenant for, by tenant for life, 65, 116
  of lease by guardians of infant, 65
    committee of lunatic, 65

INDEX. 247

RENT,
    definition of, 26, 36
    payment of, to be secured by condition of re-entry, 51
    "best," how determined, 52
    uniform except in building and mining leases, 53
    apportionment of, under building contract, 54, 56
    peppercorn may be reserved for five years in building lease, 54
    how ascertainable in mining lease, 56, 57, 193
    proportion to be set aside in mining lease, 60
    to whom payable, 62
    may be apportioned on surrender, 66
    Crown, chief, or quit, may be redeemed, 84

RENT-CHARGE,
    reservation of, on grant for building purposes, 59, 194
                  operation of, under Act of 1890, 60
    application of capital money in redemption of, 87, 187
    remedies for recovery of, 194

REPAIR OF IMPROVEMENTS,
    dedicated to the public, 72, 73
    liability of limited owners for, 107
    protection as regards waste in respect of, 111

REPAIRING LEASE
    included in building lease, 26, 55

REPEAL OF ENACTMENTS, 178, 181
    23 & 24 Vict. c. 145, Parts I. and IV.
    27 & 28 Vict. c. 114, ss. 17, 18, and 21 (in part).
    40 & 41 Vict. c. 18, s. 17
    S. L. Act, 1882, s. 15, 193

REPORT OF LAND COMMISSIONERS,
    respecting improvements, 107
    to be filed in their office, 143

RESERVATION
    of mines on sale, &c., of surface, 73

RESERVE BIDDINGS,
    tenant for life may fix, 44

RESIDENCE,
    condition as to, effect of, 150

RESTRAINT ON ANTICIPATION,
    powers of Act may be exercised notwithstanding, 169

RESTRICTIONS
    on assignment, or release of powers, 146

RESTRICTIVE COVENANTS
   may be imposed on sale of settled land, 44
   constructive notice of, binds assignee, 47
   on a general building scheme, how far binding, 47

REVERSION,
   not disposed of by settlement to be deemed to be included therein, 27, 29
   derivative settlement of, 28
   included in definition of "land," 25.
   charges on, do not affect powers, 81
   of settled leaseholds may be purchased with capital money, 84, 89
   purchase-money of, how to be apportioned, 122

RIGHTS, EASEMENTS, AND PRIVILEGES,
   sale of, by tenant for life, 38, 42
   may be re-granted on enfranchisement, 45
   how affected by enfranchisement, 48
   lease of, by tenant for life, 49
   granted or reserved on separate dealings with surface and minerals, 73
   conveyance or creation of, by deed, 77
   statutory conveyance subject to, 78
   creation of, on exchange or partition, 80, 192
   how to be made subject to settlement, 96

ROADS,
   land may be appropriated for, 71
   capital money may be expended in making, 99

ROYALTY
   included in definition of "rent," 26
   is a rent varying with the quantity of minerals extracted, 36
   outstroke, in what cases payable, 58

RULES FOR PURPOSES OF THE ACT,
   summary of, 11
   how to be made, 140
   for the Palatine Court, 141
   for Ireland, 179
      as to Civil Bill Courts, 179
   under the S. L. Act, 1882, 203

SALE,
   powers of tenant for life as to, 38
   motives of tenant for life disregarded, 39
   when restrained by injunction, 39
   purchase-money cannot be received by tenant for life 4
   what may be sold, 41
   notwithstanding decree, 41
   general regulations as to, 44
   restrictive covenants on, 44

SALE—*continued.*
    timber should be sold with land, 46
    manner of, by tenant for life, 47
    transfer of incumbrances on, 48
    of principal mansion-house restricted, 69
    dedication of streets and open spaces on, 71
    of surface and minerals separately, 73
    completion of, by conveyance, 77
    subject to incumbrances, 80
    of heirlooms under an order of the Court, 126
    notice by tenant for life of intention to make, 137
    for payment of costs, 143
    general protection of purchaser on, 154
    settlement by way of trust for, 173
    in consideration of rent-charge, 194
    to tenant for life, how effected, 197
    for dwellings for working classes, 201
    to be carried into effect out of Court, 206

SAVING CLAUSE,
    for powers conferred by settlement, 155
    as to repeal of enactments, 178

SCHEME FOR IMPROVEMENTS,
    to be submitted by tenant for life, 8, 103, 105
    how approved, 8, 103
    costs of, may be ordered to be paid out of corpus, 91
    capital money may be applied in payment for, 103
    how to be approved, 103, 104
    whether company can be required to pay for, 120
    Court may dispense with, 198
    summons for approval of, 215

SCOTLAND,
    Settled Land Act does not extend to, 24

SECURITIES,
    definition of, 27, 37
    investment of capital money on authorized, 83, 85
    power to give receipt for, 133
    trustees not liable for insufficiency of, 135

SEIGNORY
    of freehold land may be sold, 38
    sale of, an enfranchisement, 42
    may be purchased with capital money, 84

SEPARATE PROPERTY,
    married women may exercise powers in respect of, 169

SERVICE
  of proceedings, 203, 205

SERVICE OF NOTICE
  on trustees and their solicitor by registered letters, 138
  of application by trustees, on tenant for life, 140
  Court may direct, on any person, 140, 205

SETTLED ESTATES ACT,
  effect of Settled Land Act upon, 21
  cases in which it may still be used, 21
  effect of order under, upon powers of S. L. Act, 22
  definition of "settlement" in, 28
  leases under, 50, 60, 170
  mining rent set aside under, 61
  surrender of leases under, 67
  licences to copyhold tenants under, 68
  money in Court under, may be applied as capital money, 118
  And see TABLE OF STATUTES.

SETTLED LAND,
  definition of, 3, 25, 29
  time for ascertaining when land is, 25, 30
  several estates may together constitute, 29
  an undivided share may be, 30
  may be bound by restrictive covenants, 44
      the contracts of the tenant for life, 115
  transfer of incumbrances from one part of, to another, 48
  protection, or recovery of, 125
  land of an infant to be, 166
  land vested in trustees upon trust for sale to be, 173

SETTLED LAND ACT,
  general scheme of, 1
  principle on which it rests, 2
  amendments of, 3
  Settled Estates Act, how far superseded by, 21
  commencement and extent of, 24

SETTLEMENT
  of land on marriage made in two ways, 4
      by will, 5
  time when it takes effect, 5, 25
  existing, effect of Settled Land Act upon, 20
  definition of, in Settled Land Act, 24
      amended, 27, 191
      Settled Estates Act, 28
  includes marriage settlement by tenant for life, 27
  what limitations in, constitute a "succession," 28

SETTLEMENT—*continued.*
must be subsisting when powers exercised, 29
purchased land, how to be made subject to, 95
prohibition by, of exercise of powers void, 149
by way of trust for sale, express provision as to, 173, 183

SEVERANCE
of surface and mines, 73

SEWAGE WORKS
an improvement under Settled Land Act, 99
loans for, under Public Health Act, 114

SHARE,
exercise of statutory powers in case of undivided, 76

SILOS
an "authorized improvement," 101

SOLE TRUSTEE,
payment of capital money to, 132
wpoer of, to give receipts, 133

SOLICITOR
of tenant for life, not appointed trustee, 131
notice to be sent to, of intended exercise of powers, 138, 139

SPECIFIC PERFORMANCE,
with compensation for mansion house not enforced, 70
of contracts by tenant for life, 116

SQUARES,
appropriation of settled land for, 71
vesting of, in trustees, 71

STAMP DUTY
on exchange, 43
on transfer of incumbrance, 49
on building lease, not payable in respect of improvements, 55
on lease, surrender not taken into account, 67
on appointment of new trustees, 131

STATEMENT
in lease or indorsed,
    conclusive in certain cases, 51
    evidence against all the world, 54

STATUTES—*See* TABLE AT COMMENCEMENT OF VOLUME.

STEWARD OF MANOR,
    certificate of, evidence of entry of licence on Court Rolls, 68
    entry of deed on Court Rolls by, 78
    may require production of settlement, 82

STREETS AND OPEN SPACES,
    tenant for life may dedicate land for, 71
    vesting of, in trustees, 71
    inrolment of deed relating to, 72, 73
    are an "authorized improvement," 99

SUBSISTING USES,
    purchased freeholds to be conveyed to, 95

SUBSTITUTED SECURITY,
    in what cases purchased land may be made a, 95, 97

SUCCESSION DUTY,
    land freed from, on sale under the Act, 82

SUMMONS AT CHAMBERS,
    applications may be made by, 11, 140, 203
    when money paid out on, 119
    how to be entitled, 203, 209
        served, 203
    formal parts of, 209
        See FORMS, 209 et seq.

SURFACE,
    dealt with separately from mines, 73
    injury to, by mining operations, 75

SURRENDER
    of lease,
        tenant for life may accept, 66
        term destroyed by force of statute, 67
        conditions of new lease granted on, 67
        apportionment of conditions on, 67
        under the Settled Estates Act, 67
        sub-lessees unaffected by, 67
        is equivalent to payment of fine, 68
    of contract for lease,
        tenant for life may accept, 114

SURVEYOR,
    summons for appointment of, 215
    nomination of, by trustees, 216

SURVIVORS AND SURVIVOR
of "the trustees of the settlement," 129, 132

SUSPENSION OF POWERS, 147

TENANT BY THE CURTESY
is a "limited owner," 160

TENANT FOR LIFE,
summary of powers of, 6
definition of, 25
person deemed to be, notwithstanding incumbrances, 25, 30
two or more persons concurrently entitled, 25, 31
what assignments by, included in settlement, 27, 191
when entitled to possession, 30
summons to determine whether claimant is, 31
of undivided share, powers of, 31
deemed to be, notwithstanding accumulation of rents, 32
his estate must be in possession, 32
position of, as to mines, 61
of undivided share may concur with other owners, 76
when entitled to possession of deeds, 82
covenants for title by, 83
option of, as to investments, 92
bound to maintain and insure improvements, 107, 108
right of action against, in respect of improvements, 107
rights of, in respect of timber, 124
not to be appointed trustee of the settlement, 131
difference between the trustees and, may be referred to Court, 137
notice by, to trustees, 137, 182
bankruptcy of, effect on powers, 148
a trustee of his powers for all parties, 151
sale by to stop accumulations, 152
cannot purchase from himself, 153
position of, as to Statute of Limitations, 153
consent of, necessary to the exercise of powers, 155
where estate subject to determination, 163
infant absolutely entitled deemed to be, 166
must furnish information to trustees, 182
consent of one, sufficient, 183
cannot exercise powers of s. 63 without an order, 184
trustees to represent, in dealings with himself, 197
And see POWERS OF TENANT FOR LIFE.

TENANT FOR YEARS DETERMINABLE ON LIFE,
is a "limited owner," 159
has only a chattel interest, 163
mortgagee of tenant for life is generally, 163

TENANT IN FEE SIMPLE
subject to executory limitation is a "limited owner," 159, 162

INDEX

TENANT IN TAIL,
    contract by, 117
    can convey under the Act without a deed enrolled, 83, 161
    when purchased leaseholds are not to vest absolutely in, 95
    in possession to have the powers of tenant for life, 159
        even when restrained by statute from barring the entail, 159
        and when the reversion is in the Crown, 159
        not when land was bestowed by Parliament for public services, 159
    after possibility of issue extinct, is a "limited owner," 160
    powers of, independently of the Act, 161

TENANT *PUR AUTRE VIE*
    is a "limited owner," 159

TENANTS IN COMMON
    together constitute "tenant for life," 25

TIMBER
    must be sold with the estate, 42
    may be cut down for improvements, 112
    cutting and sale of, where tenant for life impeachable for waste, 124
    what trees are, 124
    form of summons for leave to sell, 212

TITHE RENT CHARGE,
    redemption of, with capital money, 84
    Acts relating to, 88

TITHES,
    an incorporeal hereditament, 36

TITLE,
    stipulations respecting, tenant for life may make, 44
    preliminary contract as to lease not part of, 115

TITLE DEEDS,
    when tenant for life entitled to, 82
    covenant for production of, when to be inserted, 82
    inspection of, right to, 82

TITLE OF HONOUR,
    an incorporeal hereditament, 36, 127

TOLL
    included in definition of "rent," 26
    is the rent payable for a wayleave, 36

TRANSFER
    of incumbrance, 48

TREES
  planted as an improvement, 99, 101
  cannot be cut down, 107

TRUST FOR SALE,
  settlement by way of, provisions as to, 4, 173
  consent of tenant for life to exercise of, 183

TRUSTEES,
  powers of leasing vested in, not taken away, 50
  authorized investments of, 85
  approval of "scheme" by, 103
  payment for "improvements" by, 103
  money in the hands of, when to be applied as capital money, 120
  power to give receipts, 133
  tenants for life to be, in the exercise of powers, 151
  saving of powers of, 153

TRUSTEES OF THE SETTLEMENT,
  definition of, 8, 25, 33
    extended by Act of 1890, 34, 199
  powers and duties of, 8, 10
  protection of, in exercise of powers, 10, 134
  a check upon the tenant for life, 33, 40
  position of, with respect to mining rent, 62
  consent of, to alienation of mansion-house, 69
    to sale of timber, 124
  capital money to be paid to, or into Court, 92
  leaseholds and copyholds to be vested in, 95
  approval of scheme by, 103
  apportionment by, of purchase-money of lease or reversion, 122
  appointment of, by the Court, 129
    under Conv. Act, 1881, 130, 200
  survivorship of the office, 129, 132
  who are fit persons to be appointed, 131
  number of, to receive capital money, 132
  power of, to give receipts, 133
  indemnity of, 134, 135
  reimbursement of, 136
  differences between, and tenant for life may be referred to the Court, 137
  notices to, by the tenant for life, 138, 182
  should appear separately from tenant for life, 142
  may exercise powers on behalf of infant, 167
  may waive notice by tenant for life, 183
  exercise of powers of tenant for life in certain cases, 197
  form of summons for appointment of, 218

UNDIVIDED SHARE,
  included in definition of "land," 26
  when "settled land," 30, 36

UNDIVIDED SHARE—*continued*.
powers of tenant for life of, 31
power of partition in the case of, 38
in mines and minerals, reservation of, 74
tenant for life of, may concur in exercise of powers, 76
of lunatic may be sold to co-owner, 77

VESTING
squares or open spaces in trustees, 72
copyholds and leaseholds in trustees, 93

VOID LEASE,
confirmation of, 63, 65

WALES
included in "England," 48, 94

WASTE,
working open mines is not, 36
leases may be granted involving, 50
lessee not liable for permissive, 51
position of tenant for life in respect of, 61, 74
"meliorating," not a ground of forfeiture, 69
permissive, remedies for, 108
in execution of improvements, 111
tenant for life impeachable for, rights in respect of timber, 124
in leases under Act of 1890, 193

WATER-SUPPLY,
capital money may be expended in procuring, 99

WAYLEAVES,
rent payable for, in mining leases, 50
on separate dealings with surface and minerals, 73

WILL,
included in "settlement," 5, 24
definition of, 27

WORKING CLASSES,
sales, &c., for dwellings of, 46, 201
dwellings for, an "authorized improvement," 102, 201
extended meaning of, in Act of 1890, 201
See HOUSING OF THE WORKING CLASSES ACT, 1890.

WRIT OR ORDER,
registration of, may be vacated, 201

www.ingramcontent.com/pod-product-compliance
Lightning Source LLC
Chambersburg PA
CBHW031342230426
43670CB00006B/416